Pharsalia: Dramatic Episodes of the Civil Wars.

Also known as:

On the Civil War

By

Lucan

Marcus Annaeus Lucanus

Cover Photograph: Albion Europe ApS

ISBN: 978-1-78139-175-4

Contents

BOOK I

THE CROSSING OF THE RUBICON

Wars worse than civil on Emathian [1] plains,
And crime let loose we sing; how Rome's high race
Plunged in her vitals her victorious sword;
Armies akin embattled, with the force
Of all the shaken earth bent on the fray;
And burst asunder, to the common guilt,
A kingdom's compact; eagle with eagle met,
Standard to standard, spear opposed to spear.

Whence, citizens, this rage, this boundless lust
To sate barbarians with the blood of Rome?   10
Did not the shade of Crassus, wandering still, [2]
Cry for his vengeance? Could ye not have spoiled,
To deck your trophies, haughty Babylon?
Why wage campaigns that send no laurels home?
What lands, what oceans might have been the prize
Of all the blood thus shed in civil strife!
Where Titan rises, where night hides the stars,
'Neath southern noons all quivering with heat,
Or where keen frost that never yields to spring
In icy fetters binds the Scythian main: 20

---

[1] 'The great Emathian conqueror' (Milton's sonnet). Emathia was part of
Macedonia, but the word is used loosely for Thessaly or Macedonia.
[2] Crassus had been defeated and slain by the Parthians in B.C. 53, four years
before this period.

Long since barbarians by the Eastern sea
And far Araxes' stream, and those who know
(If any such there be) the birth of Nile
Had felt our yoke. Then, Rome, upon thyself
With all the world beneath thee, if thou must,
Wage this nefarious war, but not till then.

Now view the houses with half-ruined walls
Throughout Italian cities; stone from stone
Has slipped and lies at length; within the home
No guard is found, and in the ancient streets so   30
Scarce seen the passer by. The fields in vain,
Rugged with brambles and unploughed for years,
Ask for the hand of man; for man is not.
Nor savage Pyrrhus nor the Punic horde
E'er caused such havoc: to no foe was given
To strike thus deep; but civil strife alone
Dealt the fell wound and left the death behind.
Yet if the fates could find no other way [1]
For Nero coming, nor the gods with ease
Gain thrones in heaven; and if the Thunderer   40
Prevailed not till the giant's war was done,
Complaint is silent. For this boon supreme
Welcome, ye gods, be wickedness and crime;
Thronged with our dead be dire Pharsalia's fields,
Be Punic ghosts avenged by Roman blood;
Add to these ills the toils of Mutina;
Perusia's dearth; on Munda's final field

---

[1] Mr. Froude in his essay entitled "Divus Caesar" hints that these famous lines may have been written in mockery. Probably the five years known as the Golden Era of Nero had passed when they were written: yet the text itself does not aid such a suggestion; and the view generally taken, namely that Lucan was in earnest, appears preferable. There were many who dreamed at the time that the disasters of the Civil War were being compensated by the wealth and prosperity of the empire under Nero; and the assurance of universal peace, then almost realised, which is expressed in lines 69-81, seems inconsistent with the idea that this passage was written in irony. (See Lecky's "European Morals from Augustus to Charlemagne", vol. i.p.240, who describes these latter verses as Written with all the fervour of a Christian poet. See also Merivale's "Roman Empire," chapter liv.)

The shock of battle joined; let Leucas' Cape
Shatter the routed navies; servile hands
Unsheath the sword on fiery Etna's slopes: 50
Still Rome is gainer by the civil war.
Thou, Caesar, art her prize. When thou shalt choose,
Thy watch relieved, to seek divine abodes,
All heaven rejoicing; and shalt hold a throne,
Or else elect to govern Phoebus' car
And light a subject world that shall not dread
To owe her brightness to a different Sun;
All shall concede thy right: do what thou wilt,
Select thy Godhead, and the central clime
Whence thou shalt rule the world with power divine.   60
And yet the Northern or the Southern Pole
We pray thee, choose not; but in rays direct
Vouchsafe thy radiance to thy city Rome.
Press thou on either side, the universe
Should lose its equipoise: take thou the midst,
And weight the scales, and let that part of heaven
Where Caesar sits, be evermore serene
And smile upon us with unclouded blue.
Then may all men lay down their arms, and peace
Through all the nations reign, and shut the gates   70
That close the temple of the God of War.
Be thou my help, to me e'en now divine!
Let Delphi's steep her own Apollo guard,
And Nysa keep her Bacchus, uninvoked.
Rome is my subject and my muse art thou!

First of such deeds I purpose to unfold
The causes -- task immense -- what drove to arms
A maddened nation, and from all the world
Struck peace away.

       By envious fate's decrees   80
Abide not long the mightiest lords of earth;
Beneath too heavy a burden great the fall.
Thus Rome o'ergrew her strength. So when that hour,
The last in all the centuries, shall sound
The world's disruption, all things shall revert
To that primaeval chaos, stars on stars

3

Shall crash; and fiery meteors from the sky
Plunge in the ocean. Earth shall then no more
Front with her bulwark the encroaching sea:
The moon, indignant at her path oblique,   90
Shall drive her chariot 'gainst her brother Sun
And claim the day for hers; and discord huge
Shall rend the spheres asunder.
                    On themselves
Great powers are dashed: such bounds the gods have placed
Upon the prosperous; nor doth Fortune lend
To any nations, so that they may strike
The sovereign power that rules the earth and sea,
The weapons of her envy. Triple reign
And baleful compact for divided power --   100
Ne'er without peril separate before --
Made Rome their victim. Oh! Ambition blind,
That stirred the leaders so to join their strength
In peace that ended ill, their prize the world!
For while the Sea on Earth and Earth on Air
Lean for support: while Titan runs his course,
And night with day divides an equal sphere,
No king shall brook his fellow, nor shall power
Endure a rival. Search no foreign lands:
These walls are proof that in their infant days   110
A hamlet, not the world, was prize enough
To cause the shedding of a brother's blood.

Concord, on discord based, brief time endured,
Unwelcome to the rivals; and alone
Crassus delayed the advent of the war.
Like to the slender neck that separates
The seas of Graecia: should it be engulfed
Then would th' Ionian and Aegean mains [1]
Break each on other: thus when Crassus fell,

---

[1] See a similar passage in the final scene of Ben Jonson's "Catiline". The cutting of the Isthmus of Corinth was proposed in Nero's reign, and actually commenced in his presence; but abandoned because it was asserted that the level of the water in the Corinthian Gulf was higher than that in the Saronic Gulf, so that, if the canal were cut, the island of Aegina would be submerged. Merivale's "Roman Empire", chapter iv.

Who held apart the chiefs, in piteous death,   120
And stained Assyria's plains with Latian blood,
Defeat in Parthia loosed the war in Rome.
More in that victory than ye thought was won,
Ye sons of Arsaces; your conquered foes
Took at your hands the rage of civil strife.
The mighty realm that earth and sea contained,
To which all peoples bowed, split by the sword,
Could not find space for two [1]. For Julia bore,
Cut off by fate unpitying[2], the bond
Of that ill-omened marriage, and the pledge   130
Of blood united, to the shades below.
Had'st thou but longer stayed, it had been thine
To keep the husband and the sire apart,
And, as the Sabine women did of old,
Dash down the threatening swords and join the hands.
With thee all trust was buried, and the chiefs
Could give their courage vent, and rushed to war.

Lest newer glories triumphs past obscure,
Late conquered Gaul the bays from pirates won,
This, Magnus, was thy fear; thy roll of fame,   140
Of glorious deeds accomplished for the state
Allows no equal; nor will Caesar's pride
A prior rival in his triumphs brook;
Which had the right 'twere impious to enquire;
Each for his cause can vouch a judge supreme;
The victor, heaven: the vanquished, Cato, thee. [3]

---

[1] Compare: "Two stars keep not their motion in one sphere;   Nor can one England brook a double reign   Of Harry Percy and the Prince of Wales."
          -- "1 Henry IV", Act v., Scene 4.
[2] This had taken place in B.C.54, about five years before the action of the poem opens.
[3] This famous line was quoted by Lamartine when addressing the French Assembly in 1848. He was advocating, against the interests of his own party (which in the Assembly was all- powerful), that the President of the Republic should be chosen by the nation, and not by the Assembly; and he ended by saying that if the course he advocated was disastrous to himself, 'Victrix causa Diis placuit, sed victa Catoni.'

Nor were they like to like: the one in years
Now verging towards decay, in times of peace
Had unlearned war; but thirsting for applause
Had given the people much, and proud of fame   150
His former glory cared not to renew,
But joyed in plaudits of the theatre, [1]
His gift to Rome: his triumphs in the past,
Himself the shadow of a mighty name.
As when some oak, in fruitful field sublime,
Adorned with venerable spoils, and gifts
Of bygone leaders, by its weight to earth
With feeble roots still clings; its naked arms
And hollow trunk, though leafless, give a shade;
And though condemned beneath the tempest's shock   160
To speedy fall, amid the sturdier trees
In sacred grandeur rules the forest still.
No such repute had Ceesar won, nor fame;
But energy was his that could not rest --
The only shame he knew was not to win.
Keen and unvanquished [2], where revenge or hope
Might call, resistless would he strike the blow
With sword unpitying: every victory won
Reaped to the full; the favour of the gods
Pressed to the utmost; all that stayed his course   170
Aimed at the summit of power, was thrust aside:
Triumph his joy, though ruin marked his track.
As parts the clouds a bolt by winds compelled,
With crack of riven air and crash of worlds,
And veils the light of day, and on mankind,
Blasting their vision with its flames oblique,
Sheds deadly fright; then turning to its home, '

---

[1] 'Plausuque sui gaudere theatri.' Quoted by Mr. Pitt, in his speech on the
address in 1783, on the occasion of peace being made with France, Spain, and
America; in allusion to Mr. Sheridan. The latter replied, 'If ever I again en-
gage in the compositions he alludes to, I may be tempted to an act of
presumption -- to attempt an improvement on one of Ben Jonson's best char-
acters -- the character of the Angry Boy in the "Alchymist."'
[2] Cicero wrote thus of Caesar: 1Have you ever read or heard of a man more
vigorous in action or more moderate in the use of victory than our Caesar?' --
Epp. ad Diversos,' viii. 15.

Nought but the air opposing, through its path
Spreads havoc, and collects its scattered fires.

Such were the hidden motives of the chiefs;   180
But in the public life the seeds of war
Their hold had taken, such as are the doom
Of potent nations: and when fortune poured
Through Roman gates the booty of a world,
The curse of luxury, chief bane of states,
Fell on her sons. Farewell the ancient ways!
Behold the pomp profuse, the houses decked
With ornament; their hunger loathed the food
Of former days; men wore attire for dames
Scarce fitly fashioned; poverty was scorned,   190
Fruitful of warriors; and from all the world
Came that which ruins nations; while the fields
Furrowed of yore by great Camillus' plough,
Or by the mattock which a Curius held,
Lost their once narrow bounds, and widening tracts
By hinds unknown were tilled. No nation this
To sheathe the sword, with tranquil peace content
And with her liberties; but prone to ire;
Crime holding light as though by want compelled:
And great the glory in the minds of men,   200
Ambition lawful even at point of sword,
To rise above their country: might their law:
Decrees are forced from Senate and from Plebs:
Consul and Tribune break the laws alike:
Bought are the fasces, and the people sell
For gain their favour: bribery's fatal curse
Corrupts the annual contests of the Field.
Then covetous usury rose, and interest
Was greedier ever as the seasons came;
Faith tottered; thousands saw their gain in war.   210

Caesar has crossed the Alps, his mighty soul
Great tumults pondering and the coming shock.
Now on the marge of Rubicon, he saw,
In face most sorrowful and ghostly guise,
His trembling country's image; huge it seemed
Through mists of night obscure; and hoary hair

7

Streamed from the lofty front with turrets crowned:
Torn were her locks and naked were her arms.
Then thus, with broken sighs the Vision spake:
"What seek ye, men of Rome? and whither hence   220
Bear ye my standards? If by right ye come,
My citizens, stay here; these are the bounds;
No further dare." But Caesar's hair was stiff
With horror as he gazed, and ghastly dread
Restrained his footsteps on the further bank.
Then spake he, "Thunderer, who from the rock
Tarpeian seest the wall of mighty Rome;
Gods of my race who watched o'er Troy of old;
Thou Jove of Alba's height, and Vestal fires,
And rites of Romulus erst rapt to heaven,   230
And God-like Rome; be friendly to my quest.
Not with offence or hostfie arms I come,
Thy Caesar, conqueror by land and sea,
Thy soldier here and wheresoe'er thou wilt:
No other's; his, his only be the guilt
Whose acts make me thy foe.' He gives the word
And bids his standards cross the swollen stream.
So in the wastes of Afric's burning clime
The lion crouches as his foes draw near,
Feeding his wrath the while, his lashing tail   240
Provokes his fury; stiff upon his neck
Bristles his mane: deep from his gaping jaws
Resounds a muttered growl, and should a lance
Or javelin reach him from the hunter's ring,
Scorning the puny scratch he bounds afield.

From modest fountain blood-red Rubicon
In summer's heat flows on; his pigmy tide
Creeps through the valleys and with slender marge
Divides the Italian peasant from the Gaul.
Then winter gave him strength, and fraught with rain   250
The third day's crescent moon; while Eastern winds
Thawed from the Alpine slopes the yielding snow.
The cavalry first form across the stream '
To break the torrent's force; the rest with ease
Beneath their shelter gain the further bank.
When Csesar crossed and trod beneath his feet

BOOK I

The soil of Italy's forbidden fields,
"Here," spake he, "peace, here broken laws be left;
Farewell to treaties. Fortune, lead me on;
War is our judge, and in the fates our trust."   260
Then in the shades of night he leads the troops
Swifter than Balearic sling or shaft
Winged by retreating Parthian, to the walls
Of threatened Rimini, while fled the stars,
Save Lucifer, before the coming sun,
Whose fires were veiled in clouds, by south wind driven,
Or else at heaven's command: and thus drew on
The first dark morning of the civil war.

Now stand the troops within the captured town,
Their standards planted; and the trumpet clang   270
Rings forth in harsh alarums, giving note
Of impious strife: roused from their sleep the men
Rush to the hall and snatch the ancient arms
Long hanging through the years of peace; the shield
With crumbling frame; dark with the tooth of rust
Their swords [1]; and javelins with blunted point.
But when the well-known signs and eagles shone,
And Caesar towering o'er the throng was seen,
They shook for terror, fear possessed their limbs,
And thoughts unuttered stirred within their souls.   280
"O miserable those to whom their home
Denies the peace that all men else enjoy!
Placed as we are beside the Northern bounds
And scarce a footstep from the restless Gaul,
We fall the first; would that our lot had been
Beneath the Eastern sky, or frozen North,
To lead a wandering life, rather than keep
The gates of Latium. Brennus sacked the town
And Hannibal, and all the Teuton hosts.
For when the fate of Rome is in the scale   290
By this path war advances." Thus they moan
Their fears but speak them not; no sound is heard

---

[1] Marlowe has it:
    "...And swords   With ugly teeth of black rust foully scarred."

9

Giving their anguish utterance: as when
In depth of winter all the fields are still,
The birds are voiceless and no sound is heard
To break the silence of the central sea.
But when the day had broken through the shades
Of chilly darkness, lo! the torch of war!
For by the hand of Fate is swift dispersed
All Caesar's shame of battle, and his mind   300
Scarce doubted more; and Fortune toiled to make
His action just and give him cause for arms.
For while Rome doubted and the tongues of men
Spoke of the chiefs who won them rights of yore,
The hostile Senate, in contempt of right,
Drove out the Tribunes. They to Caesar's camp
With Curio hasten, who of venal tongue,
Bold, prompt, persuasive, had been wont to preach
Of Freedom to the people, and to call
Upon the chiefs to lay their weapons down [1].   310
And when he saw how deeply Caesar mused,
"While from the rostrum I had power," he said,
To call the populace to aid thy cause,
By this my voice against the Senate's will
Was thy command prolonged. But silenced now
Are laws in war: we driven from our homes;
Yet is our exile willing; for thine arms
Shall make us citizens of Rome again.
Strike; for no strength as yet the foe hath gained.
Occasion calls, delay shall mar it soon: 320
Like risk, like labour, thou hast known before,
But never such reward. Could Gallia hold
Thine armies ten long years ere victory came,
That little nook of earth? One paltry fight
Or twain, fought out by thy resistless hand,

---

[1] In the Senate, Curio had proposed and carried a resolution that Pompeius and Caesar should lay their arms down simultaneously; but this was resisted by the Oligarchal party, who endeavoured, though unsuccessfully, to expel Curio from the Senate, and who placed Pompeius in command of the legions at Capua. This was in effect a declaration of war; and Curio, after a last attempt at resistance, left the city, and betook himself to Caesar. (See the close of Book IV.)

And Rome for thee shall have subdued the world:
'Tis true no triumph now would bring thee home;
No captive tribes would grace thy chariot wheels
Winding in pomp around the ancient hill.
Spite gnaws the factions; for thy conquests won   330
Scarce shalt thou be unpunished. Yet 'tis fate
Thou should'st subdue thy kinsman: share the world
With him thou canst not; rule thou canst, alone."
As when at Elis' festival a horse
In stable pent gnaws at his prison bars
Impatient, and should clamour from without
Strike on his ear, bounds furious at restraint,
So then was Caesar, eager for the fight,
Stirred by the words of Curio. To the ranks
He bids his soldiers; with majestic mien   340
And hand commanding silence as they come.
"Comrades," he cried, "victorious returned,
Who by my side for ten long years have faced,
'Mid Alpine winters and on Arctic shores,
The thousand dangers of the battle-field --
Is this our country's welcome, this her prize
For death and wounds and Roman blood outpoured?
Rome arms her choicest sons; the sturdy oaks
Are felled to make a fleet; -- what could she more
If from the Alps fierce Hannibal were come   350
With all his Punic host? By land and sea
Caesar shall fly! Fly? Though in adverse war
Our best had fallen, and the savage Gaul
Were hard upon our track, we would not fly.
And now, when fortune smiles and kindly gods
Beckon us on to glory! -- Let him come
Fresh from his years of peace, with all his crowd
Of conscript burgesses, Marcellus' tongue [1]
And Cato's empty name! We will not fly.
Shall Eastern hordes and greedy hirelings keep   360
Their loved Pompeius ever at the helm?
Shall chariots of triumph be for him
Though youth and law forbad them? Shall he seize

---

[1] Marcus Marcellus, Consul in B.C. 51.

11

On Rome's chief honours ne'er to be resigned?
And what of harvests [1] blighted through the world
And ghastly famine made to serve his ends?
Who hath forgotten how Pompeius' bands
Seized on the forum, and with glittering arms
Made outraged justice tremble, while their swords
Hemmed in the judgment-seat where Milo [2] stood?   370
And now when worn and old and ripe for rest [3],
Greedy of power, the impious sword again
He draws. As tigers in Hyrcanian woods
Wandering, or in the caves that saw their birth,
Once having lapped the blood of slaughtered kine,
Shall never cease from rage; e'en so this whelp
Of cruel Sulla, nursed in civil war,
Outstrips his master; and the tongue which licked
That reeking weapon ever thirsts for more.
Stain once the lips with blood, no other meal   380
They shall enjoy. And shall there be no end
Of these long years of power and of crime?
Nay, this one lesson, e'er it be too late,
Learn of thy gentle Sulla -- to retire!
Of old his victory o'er Cilician thieves
And Pontus' weary monarch gave him fame,
By poison scarce attained. His latest prize
Shall I be, Caesar, I, who would not quit
My conquering eagles at his proud command?
Nay, if no triumph is reserved for me,   390
Let these at least of long and toilsome war
'Neath other leaders the rewards enjoy.
Where shall the weary soldier find his rest?
What cottage homes their joys, what fields their fruit
Shall to our veterans yield? Will Magnus say

---

[1] Plutarch, "Pomp.", 49. The harbours and places of trade were placed under
his control in order that he might find a remedy for the scarcity of grain. But
his enemies said that he had caused the scarcity in order to get the power.
[2] Milo was brought to trial for the murder of Clodius in B.C.52, about three
years before this. Pompeius, then sole Consul, had surrounded the tribunal
with soldiers, who at one time charged the crowd. Milo was sent into exile at
Massilia.
[3] See Book II., 630.

That pirates only till the fields alight?
Unfurl your standards; victory gilds them yet,
As through those glorious years. Deny our rights!
He that denies them makes our quarrel just.
Nay! use the strength that we have made our own.   400
No booty seek we, nor imperial power.
This would-be ruler of subservient Rome
We force to quit his grasp; and Heaven shall smile
On those who seek to drag the tyrant down."

Thus Caesar spake; but doubtful murmurs ran
Throughout the listening crowd, this way and that
Their wishes urging them; the thoughts of home
And household gods and kindred gave them pause:
But fear of Caesar and the pride of war
Their doubts resolved. Then Laelius, who wore   410
The well-earned crown for Roman life preserved,
The foremost Captain of the army, spake:
"O greatest leader of the Roman name,
If 'tis thy wish the very truth to hear
'Tis mine to speak it; we complain of this,
That gifted with such strength thou did'st refrain
From using it. Had'st thou no trust in us?
While the hot life-blood fills these glowing veins,
While these strong arms avail to hurl the lance,
Wilt thou make peace and bear the Senate's rule?   420
Is civil conquest then so base and vile?
Lead us through Scythian deserts, lead us where
The inhospitable Syrtes line the shore
Of Afric's burning sands, or where thou wilt:
This hand, to leave a conquered world behind,
Held firm the oar that tamed the Northern Sea
And Rhine's swift torrent foaming to the main.
To follow thee fate gives me now the power:
The will was mine before. No citizen
I count the man 'gainst whom thy trumpets sound.   430
By ten campaigns of victory, I swear,
By all thy world-wide triumphs, though with hand
Unwilling, should'st thou now demand the life
Of sire or brother or of faithful spouse,
Caesar, the life were thine. To spoil the gods

13

And sack great Juno's temple on the hill,
To plant our arms o'er Tiber's yellow stream,
To measure out the camp, against the wall
To drive the fatal ram, and raze the town,
This arm shall not refuse, though Rome the prize."   440

His comrades swore consent with lifted hands
And vowed to follow wheresoe'er he led.
And such a clamour rent the sky as when
Some Thracian blast on Ossa's pine-clad rocks
Falls headlong, and the loud re-echoing woods,
Or bending, or rebounding from the stroke,
In sounding chorus lift the roar on high.

When Csesar saw them welcome thus the war
And Fortune leading on, and favouring fates,
He seized the moment, called his troops from Gaul,   450
And breaking up his camp set on for Rome.

The tents are vacant by Lake Leman's side;
The camps upon the beetling crags of Vosges
No longer hold the warlike Lingon down,
Fierce in his painted arms; Isere is left,
Who past his shallows gliding, flows at last
Into the current of more famous Rhone,
To reach the ocean in another name.
The fair-haired people of Cevennes are free:
Soft Aude rejoicing bears no Roman keel,   460
Nor pleasant Var, since then Italia's bound;
The harbour sacred to Alcides' name
Where hollow crags encroach upon the sea,
Is left in freedom: there nor Zephyr gains
Nor Caurus access, but the Circian blast [1]
Forbids the roadstead by Monaecus' hold.
And others left the doubtful shore, which sea
And land alternate claim, whene'er the tide
Pours in amain or when the wave rolls back --

---

[1] The north-west wind. Circius was a violent wind from about the same quarter, but peculiar to the district.

BOOK I

Be it the wind which thus compels the deep   470
From furthest pole, and leaves it at the flood;
Or else the moon that makes the tide to swell,
Or else, in search of fuel [1] for his fires,
The sun draws heavenward the ocean wave; --
Whate'er the cause that may control the main
I leave to others; let the gods for me
Lock in their breasts the secrets of the world.

Those who kept watch beside the western shore
Have moved their standards home; the happy Gaul
Rejoices in their absence; fair Garonne   480
Through peaceful meads glides onward to the sea.
And where the river broadens, neath the cape
Her quiet harbour sleeps. No outstretched arm
Except in mimic war now hurls the lance.
No skilful warrior of Seine directs
The scythed chariot 'gainst his country's foe.
Now rest the Belgians, and the Arvernian race
That boasts our kinship by descent from Troy;
And those brave rebels whose undaunted hands
Were dipped in Cotta's blood, and those who wear   490
Sarmatian garb. Batavia's warriors fierce
No longer listen for the bugle call,
Nor those who dwell where Rhone's swift eddies sweep
Saone to the ocean; nor the mountain tribes
Who dwell about its source. Thou, too, oh Treves,
Rejoicest that the war has left thy bounds.
Ligurian tribes, now shorn, in ancient days
First of the long-haired nations, on whose necks
Once flowed the auburn locks in pride supreme;
And those who pacify with blood accursed   500
Savage Teutates, Hesus' horrid shrines,
And Taranis' altars cruel as were those
Loved by Diana [2], goddess of the north;

---

[1] This idea that the sun found fuel in the clouds appears again in Book VII.,
line 7; Book IX., line 379; and Book X., line 317.
[2] This Diana was worshipped by the Tauri, a people who dwelt in the Crimea;
and, according to legend, was propitiated by human sacrifices. Orestes on his

15

Pharsalia: Dramatic Episodes of the Civil Wars

All these now rest in peace. And you, ye Bards,
Whose martial lays send down to distant times
The fame of valorous deeds in battle done,
Pour forth in safety more abundant song.
While you, ye Druids [1], when the war was done,
To mysteries strange and hateful rites returned:
To you alone 'tis given the gods and stars   510
To know or not to know; secluded groves
Your dwelling-place, and forests far remote.
If what ye sing be true, the shades of men
Seek not the dismal homes of Erebus
Or death's pale kingdoms; but the breath of life
Still rules these bodies in another age --
Life on this hand and that, and death between.
Happy the peoples 'neath the Northern Star
In this their false belief; for them no fear
Of that which frights all others: they with hands   520
And hearts undaunted rush upon the foe
And scorn to spare the life that shall return.
Ye too depart who kept the banks of Rhine
Safe from the foe, and leave the Teuton tribes
Free at their will to march upon the world.

Caesar, with strength increased and gathered troops
New efforts daring, spreads his bands afar
Through Italy, and fills the neighbouring towns.
Then empty rumour to well-grounded fear

---

return from his expiatory wanderings brought her image to Greece, and the Greeks identified her with their Artemis. (Compare Book VI., 93.)
[1] The horror of the Druidical groves is again alluded to in Book III., lines 462-489. Dean Merivale remarks (chapter li.) on this passage, that in the despair of another life which pervaded Paganism at the time, the Roman was exasperated at the Druids' assertion of the transmigration of souls. But the passage seems also to betray a lingering suspicion that the doctrine may in some shape be true, however horrible were the rites and sacrifices. The reality of a future life was a part of Lucan's belief, as a state of reward for heroes. (See the passage at the beginning of Book IX.; and also Book VI., line 933). But all was vague and uncertain, and he appears to have viewed the Druidical transmigration rather with doubt and unbelief, as a possible form of future or recurring life, than with scorn as an absurdity.

Gave strength, and heralding the coming war   530
In hundred voices 'midst the people spread.
One cries in terror, "Swift the squadrons come
Where Nar with Tiber joins: and where, in meads
By oxen loved, Mevania spreads her walls,
Fierce Caesar hurries his barbarian horse.
Eagles and standards wave above his head,
And broad the march that sweeps across the land."
Nor is he pictured truly; greater far
More fierce and pitiless -- from conquered foes
Advancing; in his rear the peoples march.   540
Snatched from their homes between the Rhine and Alps,
To pillage Rome while Roman chiefs look on.
Thus each man's panic thought swells rumour's lie:
They fear the phantoms they themselves create.
Nor does the terror seize the crowd alone:
But fled the Fathers, to the Consuls [1] first
Issuing their hated order, as for war;
And doubting of their safety, doubting too
Where lay the peril, through the choking gates,
Each where he would, rushed all the people forth.   550
Thou would'st believe that blazing to the torch
Were men's abodes, or nodding to their fall.
So streamed they onwards, frenzied with affright,
As though in exile only could they find
Hope for their country. So, when southern blasts
From Libyan whirlpools drive the boundless main,
And mast and sail crash down upon a ship
With ponderous weight, but still the frame is sound,
Her crew and captain leap into the sea,
Each making shipwreck for himself. 'Twas thus   560
They passed the city gates and fled to war.
No aged parent now could stay his son;
Nor wife her spouse, nor did they pray the gods
To grant the safety of their fatherland.
None linger on the threshold for a look
Of their loved city, though perchance the last.

---

[1] Plutarch says the Consuls fled without making the sacrifices usual before wars. ("Pomp." 61.)

Ye gods, who lavish priceless gifts on men,
Nor care to guard them, see victorious Rome
Teeming with life, chief city of the world,
With ample walls that all mankind might hold,   570
To coming Caesar left an easy prey.
The Roman soldier, when in foreign lands
Pressed by the enemy, in narrow trench
And hurried mound finds guard enough to make
His slumber safe; but thou, imperial Rome,
Alone on rumour of advancing foes
Art left a desert, and thy battlements
They trust not for one night. Yet for their fear
This one excuse was left; Pompeius fled.
Nor found they room for hope; for nature gave   580
Unerring portents of worse ills to come.
The angry gods filled earth and air and sea
With frequent prodigies; in darkest nights
Strange constellations sparkled through the gloom:
The pole was all afire, and torches flew
Across the depths of heaven; with horrid hair
A blazing comet stretched from east to west
And threatened change to kingdoms. From the blue
Pale lightning flashed, and in the murky air
The fire took divers shapes; a lance afar   590
Would seem to quiver or a misty torch;
A noiseless thunderbolt from cloudless sky
Rushed down, and drawing fire in northern parts
Plunged on the summit of the Alban mount.
The stars that run their courses in the night
Shone in full daylight; and the orbed moon,
Hid by the shade of earth, grew pale and wan.
The sun himself, when poised in mid career,
Shrouded his burning car in blackest gloom
And plunged the world in darkness, so that men   600
Despaired of day -- like as he veiled his light
From that fell banquet which Mycenae saw [1].

---

[1] Compare Ben Jonson's "Catiline," I. 1: --   Lecca: The day goes back,
      Or else my senses.   Curius: As at Atreus' feast.

The jaws of Etna were agape with flame
That rose not heavenwards, but headlong fell
In smoking stream upon the Italian flank.
Then black Charybdis, from her boundless depth,
Threw up a gory sea. In piteous tones
Howled the wild dogs; the Vestal fire was snatched
From off the altar; and the flame that crowned
The Latin festival was split in twain,   610
As on the Theban pyre [1], in ancient days;
Earth tottered on its base: the mighty Alps
From off their summits shook th' eternal snow [2].
In huge upheaval Ocean raised his waves
O'er Calpe's rock and Atlas' hoary head.
The native gods shed tears, and holy sweat
Dropped from the idols; gifts in temples fell:
Foul birds defiled the day; beasts left the woods
And made their lair among the streets of Rome.
All this we hear; nay more: dumb oxen spake;   620
Monsters were brought to birth and mothers shrieked
At their own offspring; words of dire import
From Cumae's prophetess were noised abroad.
Bellona's priests with bleeding arms, and slaves
Of Cybele's worship, with ensanguined hair,
Howled chants of havoc and of woe to men.
Arms clashed; and sounding in the pathless woods
Were heard strange voices; spirits walked the earth:
And dead men's ashes muttered from the urn.
Those who live near the walls desert their homes,   630
For lo! with hissing serpents in her hair,
Waving in downward whirl a blazing pine,
A fiend patrols the town, like that which erst
At Thebes urged on Agave [3], or which hurled
Lycurgus' bolts, or that which as he came

---

[1] When the Theban brothers, Eteocles and Polynices, were being burned on the same pyre, the flame shot up in two separate tongues, indicating that even in death they could not be reconciled. (Mr. Haskins' note, citing Statius, "Thebiad")
[2] "Shook the old snow from off their trembling laps." (Marlowe.) The Latin word is "jugis".
[3] Book VI., 420.

From Hades seen, at haughty Juno's word,
Brought terror to the soul of Hercules.
Trumpets like those that summon armies forth
Were heard re-echoing in the silent night:
And from the earth arising Sulla's [1] ghost   640
Sang gloomy oracles, and by Anio's wave
All fled the homesteads, frighted by the shade
Of Marius waking from his broken tomb.

In such dismay they summon, as of yore,
The Tuscan sages to the nation's aid.
Aruns, the eldest, leaving his abode
In desolate Luca, came, well versed in all
The lore of omens; knowing what may mean
The flight of hovering bird, the pulse that beats
In offered victims, and the levin bolt.   650
All monsters first, by most unnatural birth
Brought into being, in accursd flames
He bids consume [2]. Then round the walls of Rome
Each trembling citizen in turn proceeds.
The priests, chief guardians of the public faith,
With holy sprinkling purge the open space
That borders on the wall; in sacred garb
Follows the lesser crowd: the Vestals come
By priestess led with laurel crown bedecked,
To whom alone is given the right to see   660
Minerva's effigy that came from Troy [3].
Next come the keepers of the sacred books
And fate's predictions; who from Almo's brook
Bring back Cybebe laved; the augur too
Taught to observe sinister flight of birds;
And those who serve the banquets to the gods;
And Titian brethren; and the priest of Mars,

---

[1] Sulla was buried in the Campus Martius. (Plutarch, "Sulla,".) The corpse of Marius was dragged from his tomb by Sulla's order, and thrown into the Anio.
[2] Such a ceremonial took place in A.D. 56 under Nero, after the temples of Jupiter and Minerva had been struck by lightning, and was probably witnessed by Lucan himself. (See Merivale's "History of the Roman Empire," chapter lii.)
[3] See Book IX., 1178.

Proud of the buckler that adorns his neck;
By him the Flamen, on his noble head
The cap of office. While they tread the path   670
That winds around the walls, the aged seer
Collects the thunderbolts that fell from heaven,
And lays them deep in earth, with muttered words
Naming the spot accursed. Next a steer,
Picked for his swelling neck and beauteous form,
He leads to the altar, and with slanting knife
Spreads on his brow the meal, and pours the wine.
The victim's struggles prove the gods averse;
But when the servers press upon his horns

He bends the knee and yields him to the blow.   680
No crimson torrent issued at the stroke,
But from the wound a dark empoisoned stream
Ebbed slowly downward. Aruns at the sight
Aghast, upon the entrails of the beast
Essayed to read the anger of the gods.
Their very colour terrified the seer;
Spotted they were and pale, with sable streaks
Of lukewarm gore bespread; the liver damp
With foul disease, and on the hostile part
The angry veins defiant; of the lungs   690
The fibre hid, and through the vital parts
The membrane small; the heart had ceased to throb;
Blood oozes through the ducts; the caul is split:
And, fatal omen of impending ill,
One lobe o'ergrows the other; of the twain
The one lies flat and sick, the other beats
And keeps the pulse in rapid strokes astir.

Disaster's near approach thus learned, he cries --
"Whate'er may be the purpose of the gods,
'Tis not for me to tell; this offered beast   700
Not Jove possesses, but the gods below.
We dare not speak our fears, yet fear doth make
The future worse than fact. May all the gods
Prosper the tokens, and the sacrifice
Be void of truth, and Tages (famous seer)
Have vainly taught these mysteries." Such his words

Involved, mysterious. Figulus, to whom
For knowledge of the secret depths of space
And laws harmonious that guide the stars,
Memphis could find no peer, then spake at large: 710
"Either," he said, "the world and countless orbs
Throughout the ages wander at their will;
Or, if the fates control them, ruin huge
Hangs o'er this city and o'er all mankind.
Shall Earth yawn open and engulph the towns?
Shall scorching heat usurp the temperate air
And fields refuse their timely fruit? The streams
Flow mixed with poison? In what plague, ye gods,
In what destruction shall ye wreak your ire?
Whate'er the truth, the days in which we live   720
Shall find a doom for many. Had the star
Of baleful Saturn, frigid in the height,
Kindled his lurid fires, the sky had poured
Its torrents forth as in Deucalion's time,
And whelmed the world in waters. Or if thou,
Phoebus, beside the Nemean lion fierce
Wert driving now thy chariot, flames should seize
The universe and set the air ablaze.
These are at peace; but, Mars, why art thou bent
On kindling thus the Scorpion, his tail   730
Portending evil and his claws aflame?
Deep sunk is kindly Jupiter, and dull
Sweet Venus' star, and rapid Mercury
Stays on his course: Mars only holds the sky.
Why does Orion's sword too brightly shine?
Why planets leave their paths and through the void
Thus journey on obscure? 'Tis war that comes,
Fierce rabid war: the sword shall bear the rule
Confounding justice; hateful crime usurp
The name of virtue; and the havoc spread   740
Through many a year. But why entreat the gods?
The end Rome longs for and the final peace
Comes with a despot. Draw thou out thy chain
Of lengthening slaughter, and (for such thy fate)
Make good thy liberty through civil war."

The frightened people heard, and as they heard

His words prophetic made them fear the more.
But worse remained; for as on Pindus' slopes
Possessed with fury from the Theban god
Speeds some Bacchante, thus in Roman streets   750
Behold a matron run, who, in her trance,
Relieves her bosom of the god within.

"Where dost thou snatch me, Paean, to what shore
Through airy regions borne? I see the snows
Of Thracian mountains; and Philippi's plains
Lie broad beneath. But why these battle lines,
No foe to vanquish -- Rome on either hand?
Again I wander 'neath the rosy hues
That paint thine eastern skies, where regal Nile
Meets with his flowing wave the rising tide.   760
Known to mine eyes that mutilated trunk
That lies upon the sand! Across the seas
By changing whirlpools to the burning climes
Of Libya borne, again I see the hosts
From Thracia brought by fate's command. And now
Thou bear'st me o'er the cloud-compelling Alps
And Pyrenean summits; next to Rome.
There in mid-Senate see the closing scene
Of this foul war in foulest murder done.
Again the factions rise; through all the world   770
Once more I pass; but give me some new land,
Some other region, Phoebus, to behold!
Washed by the Pontic billows! for these eyes
Already once have seen Philippi's plains!" [1]

The frenzy left her and she speechless fell.

---

[1] The confusion between the site of the battle of Philippi and that of the battle of Pharsalia is common among the Roman writers. (See the note to Merivale, chapter xxvi.)

BOOK II

THE FLIGHT OF POMPEIUS

This was made plain the anger of the gods;
The universe gave signs Nature reversed
In monstrous tumult fraught with prodigies
Her laws, and prescient spake the coming guilt.

How seemed it just to thee, Olympus' king,
That suffering mortals at thy doom should know
By omens dire the massacre to come?
Or did the primal parent of the world
When first the flames gave way and yielding left
Matter unformed to his subduing hand,   10
And realms unbalanced, fix by stern decree'
Unalterable laws to bind the whole
(Himself, too, bound by law), so that for aye
All Nature moves within its fated bounds?
Or, is Chance sovereign over all, and we
The sport of Fortune and her turning wheel?
Whate'er be truth, keep thou the future veiled
From mortal vision, and amid their fears
May men still hope.

    Thus known how great the woes   20
The world should suffer, from the truth divine,
A solemn fast was called, the courts were closed,
All men in private garb; no purple hem
Adorned the togas of the chiefs of Rome;
No plaints were uttered, and a voiceless grief

Lay deep in every bosom: as when death
Knocks at some door but enters not as yet,
Before the mother calls the name aloud
Or bids her grieving maidens beat the breast,
While still she marks the glazing eye, and soothes   30
The stiffening limbs and gazes on the face,
In nameless dread, not sorrow, and in awe
Of death approaching: and with mind distraught
Clings to the dying in a last embrace.

The matrons laid aside their wonted garb:
Crowds filled the temples -- on the unpitying stones
Some dashed their bosoms; others bathed with tears
The statues of the gods; some tore their hair
Upon the holy threshold, and with shrieks
And vows unceasing called upon the names   40
Of those whom mortals supplicate. Nor all
Lay in the Thunderer's fane: at every shrine
Some prayers are offered which refused shall bring
Reproach on heaven. One whose livid arms
Were dark with blows, whose cheeks with tears bedewed
And riven, cried, "Beat, mothers, beat the breast,
Tear now the lock; while doubtful in the scales
Still fortune hangs, nor yet the fight is won,
You still may grieve: when either wins rejoice."
Thus sorrow stirs itself.   50

                    Meanwhile the men
Seeking the camp and setting forth to war,
Address the cruel gods in just complaint.
"Happy the youths who born in Punic days
On Cannae's uplands or by Trebia's stream
Fought and were slain! What wretched lot is ours!
No peace we ask for: let the nations rage;
Rouse fiercest cities! may the world find arms
To wage a war with Rome: let Parthian hosts
Rush forth from Susa; Scythian Ister curb   60
No more the Massagete: unconquered Rhine
Let loose from furthest North her fair-haired tribes:
Elbe, pour thy Suevians forth! Let us be foes
Of all the peoples. May the Getan press

25

Here, and the Dacian there; Pompeius meet
The Eastern archers, Caesar in the West
Confront th' Iberian. Leave to Rome no hand
To raise against herself in civil strife.
Or, if Italia by the gods be doomed,
Let all the sky, fierce Parent, be dissolved   70
And falling on the earth in flaming bolts,
Their hands still bloodless, strike both leaders down,
With both their hosts! Why plunge in novel crime
To settle which of them shall rule in Rome?
Scarce were it worth the price of civil war
To hinder either." Thus the patriot voice
Still found an utterance, soon to speak no more.

Meantime, the aged fathers o'er their fates
In anguish grieved, detesting life prolonged
That brought with it another civil war.   80
And thus spake one, to justify his fears:
"No other deeds the fates laid up in store
When Marius [1], victor over Teuton hosts,
Afric's high conqueror, cast out from Rome,
Lay hid in marshy ooze, at thy behest,
O Fortune! by the yielding soil concealed
And waving rushes; but ere long the chains
Of prison wore his weak and aged frame,
And lengthened squalor: thus he paid for crime
His punishment beforehand; doomed to die   90
Consul in triumph over wasted Rome.
Death oft refused him; and the very foe,
In act to murder, shuddered in the stroke
And dropped the weapon from his nerveless hand.
For through the prison gloom a flame of light
He saw; the deities of crime abhorred;

---

[1] When dragged from his hiding place in the marsh, Marius was sent by the magistrates of Minturnae to the house of a woman named Fannia, and there locked up in a dark apartment. It does not appear that he was there long. A Gallic soldier was sent to kill him; "and the eyes of Marius appeared to him to dart a strong flame, and a loud voice issued from the gloom, 'Man, do you dare to kill Caius Marius?'" He rushed out exclaiming, "I cannot kill Caius Marius." (Plutarch, "Marius", 38.)

BOOK II

The Marius to come. A voice proclaimed
Mysterious, 'Hold! the fates permit thee not
That neck to sever. Many a death he owes
To time's predestined laws ere his shall come;   100
Cease from thy madness. If ye seek revenge
For all the blood shed by your slaughtered tribes to
Let this man, Cimbrians, live out all his days.'
Not as their darling did the gods protect
The man of blood, but for his ruthless hand
Fit to prepare that sacrifice of gore
Which fate demanded. By the sea's despite
Borne to our foes, Jugurtha's wasted realm
He saw, now conquered; there in squalid huts
Awhile he lay, and trod the hostile dust   110
Of Carthage, and his ruin matched with hers:
Each from the other's fate some solace drew,
And prostrate, pardoned heaven. On Libyan soil [1]
Fresh fury gathering [2], next, when Fortune smiled
The prisons he threw wide and freed the slaves.
Forth rushed the murderous bands, their melted chains
Forged into weapons for his ruffian needs.
No charge he gave to mere recruits in guilt
Who brought not to the camp some proof of crime.
How dread that day when conquering Marius seized   120
The city's ramparts! with what fated speed
Death strode upon his victims! plebs alike
And nobles perished; far and near the sword
Struck at his pleasure, till the temple floors
Ran wet with slaughter and the crimson stream
Befouled with slippery gore the holy walls.
No age found pity men of failing years,
Just tottering to the grave, were hurled to death;
From infants, in their being's earliest dawn [1],

---

[1] The Governor of Libya sent an officer to Marius, who had landed in the
neighbourhood of Carthage. The officer delivered his message, and Marius
replied, "Tell the Governor you have seen Caius Marius, a fugitive sitting on
the ruins of Carthage," a reply in which he not inaptly compared the fate of
that city and his own changed fortune. (Plutarch, "Marius", 40.)
[2] In the "gathering of fresh fury on Libyan soil", there appears to be an allu-
sion to the story of Antruns, in Book IV.

27

The growing life was severed. For what crime?   130
Twas cause enough for death that they could die.
The fury grew: soon 'twas a sluggard's part
To seek the guilty: hundreds died to swell
The tale of victims. Shamed by empty hands,
The bloodstained conqueror snatched a reeking head
From neck unknown. One way of life remained,
To kiss with shuddering lips the red right hand [2].
Degenerate people! Had ye hearts of men,
Though ye were threatened by a thousand swords,
Far rather death than centuries of life   140
Bought at such price; much more that breathing space
Till Sulla comes again [3]. But time would fail
In weeping for the deaths of all who fell.
Encircled by innumerable bands
Fell Baebius, his limbs asunder torn,
His vitals dragged abroad. Antonius too,
Prophet of ill, whose hoary head [4] was placed,
Dripping with blood, upon the festal board.
There headless fell the Crassi; mangled frames
'Neath Fimbria's falchion: and the prison cells   150
Were wet with tribunes' blood. Hard by the fane
Where dwells the goddess and the sacred fire,
Fell aged Scaevola, though that gory hand [5]
Had spared him, but the feeble tide of blood
Still left the flame alive upon the hearth.
That selfsame year the seventh time restored [1]

---

[1] See Ben Jonson's "Catiline", Act i., scene 1, speaking of the Sullan massacre.   Cethegus: Not infants in the porch of life were free.   ....   Catiline: 'Twas crime enough that they had lives: to   strike but only those that could do hurt was dull and   poor: some fell to make the number as some the prey.
[2] Whenever he did not salute a man, or return his salute, this was a signal for massacre. (Plutarch, "Marius", 49.)
[3] The Marian massacre was in B.C. 87-86; the Sullan in 82-81.
[4] The head of Antonius was struck off and brought to Marius at supper. He was the grandfather of the triumvir.
[5] Scaevola, it would appear, was put to death after Marius the elder died, by the younger Marius. He was Pontifex Maximus, and slain by the altar of Vesta.

28

The Consul's rods; that year to Marius brought
The end of life, when he at Fortune's hands
All ills had suffered; all her goods enjoyed.

"And what of those who at the Sacriport [2]   160
And Colline gate were slain, then, when the rule
Of Earth and all her nations almost left
This city for another, and the chiefs
Who led the Samnite hoped that Rome might bleed
More than at Caudium's Forks she bled of old?
Then came great Sulla to avenge the dead,
And all the blood still left within her frame
Drew from the city; for the surgeon knife
Which shore the cancerous limbs cut in too deep,
And shed the life stream from still healthy veins.   170
True that the guilty fell, but not before
All else had perished. Hatred had free course
And anger reigned unbridled by the law.
The victor's voice spake once; but each man struck
Just as he wished or willed. The fatal steel
Urged by the servant laid the master low.
Sons dripped with gore of sires; and brothers fought
For the foul trophy of a father slain,
Or slew each other for the price of blood.
Men sought the tombs and, mingling with the dead,   180
Hoped for escape; the wild beasts' dens were full.
One strangled died; another from the height
Fell headlong down upon the unpitying earth,
And from the encrimsoned victor snatched his death:
One built his funeral pyre and oped his veins,
And sealed the furnace ere his blood was gone.
Borne through the trembling town the leaders' heads
Were piled in middle forum: hence men knew

---

[1] B.C. 86, Marius and Cinna were Consuls. Marius died seventeen days afterwards, in the seventieth year of his age.
[2] The Battle of Sacriportus was fought between Marius the younger and the Sullan army in B.C. 82. Marius was defeated with great loss, and fled to Praeneste, a town which afterwards submitted to Sulla, who put all the inhabitants to death (line 216). At the Colline gate was fought the decisive battle between Sulla and the Saranires, who, after a furious contest, were defeated.

Of murders else unpublished. Not on gates
Of Diomedes [1], tyrant king of Thrace,   190
Nor of Antaeus, Libya's giant brood,
Were hung such horrors; nor in Pisa's hall
Were seen and wept for when the suitors died.
Decay had touched the features of the slain
When round the mouldering heap, with trembling steps
The grief-struck parents sought and stole their dead.
I, too, the body of my brother slain
Thought to remove, my victim to the peace
Which Sulla made, and place his loved remains
On the forbidden pyre. The head I found,   200
But not the butchered corse.

             "Why now renew
The tale of Catulus's shade appeased?
And those dread tortures which the living frame
Of Marius [2] suffered at the tomb of him
Who haply wished them not? Pierced, mangled, torn --
Nor speech nor grasp was left: his every limb
Maimed, hacked and riven; yet the fatal blow
The murderers with savage purpose spared.
'Twere scarce believed that one poor mortal frame   210
Such agonies could bear e'er death should come.
Thus crushed beneath some ruin lie the dead;
Thus shapeless from the deep are borne the drowned.
Why spoil delight by mutilating thus,
The head of Marius? To please Sulla's heart
That mangled visage must be known to all.
Fortune, high goddess of Praeneste's fane,
Saw all her townsmen hurried to their deaths
In one fell instant. All the hope of Rome,
The flower of Latium, stained with blood the field   220
Where once the peaceful tribes their votes declared.

---

[1] Diomedes was said to feed his horses on human flesh. (For Antaeus see
Book IV., 660.) Enomaus was king of Pisa in Elis. Those who came to sue
for his daughter's hand had to compete with him in a chariot race, and if de-
feated were put to death.
[2] The brother of the Consul.

Famine and Sword, the raging sky and sea,
And Earth upheaved, have laid such numbers low:
But ne'er one man's revenge. Between the slain
And living victims there was space no more,
Death thus let slip, to deal the fatal blow.
Hardly when struck they fell; the severed head
Scarce toppled from the shoulders; but the slain
Blent in a weighty pile of massacre
Pressed out the life and helped the murderer's arm.   230
Secure from stain upon his lofty throne,
Unshuddering sat the author of the whole,
Nor feared that at his word such thousands fell.
At length the Tuscan flood received the dead
The first upon his waves; the last on those
That lay beneath them; vessels in their course
Were stayed, and while the lower current flowed
Still to the sea, the upper stood on high
Dammed back by carnage. Through the streets meanwhile
In headlong torrents ran a tide of blood,   240
Which furrowing its path through town and field
Forced the slow river on. But now his banks
No longer held him, and the dead were thrown
Back on the fields above. With labour huge
At length he struggled to his goal and stretched
In crimson streak across the Tuscan Sea.

"For deeds like these, shall Sulla now be styled
'Darling of Fortune', 'Saviour of the State'?
For these, a tomb in middle field of Mars
Record his fame? Like horrors now return   250
For us to suffer; and the civil war
Thus shall be waged again and thus shall end.
Yet worse disasters may our fears suggest,
For now with greater carnage of mankind
The rival hosts in weightier battle meet.
To exiled Marius, successful strife
Was Rome regained; triumphant Sulla knew
No greater joy than on his hated foes
To wreak his vengeance with unsparing sword.
But these more powerful rivals Fortune calls   260
To worse ambitions; nor would either chief

31

For such reward as Sulla's wage the war."
Thus, mindful of his youth, the aged man
Wept for the past, but feared the coming days.

Such terrors found in haughty Brutus' breast
No home. When others sat them down to fear
He did not so, but in the dewy night
When the great wain was turning round the pole
He sought his kinsman Cato's humble home.
Him sleepless did he find, not for himself   270
Fearing, but pondering the fates of Rome,
And deep in public cares. And thus he spake:
"O thou in whom that virtue, which of yore
Took flight from earth, now finds its only home,
Outcast to all besides, but safe with thee:
Vouchsafe thy counsel to my wavering soul
And make my weakness strength. While Caesar some,
Pompeius others, follow in the fight,
Cato is Brutus' guide. Art thou for peace,
Holding thy footsteps in a tottering world   280
Unshaken? Or wilt thou with the leaders' crimes
And with the people's fury take thy part,
And by thy presence purge the war of guilt?
In impious battles men unsheath the sword;
But each by cause impelled: the household crime;
Laws feared in peace; want by the sword removed;
And broken credit, that its ruin hides
In general ruin. Drawn by hope of gain,
And not by thirst for blood, they seek the camp.
Shall Cato for war's sake make war alone?   290
What profits it through all these wicked years
That thou hast lived untainted? This were all
Thy meed of virtue, that the wars which find
Guilt in all else, shall make thee guilty too.
Ye gods, permit not that this fatal strife
Should stir those hands to action! When the clouds
Of flying javelins hiss upon the air,
Let not a dart be thine; nor spent in vain
Such virtue! All the fury of the war
Shall launch itself on thee, for who, when faint   300
And wounded, would not rush upon thy sword,

BOOK II

Take thence his death, and make the murder thine?
Do thou live on thy peaceful life apart
As on their paths the stars unshaken roll.
The lower air that verges on the earth
Gives flame and fury to the levin bolt;
The deeps below the world engulph the winds
And tracts of flaming fire. By Jove's decree
Olympus rears his summit o'er the clouds:
In lowlier valleys storms and winds contend,   310
But peace eternal reigns upon the heights.
What joy for Caesar, if the tidings come
That such a citizen has joined the war?
Glad would he see thee e'en in Magnus' tents;
For Cato's conduct shall approve his own.
Pompeius, with the Consul in his ranks,
And half the Senate and the other chiefs,
Vexes my spirit; and should Cato too
Bend to a master's yoke, in all the world
The one man free is Caesar. But if thou   310
For freedom and thy country's laws alone
Be pleased to raise the sword, nor Magnus then
Nor Caesar shall in Brutus find a foe.
Not till the fight is fought shall Brutus strike,
Then strike the victor."

       Brutus thus; but spake
Cato from inmost breast these sacred words:
"Chief in all wickedness is civil war,
Yet virtue in the paths marked out by fate
Treads on securely. Heaven's will be the crime   330
To have made even Cato guilty. Who has strength
To gaze unawed upon a toppling world?
When stars and sky fall headlong, and when earth
Slips from her base, who sits with folded hands?
Shall unknown nations, touched by western strife,
And monarchs born beneath another clime
Brave the dividing seas to join the war?
Shall Scythian tribes desert their distant north,
And Getae haste to view the fall of Rome,
And I look idly on? As some fond sire,   340
Reft of his sons, compelled by grief, himself

33

Marshals the long procession to the tomb,
Thrusts his own hand within the funeral flames,
Soothing his heart, and, as the lofty pyre
Rises on high, applies the kindled torch:
Nought, Rome, shall tear thee from me, till I hold
Thy form in death embraced; and Freedom's name,
Shade though it be, I'll follow to the grave.
Yea! let the cruel gods exact in full
Rome's expiation: of no drop of blood   350
The war be robbed. I would that, to the gods
Of heaven and hell devoted, this my life
Might satisfy their vengeance. Decius fell,
Crushed by the hostile ranks. When Cato falls
Let Rhine's fierce barbarous hordes and both the hosts
Thrust through my frame their darts! May I alone
Receive in death the wounds of all the war!
Thus may the people be redeemed, and thus
Rome for her guilt pay the atonement due.
Why should men die who wish to bear the yoke   360
And shrink not from the tyranny to come?
Strike me, and me alone, of laws and rights
In vain the guardian: this vicarious life
Shall give Hesperia peace and end her toils.
Who then will reign shall find no need for war.
You ask, 'Why follow Magnus? If he wins [1]
He too will claim the Empire of the world.'
Then let him, conquering with my service, learn
Not for himself to conquer." Thus he spoke
And stirred the blood that ran in Brutus' veins   370
Moving the youth to action in the war.

Soon as the sun dispelled the chilly night,
The sounding doors flew wide, and from the tomb
Of dead Hortensius grieving Marcia came [2].

---

[1] So Cicero: "Our Cnaeus is wonderfully anxious for such a royalty as Sulla's.
I who tell you know it." ("Ep. ad Att.", ix. 7.)
[2] Marcia was first married to Cato, and bore him three sons; he then yielded
her to Hortensius. On his death she returned to Cato. (Plutarch, "Cato", 25,
52.) It was in reference to this that Caesar charged him with making a traffic
of his marriage; but Plutarch says "to accuse Cato of filthy lucre is like up-

First joined in wedlock to a greater man
Three children did she bear to grace his home:
Then Cato to Hortensius gave the dame
To be a fruitful mother of his sons
And join their houses in a closer tie.
And now the last sad offices were done   380
She came with hair dishevelled, beaten breast,
And ashes on her brow, and features worn
With grief; thus only pleasing to the man.
"When youth was in me and maternal power
I did thy bidding, Cato, and received
A second husband: now in years grown old
Ne'er to be parted I return to thee.
Renew our former pledges undefiled:
Give back the name of wife: upon my tomb
Let 'Marcia, spouse to Cato,' be engraved.   390
Nor let men question in the time to come,
Did'st thou compel, or did I willing leave
My first espousals. Not in happy times,
Partner of joys, I come; but days of care
And labour shall be mine to share with thee.
Nor leave me here, but take me to the camp,
Thy fond companion: why should Magnus' wife
Be nearer, Cato, to the wars than thine?"

Although the times were warlike and the fates
Called to the fray, he lent a willing ear.   400
Yet must they plight their faith in simple form
Of law; their witnesses the gods alone.
No festal wreath of flowers crowned the gate
Nor glittering fillet on each post entwined;
No flaming torch was there, nor ivory steps,
No couch with robes of broidered gold adorned;
No comely matron placed upon her brow
The bridal garland, or forbad the foot [1]

---

braiding Hercules with cowardice." After the marriage Marcia remained at
Rome while Cato hurried after Pompeius.
[1] The bride was carried over the threshold of her new home, for to stumble on
it would be of evil omen. Plutarch ("Romulus") refers this custom to the rape

To touch the threshold stone; no saffron veil
Concealed the timid blushes of the bride;   410
No jewelled belt confined her flowing robe [1]
Nor modest circle bound her neck; no scarf
Hung lightly on the snowy shoulder's edge
Around the naked arm. Just as she came,
Wearing the garb of sorrow, while the wool
Covered the purple border of her robe,
Thus was she wedded. As she greets her sons
So doth she greet her husband. Festal games
Graced not their nuptials, nor were friends and kin
As by the Sabines bidden: silent both   420
They joined in marriage, yet content, unseen
By any save by Brutus. Sad and stern
On Cato's lineaments the marks of grief
Were still unsoftened, and the hoary hair
Hung o'er his reverend visage; for since first
Men flew to arms, his locks were left unkempt
To stream upon his brow, and on his chin
His beard untended grew. 'Twas his alone
Who hated not, nor loved, for all mankind
To mourn alike. Nor did their former couch   430
Again receive them, for his lofty soul
E'en lawful love resisted. 'Twas his rule
Inflexible, to keep the middle path
Marked out and bounded; to observe the laws
Of natural right; and for his country's sake
To risk his life, his all, as not for self
Brought into being, but for all the world:
Such was his creed. To him a sumptuous feast
Was hunger conquered, and the lowly hut,
Which scarce kept out the winter, was a home   440
Equal to palaces: a robe of price
Such hairy garments as were worn of old:

---

of the Sabine women, who were "so lift up and carried away by force."
(North, volume i., p. 88, Edition by Windham.) I have read "vetuit" in this
passage, though "vitat" appears to be a better variation according to the man-
uscripts.
[1] The bride was dressed in a long white robe, bound round the waist with a
girdle. She had a veil of bright yellow colour. ("Dict. Antiq.")

BOOK II

The end of marriage, offspring. To the State
Father alike and husband, right and law
He ever followed with unswerving step:
No thought of selfish pleasure turned the scale
In Cato's acts, or swayed his upright soul.

Meanwhile Pompeius led his trembling host
To fields Campanian, and held the walls
First founded by the chief of Trojan race [1].   450
These chose he for the central seat of war,
Some troops despatching who might meet the foe
Where shady Apennine lifts up the ridge
Of mid Italia; nearest to the sky
Upsoaring, with the seas on either hand,
The upper and the lower. Pisa's sands
Breaking the margin of the Tuscan deep,
Here bound his mountains: there Ancona's towers
Laved by Dalmatian waves. Rivers immense,
In his recesses born, pass on their course,   460
To either sea diverging. To the left
Metaurus, and Crustumium's torrent, fall
And Sena's streams and Aufidus who bursts
On Adrian billows; and that mighty flood
Which, more than all the rivers of the earth,
Sweeps down the soil and tears the woods away
And drains Hesperia's springs. In fabled lore
His banks were first by poplar shade enclosed: [2]
And when by Phaethon the waning day
Was drawn in path transverse, and all the heaven   470
Blazed with his car aflame, and from the depths
Of inmost earth were rapt all other floods,
Padus still rolled in pride of stream along.
Nile were no larger, but that o'er the sand
Of level Egypt he spreads out his waves;

---

[1] Capua, supposed to be founded by Capys, the Trojan hero. (Virgil, "Aeneid", x., 145.)
[2] Phaethon's sisters, who yoked the horses of the Sun to the chariot for their brother, were turned into poplars. Phaethon was flung by Jupiter into the river Po.

Nor Ister, if he sought the Scythian main
Unhelped upon his journey through the world
By tributary waters not his own.
But on the right hand Tiber has his source,
Deep-flowing Rutuba, Vulturnus swift,   480
And Sarnus breathing vapours of the night
Rise there, and Liris with Vestinian wave
Still gliding through Marica's shady grove,
And Siler flowing through Salernian meads:
And Macra's swift unnavigable stream
By Luna lost in Ocean. On the Alps
Whose spurs strike plainwards, and on fields of Gaul
The cloudy heights of Apennine look down
In further distance: on his nearer slopes
The Sabine turns the ploughshare; Umbrian kine   490
And Marsian fatten; with his pineclad rocks
He girds the tribes of Latium, nor leaves
Hesperia's soil until the waves that beat
On Scylla's cave compel. His southern spurs
Extend to Juno's temple, and of old
Stretched further than Italia, till the main
O'erstepped his limits and the lands repelled.
But, when the seas were joined, Pelorus claimed
His latest summits for Sicilia's isle.

Caesar, in rage for war, rejoicing found   500
Foes in Italia; no bloodless steps
Nor vacant homes had pleased him [1]; so his march
Were wasted: now the coming war was joined
Unbroken to the past; to force the gates
Not find them open, fire and sword to bring
Upon the harvests, not through fields unharmed
To pass his legions -- this was Caesar's joy;
In peaceful guise to march, this was his shame.
Italia's cities, doubtful in their choice,
Though to the earliest onset of the war   510
About to yield, strengthened their walls with mounds

---

[1] See the note to Book I., 164. In reality Caesar found little resistance, and
did not ravage the country.

And deepest trench encircling: massive stones
And bolts of war to hurl upon the foe
They place upon the turrets. Magnus most
The people's favour held, yet faith with fear
Fought in their breasts. As when, with strident blast,
A southern tempest has possessed the main
And all the billows follow in its track:
Then, by the Storm-king smitten, should the earth
Set Eurus free upon the swollen deep, 520
It shall not yield to him, though cloud and sky
Confess his strength; but in the former wind
Still find its master. But their fears prevailed,
And Caesar's fortune, o'er their wavering faith.
For Libo fled Etruria; Umbria lost
Her freedom, driving Thermus [1] from her bounds;
Great Sulla's son, unworthy of his sire,
Feared at the name of Caesar: Varus sought
The caves and woods, when smote the hostile horse
The gates of Auximon; and Spinther driven 530
From Asculum, the victor on his track,
Fled with his standards, soldierless; and thou,
Scipio, did'st leave Nuceria's citadel
Deserted, though by bravest legions held
Sent home by Caesar for the Parthian war [2];
Whom Magnus earlier, to his kinsman gave
A loan of Roman blood, to fight the Gaul.

But brave Domitius held firm his post [3]
Behind Corfinium's ramparts; his the troops
Who newly levied kept the judgment hall 540
At Milo's trial [1]. When from far the plain

---

[1] Thermus. to whom Iguvium had been entrusted by the Senate, was compelled to quit it owing to the disaffection of the inhabitants. (Merivale, chapter xiv.) Auximon in a similar way rose against Varus.
[2] After Caesar's campaign with the Nervii, Pompeius had lent him a legion. When the Parthian war broke out and the Senate required each of the two leaders to supply a legion for it, Pompeius demanded the return of the legion which he had sent to Gaul; and Caesar returned it, together with one of his own. They were, however, retained in Italy.
[3] See Book VII., 695.

Rolled up a dusty cloud, beneath whose veil
The sheen of armour glistening in the sun,
Revealed a marching host. "Dash down," he cried,
Swift; as ye can, the bridge that spans the stream;
And thou, O river, from thy mountain source
With all thy torrents rushing, planks and beams
Ruined and broken on thy foaming breast
Bear onward to the sea. The war shall stop
Here, to our triumph; for this headlong chief   550
Here first at our firm bidding shall be stayed."
He bade his squadrons, speeding from the walls,
Charge on the bridge: in vain: for Caesar saw
They sought to free the river from his chains [2]
And bar his march; and roused to ire, he cried:
"Were not the walls sufficient to protect
Your coward souls? Seek ye by barricades
And streams to keep me back? What though the flood
Of swollen Ganges were across my path?
Now Rubicon is passed, no stream on earth   560
Shall hinder Caesar! Forward, horse and foot,
And ere it totters rush upon the bridge."
Urged in their swiftest gallop to the front
Dashed the light horse across the sounding plain;
And suddenly, as storm in summer, flew
A cloud of javelins forth, by sinewy arms
Hurled at the foe; the guard is put to flight,
And conquering Caesar, seizing on the bridge,
Compels the enemy to keep the walls.
Now do the mighty engines, soon to hurl   570
Gigantic stones, press forward, and the ram
Creeps 'neath the ramparts; when the gates fly back,
And lo! the traitor troops, foul crime in war,
Yield up their leader. Him they place before

His proud compatriot; yet with upright form,
And scornful features and with noble mien,

---

[1] See Book I., 368.
[2] That is to say, by the breaking of the bridge, the river would become a serious obstacle to Caesar.

He asks his death. But Caesar knew his wish
Was punishment, and pardon was his fear:
"Live though thou would'st not," so the chieftain spake,
"And by my gift, unwilling, see the day: 580
Be to my conquered foes the cause of hope,
Proof of my clemency -- or if thou wilt
Take arms again -- and should'st thou conquer, count
This pardon nothing." Thus he spake, and bade
Let loose the bands and set the captive free.
Ah! better had he died, and fortune spared
The Roman's last dishonour, whose worse doom
It is, that he who joined his country's camp
And fought with Magnus for the Senate's cause
Should gain for this -- a pardon! Yet he curbed   590
His anger, thinking, "Wilt thou then to Rome
And peaceful scenes, degenerate? Rather war,
The furious battle and the certain end!
Break with life's ties: be Caesar's gift in vain."

Pompeius, ignorant that his captain thus
Was taken, armed his levies newly raised
To give his legions strength; and as he thought
To sound his trumpets with the coming dawn,
To test his soldiers ere he moved his camp
Thus in majestic tones their ranks addressed: 600
"Soldiers of Rome! Avengers of her laws!
To whom the Senate gives no private arms,
Ask by your voices for the battle sign.
Fierce falls the pillage on Hesperian fields,
And Gallia's fury o'er the snowy Alps [1]
Is poured upon us. Caesar's swords at last
Are red with Roman blood. But with the wound
We gain the better cause; the crime is theirs.
No war is this, but for offended Rome
We wreak the vengeance; as when Catiline   610
Lifted against her roofs the flaming brand
And, partner in his fury, Lentulus,
And mad Cethegus [1] with his naked arm.

---

[1] See line 497.

41

Is such thy madness, Caesar? when the Fates
With great Camillus' and Metellus' names
Might place thine own, dost thou prefer to rank
With Marius and Cinna? Swift shall be
Thy fall: as Lepidus before the sword
Of Catulus; or who my axes felt,
Carbo [2], now buried in Sicanian tomb;   620
Or who, in exile, roused Iberia's hordes,
Sertorius -- yet, witness Heaven, with these
I hate to rank thee; hate the task that Rome
Has laid upon me, to oppose thy rage.
Would that in safety from the Parthian war
And Scythian steppes had conquering Crassus come!
Then haply had'st thou fallen by the hand
That smote vile Spartacus the robber foe.
But if among my triumphs fate has said
Thy conquest shall be written, know this heart   630
Still sends the life blood coursing: and this arm [3]
Still vigorously flings the dart afield.
He deems me slothful. Caesar, thou shalt learn
We brook not peace because we lag in war.
Old, does he call me? Fear not ye mine age.
Let me be elder, if his soldiers are.
The highest point a citizen can reach
And leave his people free, is mine: a throne
Alone were higher; whoso would surpass
Pompeius, aims at that. Both Consuls stand   640
Here; here for battle stand your lawful chiefs:
And shall this Caesar drag the Senate down?
Not with such blindness, not so lost to shame
Does Fortune rule. Does he take heart from Gaul:
For years on years rebellious, and a life
Spent there in labour? or because he fled

---

[1] This family is also alluded to by Horace ("Ars Poetica,") as having worn a
garment of ancient fashion leaving their arms bare. (See also Book VI., 945.)
[2] In B.C. 77, after the death of Sulla, Carbo had been defeated by Pompeius in
81 B.C., in which occasion Pompeius had, at the early age of twenty-five,
demanded and obtained his first triumph. The war with Sertorius lasted till
71 B.C., when Pompeius and Metellus triumphed in respect of his overthrow.
[3] See Book I., line 369.

Rhine's icy torrent and the shifting pools
He calls an ocean? or unchallenged sought
Britannia's cliffs; then turned his back in flight?
Or does he boast because his citizens   650
Were driven in arms to leave their hearths and homes?
Ah, vain delusion! not from thee they fled:
My steps they follow -- mine, whose conquering signs
Swept all the ocean [1], and who, ere the moon
Twice filled her orb and waned, compelled to flight
The pirate, shrinking from the open sea,
And humbly begging for a narrow home
In some poor nook on shore. 'Twas I again
Who, happier far than Sulla, drave to death [2]
That king who, exiled to the deep recess   660
Of Scythian Pontus, held the fates of Rome
Still in the balances. Where is the land
That hath not seen my trophies? Icy waves
Of northern Phasis, hot Egyptian shores,
And where Syene 'neath its noontide sun
Knows shade on neither hand [3]: all these have learned
To fear Pompeius: and far Baetis' [4] stream,
Last of all floods to join the refluent sea.
Arabia and the warlike hordes that dwell
Beside the Euxine wave: the famous land   670
That lost the golden fleece; Cilician wastes,
And Cappadocian, and the Jews who pray
Before an unknown God; Sophene soft --
All felt my yoke. What conquests now remain,

---

[1] In B.C. 67, Pompeius swept the pirates off the seas. The whole campaign did not last three months.
[2] From B.C. 66 to B.C. 63, Pompeius conquered Mithridates, Syria and the East, except Parthia.
[3] Being (as was supposed) exactly under the Equator. Syene (the modern Assouan) is the town mentioned by the priest of Sais, who told Herodotus that "between Syene and Elephantine are two hills with conical tops. The name of one of them is Crophi, and of the other, Mophi. Midway between them are the fountains of the Nile." (Herod., II., chapter 28.) And see "Paradise Regained," IV., 70: -- "Syene, and where the shadow both way falls, "Meroe, Nilotick isle;..."
[4] Baetis is the Guadalquivir.

What wars not civil can my kinsman wage?"

No loud acclaim received his words, nor shout
Asked for the promised battle: and the chief
Drew back the standards, for the soldier's fears
Were in his soul alike; nor dared he trust
An army, vanquished by the fame alone   680
Of Caesar's powers, to fight for such a prize.
And as some bull, his early combat lost,
Forth driven from the herd, in exile roams
Through lonely plains or secret forest depths,
Whets on opposing trunks his growing horn,
And proves himself for battle, till his neck
Is ribbed afresh with muscle: then returns,
Defiant of the hind, and victor now
Leads wheresoe'er he will his lowing bands:
Thus Magnus, yielding to a stronger foe,   690
Gave up Italia, and sought in flight
Brundusium's sheltering battlements.

                    Here of old
Fled Cretan settlers when the dusky sail [1]
Spread the false message of the hero dead;
Here, where Hesperia, curving as a bow,
Draws back her coast, a little tongue of land
Shuts in with bending horns the sounding main.
Yet insecure the spot, unsafe in storm,
Were it not sheltered by an isle on which   700
The Adriatic billows dash and fall,
And tempests lose their strength: on either hand
A craggy cliff opposing breaks the gale
That beats upon them, while the ships within
Held by their trembling cables ride secure.
Hence to the mariner the boundless deep
Lies open, whether for Corcyra's port
He shapes his sails, or for Illyria's shore,
And Epidamnus facing to the main

---

[1] Theseus, on returning from his successful exploit in Crete, hoisted by mistake black sails instead of white, thus spreading false intelligence of disaster.

44

Ionian. Here, when raging in his might   710
Fierce Adria whelms in foam Calabria's coast,
When clouds tempestuous veil Ceraunus' height,
The sailor finds a haven.

           When the chief
Could find no hope in battle on the soil
He now was quitting, and the lofty Alps
Forbad Iberia, to his son he spake,
The eldest scion of that noble stock:
"Search out the far recesses of the earth,
Nile and Euphrates, wheresoe'er the fame   720
Of Magnus lives, where, through thy father's deeds,
The people tremble at the name of Rome.
Lead to the sea again the pirate bands;
Rouse Egypt's kings; Tigranes, wholly mine,
And Pharnaces and all the vagrant tribes
Of both Armenias; and the Pontic hordes,
Warlike and fierce; the dwellers on the hills
Rhipaean, and by that dead northern marsh
Whose frozen surface bears the loaded wain.
Why further stay thee? Let the eastern world   730
Sound with the war, all cities of the earth
Conquered by me, as vassals, to my camp
Send all their levied hosts. And you whose names
Within the Latian book recorded stand,
Strike for Epirus with the northern wind;
And thence in Greece and Macedonian tracts,
(While winter gives us peace) new strength acquire
For coming conflicts." They obey his words
And loose their ships and launch upon the main.

But Caesar's might, intolerant of peace   740
Or lengthy armistice, lest now perchance
The fates might change their edicts, swift pursued
The footsteps of his foe. To other men,
So many cities taken at a blow,
So many strongholds captured, might suffice;
And Rome herself, the mistress of the world,
Lay at his feet, the greatest prize of all.
Not so with Caesar: instant on the goal

He fiercely presses; thinking nothing done
While aught remained to do. Now in his grasp   750
Lay all Italia; -- but while Magnus stayed
Upon the utmost shore, his grieving soul
Deemed all was shared with him. Yet he essayed
Escape to hinder, and with labour vain
Piled in the greedy main gigantic rocks:
Mountains of earth down to the sandy depths
Were swallowed by the vortex of the sea;
Just as if Eryx and its lofty top
Were cast into the deep, yet not a speck
Should mark the watery plain; or Gaurus huge   760
Split from his summit to his base, were plunged
In fathomless Avernus' stagnant pool.
The billows thus unstemmed, 'twas Caesar's will
To hew the stately forests and with trees
Enchained to form a rampart. Thus of old
(If fame be true) the boastful Persian king
Prepared a way across the rapid strait
'Twixt Sestos and Abydos, and made one
The European and the Trojan shores;
And marched upon the waters, wind and storm   770
Counting as nought, but trusting his emprise
To one frail bridge, so that his ships might pass
Through middle Athos. Thus a mighty mole
Of fallen forests grew upon the waves,
Free until then, and lofty turrets rose,
And land usurped the entrance to the main.

This when Pompeius saw, with anxious care
His soul was filled; yet hoping to regain
The exit lost, and win a wider world
Wherein to wage the war, on chosen ships   780
He hoists the sails; these, driven by the wind
And drawn by cables fastened to their prows,
Scattered the beams asunder; and at night
Not seldom engines, worked by stalwart arms,
Flung flaming torches forth. But when the time
For secret flight was come, no sailor shout
Rang on the shore, no trumpet marked the hour,
No bugle called the armament to sea.

Already shone the Virgin in the sky
Leading the Scorpion in her course, whose claws   790
Foretell the rising Sun, when noiseless all
They cast the vessels loose; no song was heard
To greet the anchor wrenched from stubborn sand;
No captain's order, when the lofty mast
Was raised, or yards were bent; a silent crew
Drew down the sails which hung upon the ropes,
Nor shook the mighty cables, lest the wind
Should sound upon them. But the chief, in prayer,
Thus spake to Fortune: "Thou whose high decree
Has made us exiles from Italia's shores,   800
Grant us at least to leave them." Yet the fates
Hardly permitted, for a murmur vast
Came from the ocean, as the countless keels
Furrowed the waters, and with ceaseless splash
The parted billows rose again and fell.
Then were the gates thrown wide; for with the fates
The city turned to Caesar: and the foe,
Seizing the town, rushed onward by the pier
That circled in the harbour; then they knew
With shame and sorrow that the fleet was gone   810
And held the open: and Pompeius' flight
Gave a poor triumph.

        Yet was narrower far
The channel which gave access to the sea
Than that Euboean strait [1] whose waters lave
The shore by Chalcis. Here two ships stuck fast
Alone, of all the fleet; the fatal hook
Grappled their decks and drew them to the land,
And the first bloodshed of the civil war
Here left a blush upon the ocean wave.   820
As when the famous ship [2] sought Phasis' stream
The rocky gates closed in and hardly gripped
Her flying stern; then from the empty sea
The cliffs rebounding to their ancient seat

---

[1] It seems that the Euripus was bridged over. (Mr. Haskins' note.)
[2] The "Argo".

Were fixed to move no more. But now the steps
Of morn approaching tinged the eastern sky
With roseate hues: the Pleiades were dim,
The wagon of the Charioteer grew pale,
The planets faded, and the silvery star
Which ushers in the day, was lost in light.   830

Then Magnus, hold'st the deep; yet not the same
Now are thy fates, as when from every sea
Thy fleet triumphant swept the pirate pest.
Tired of thy conquests, Fortune now no more
Shall smile upon thee. With thy spouse and sons,
Thy household gods, and peoples in thy train,
Still great in exile, in a distant land
Thou seek'st thy fated fall; not that the gods,
Wishing to rob thee of a Roman grave,
Decreed the strands of Egypt for thy tomb: 840
'Twas Italy they spared, that far away
Fortune on shores remote might hide her crime,
And Roman soil be pure of Magnus' blood.

BOOK III

MASSILIA

With canvas yielding to the western wind
The navy sailed the deep, and every eye
Gazed on Ionian billows. But the chief
Turned not his vision from his native shore
Now left for ever, while the morning mists
Drew down upon the mountains, and the cliffs
Faded in distance till his aching sight
No longer knew them. Then his wearied frame
Sank in the arms of sleep. But Julia's shape,
In mournful guise, dread horror on her brow,   10
Rose through the gaping earth, and from her tomb
Erect [1], in form as of a Fury spake:
"Driven from Elysian fields and from the plains
The blest inhabit, when the war began,
I dwell in Stygian darkness where abide
The souls of all the guilty. There I saw
Th' Eumenides with torches in their hands
Prepared against thy battles; and the fleets [2]
Which by the ferryman of the flaming stream
Were made to bear thy dead: while Hell itself   20
Relaxed its punishments; the sisters three

---

[1] Reading adscenso, as Francken (Leyden, 1896).
[2] So: "The rugged Charon fainted,   And asked a navy, rather than a
boat,   To ferry over the sad world that came."
            (Ben Jonson, "Catiline", Act i., scene 1.)

With busy fingers all their needful task
Could scarce accomplish, and the threads of fate
Dropped from their weary hands. With me thy wife,
Thou, Magnus, leddest happy triumphs home:
New wedlock brings new luck. Thy concubine,
Whose star brings all her mighty husbands ill,
Cornelia, weds in thee a breathing tomb. [1]
Through wars and oceans let her cling to thee
So long as I may break thy nightly rest: 30
No moment left thee for her love, but all
By night to me, by day to Caesar given.
Me not the oblivious banks of Lethe's stream
Have made forgetful; and the kings of death
Have suffered me to join thee; in mid fight
I will be with thee, and my haunting ghost
Remind thee Caesar's daughter was thy spouse.
Thy sword kills not our pledges; civil war
Shall make thee wholly mine." She spake and fled.
But he, though heaven and hell thus bode defeat,   40
More bent on war, with mind assured of ill,
"Why dread vain phantoms of a dreaming brain?
Or nought of sense and feeling to the soul
Is left by death; or death itself is nought."

Now fiery Titan in declining path
Dipped to the waves, his bright circumference
So much diminished as a growing moon
Not yet full circled, or when past the full;
When to the fleet a hospitable coast
Gave access, and the ropes in order laid,   50
The sailors struck the masts and rowed ashore.

When Caesar saw the fleet escape his grasp
And hidden from his view by lengthening seas,
Left without rival on Hesperian soil,
He found no joy in triumph; rather grieved
That thus in safety Magnus' flight was sped.

---

[1] I take "tepido busto" as the dative case; and, as referring to Pompeius,
doomed, like Cornelia's former husband, to defeat and death.

Not any gifts of Fortune now sufficed
His fiery spirit; and no victory won,
Unless the war was finished with the stroke.
Then arms he laid aside, in guise of peace   60
Seeking the people's favour; skilled to know
How to arouse their ire, and how to gain
The popular love by corn in plenty given.
For famine only makes a city free;
By gifts of food the tyrant buys a crowd
To cringe before him: but a people starved
Is fearless ever.

       Curio he bids
Cross over to Sicilian cities, where
Or ocean by a sudden rise o'erwhelmed   70
The land, or split the isthmus right in twain,
Leaving a path for seas. Unceasing tides
There labour hugely lest again should meet
The mountains rent asunder. Nor were left
Sardinian shores unvisited: each isle
Is blest with noble harvests which have filled
More than all else the granaries of Rome,
And poured their plenty on Hesperia's shores.
Not even Libya, with its fertile soil,
Their yield surpasses, when the southern wind   80
Gives way to northern and permits the clouds
To drop their moisture on the teeming earth.
This ordered, Caesar leads his legions on,
Not armed for war, but as in time of peace
Returning to his home. Ah! had he come
With only Gallia conquered and the North [1],
What long array of triumph had he brought!
What pictured scenes of battle! how had Rhine
And Ocean borne his chains! How noble Gaul,
And Britain's fair-haired chiefs his lofty car   90
Had followed! Such a triumph had he lost

---

[1] It may be remarked that, in B.C. 46, Caesar, after the battle of Thapsus, celebrated four triumphs: for his victories over the Gauls, Ptolemaeus, Pharnaces, and Juba.

By further conquest. Now in silent fear
They watched his marching troops, nor joyful towns
Poured out their crowds to welcome his return.
Yet did the conqueror's proud soul rejoice,
Far more than at their love, at such a fear.

Now Anxur's hold was passed, the oozy road
That separates the marsh, the grove sublime [1]
Where reigns the Scythian goddess, and the path
By which men bear the fasces to the feast   100
On Alba's summit. From the height afar --
Gazing in awe upon the walls of Rome
His native city, since the Northern war
Unseen, unvisited -- thus Caesar spake:
"Who would not fight for such a god-like town?
And have they left thee, Rome, without a blow?
Thank the high gods no eastern hosts are here
To wreak their fury; nor Sarmatian horde
With northern tribes conjoined; by Fortune's gift
This war is civil: else this coward chief   110
Had been thy ruin."

       Trembling at his feet
He found the city: deadly fire and flame,
As from a conqueror, gods and fanes dispersed;
Such was the measure of their fear, as though
His power and wish were one. No festal shout
Greeted his march, no feigned acclaim of joy.
Scarce had they time for hate. In Phoebus' hall
Their hiding places left, a crowd appeared
Of Senators, uncalled, for none could call.   120
No Consul there the sacred shrine adorned
Nor Praetor next in rank, and every seat
Placed for the officers of state was void:
Caesar was all; and to his private voice [2]
All else were listeners. The fathers sat
Ready to grant a temple or a throne,

---

[1] Near Aricia. (See Book VI., 92.)
[2] He held no office at the time.

If such his wish; and for themselves to vote
Or death or exile. Well it was for Rome

That Caesar blushed to order what they feared.
Yet in one breast the spirit of freedom rose   130
Indignant for the laws; for when the gates
Of Saturn's temple hot Metellus saw,
Were yielding to the shock, he clove the ranks
Of Caesar's troops, and stood before the doors
As yet unopened. 'Tis the love of gold
Alone that fears not death; no hand is raised
For perished laws or violated rights:
But for this dross, the vilest cause of all,
Men fight and die. Thus did the Tribune bar
The victor's road to rapine, and with voice   140
Clear ringing spake: "Save o'er Metellus dead
This temple opens not; my sacred blood
Shall flow, thou robber, ere the gold be thine.
And surely shall the Tribune's power defied
Find an avenging god; this Crassus knew [1],
Who, followed by our curses, sought the war
And met disaster on the Parthian plains.
Draw then thy sword, nor fear the crowd that gapes
To view thy crimes: the citizens are gone.
Not from our treasury reward for guilt   150
Thy hosts shall ravish: other towns are left,
And other nations; wage the war on them --
Drain not Rome's peace for spoil." The victor then,
Incensed to ire: "Vain is thy hope to fall
In noble death, as guardian of the right;
With all thine honours, thou of Caesar's rage
Art little worthy: never shall thy blood
Defile his hand. Time lowest things with high
Confounds not yet so much that, if thy voice
Could save the laws, it were not better far   160
They fell by Caesar." Such his lofty words.

---

[1] The tribune Ateius met Crassus as he was setting out from Rome and de-
nounced him with mysterious and ancient curses. (Plutarch, "Crassus", 16.)

But as the Tribune yielded not, his rage
Rose yet the more, and at his soldiers' swords
One look he cast, forgetting for the time
What robe he wore; but soon Metellus heard
These words from Cotta: "When men bow to power
Freedom of speech is only Freedom's bane [1],
Whose shade at least survives, if with free will
Thou dost whate'er is bidden thee. For us
Some pardon may be found: a host of ills   170
Compelled submission, and the shame is less
That to have done which could not be refused.
Yield, then, this wealth, the seeds of direful war.
A nation's anger is by losses stirred,
When laws protect it; but the hungry slave
Brings danger to his master, not himself."

At this Metellus yielded from the path;
And as the gates rolled backward, echoed loud
The rock Tarpeian, and the temple's depths
Gave up the treasure which for centuries   180
No hand had touched: all that the Punic foe
And Perses and Philippus conquered gave,
And all the gold which Pyrrhus panic-struck
Left when he fled: that gold [2], the price of Rome,
Which yet Fabricius sold not, and the hoard
Laid up by saving sires; the tribute sent
By Asia's richest nations; and the wealth
Which conquering Metellus brought from Crete,
And Cato [3] bore from distant Cyprus home;
And last, the riches torn from captive kings   190
And borne before Pompeius when he came
In frequent triumph. Thus was robbed the shrine,
And Caesar first brought poverty to Rome.

---

[1] That is, the liberty remaining to the people is destroyed by speaking freely
to the tyrant.
[2] That is, the gold offered by Pyrrhus, and refused by Fabricius, which, after
the final defeat of Pyrrhus, came into the possession of the victors.
[3] See Plutarch, "Cato", 34, 39.

BOOK III

Meanwhile all nations of the earth were moved
To share in Magnus' fortunes and the war,
And in his fated ruin. Graecia sent,
Nearest of all, her succours to the host.
From Cirrha and Parnassus' double peak
And from Amphissa, Phocis sent her youth:
Boeotian leaders muster in the meads   200
By Dirce laved, and where Cephisus rolls
Gifted with fateful power his stream along:
And where Alpheus, who beyond the sea [1]
In fount Sicilian seeks the day again.
Pisa deserted stands, and Oeta, loved
By Hercules of old; Dodona's oaks
Are left to silence by the sacred train,
And all Epirus rushes to the war.
And proud Athena, mistress of the seas,
Sends three poor ships (alas! her all) to prove   210
Her ancient victory o'er the Persian King.
Next seek the battle Creta's hundred tribes
Beloved of Jove and rivalling the east
In skill to wing the arrow from the bow.
The walls of Dardan Oricum, the woods
Where Athamanians wander, and the banks
Of swift Absyrtus foaming to the main
Are left forsaken. Enchelaean tribes
Whose king was Cadmus, and whose name records
His transformation [2], join the host; and those   220
Who till Penean fields and turn the share
Above Iolcos in Thessalian lands."
There first men steeled their hearts to dare the waves [3]
And 'gainst the rage of ocean and the storm
To match their strength, when the rude Argo sailed
Upon that distant quest, and spurned the shore,

---

[1] It was generally believed that the river Alpheus of the Peloponnesus passed under the sea and reappeared in the fountain of Arethusa at Syracuse. A goblet was said to have been thrown into the river in Greece, and to have reappeared in the Sicilian fountain. See the note in Grote's "History of Greece", Edition 1863, vol. ii., p. 8.)
[2] As a serpent. XXXXX is the Greek word for serpent.
[3] Conf. Book VI., 473.

Joining remotest nations in her flight,
And gave the fates another form of death.
Left too was Pholoe; pretended home
Where dwelt the fabled race of double form [1];   230
Arcadian Maenalus; the Thracian mount
Named Haemus; Strymon whence, as autumn falls,
Winged squadrons seek the banks of warmer Nile;
And all the isles the mouths of Ister bathe
Mixed with the tidal wave; the land through which
The cooling eddies of Caicus flow
Idalian; and Arisbe bare of glebe.
The hinds of Pitane, and those who till
Celaenae's fields which mourned of yore the gift
Of Pallas [2], and the vengeance of the god,   240
All draw the sword; and those from Marsyas' flood
First swift, then doubling backwards with the stream
Of sinuous Meander: and from where
Pactolus leaves his golden source and leaps
From Earth permitting; and with rival wealth
Rich Hermus parts the meads. Nor stayed the bands
Of Troy, but (doomed as in old time) they joined
Pompeius' fated camp: nor held them back
The fabled past, nor Caesar's claimed descent
From their Iulus. Syrian peoples came   250
From palmy Idumea and the walls
Of Ninus great of yore; from windy plains
Of far Damascus and from Gaza's hold,
From Sidon's courts enriched with purple dye,
And Tyre oft trembling with the shaken earth.
All these led on by Cynosura's light [3]

---

[1] The Centaurs.

[2] Probably the flute thrown away by Pallas, which Marsyas picked up and
then challenged Apollo to a musical contest. For his presumption the god had
him flayed alive.

[3] That is, the Little Bear, by which the Phoenicians steered, while the Greeks
steered by the Great Bear. (See Sir G. Lewis's "Astronomy of the Ancients",
p. 447.) In Book VI., line 193, the pilot declares that he steers by the pole
star itself, which is much nearer to the Little than to the Great Bear, and is (I
believe) reckoned as one of the stars forming the group known by that name.
He may have been a Phoenician.

Furrow their certain path to reach the war.

Phoenicians first (if story be believed)
Dared to record in characters; for yet
Papyrus was not fashioned, and the priests   260
Of Memphis, carving symbols upon walls
Of mystic sense (in shape of beast or fowl)
Preserved the secrets of their magic art.

Next Persean Tarsus and high Taurus' groves
Are left deserted, and Corycium's cave;
And all Cilicia's ports, pirate no more,
Resound with preparation. Nor the East
Refused the call, where furthest Ganges dares,
Alone of rivers, to discharge his stream
Against the sun opposing; on this shore [1]   270
The Macedonian conqueror stayed his foot
And found the world his victor; here too rolls
Indus his torrent with Hydaspes joined
Yet hardly feels it; here from luscious reed
Men draw sweet liquor; here they dye their locks
With tints of saffron, and with coloured gems
Bind down their flowing garments; here are they,
Who satiate of life and proud to die,
Ascend the blazing pyre, and conquering fate,
Scorn to live longer; but triumphant give   280
The remnant of their days in flame to heaven. [2]

Nor fails to join the host a hardy band
Of Cappadocians, tilling now the soil,
Once pirates of the main: nor those who dwell
Where steep Niphates hurls the avalanche,
And where on Median Coatra's sides
The giant forest rises to the sky.

---

[1] He did not in fact reach the Ganges, as is well known.
[2] Perhaps in allusion to the embassy from India to Augustus in B.C. 19, when
Zarmanochanus, an Indian sage, declaring that he had lived in happiness and
would not risk the chance of a reverse, burnt himself publicly. (Merivale,
chapter xxxiv.)

And you, Arabians, from your distant home
Came to a world unknown, and wondering saw
The shadows fall no longer to the left. [1]   290
Then fired with ardour for the Roman war
Oretas came, and far Carmania's chiefs,
Whose clime lies southward, yet men thence descry
Low down the Pole star, and Bootes runs
Hasting to set, part seen, his nightly course;
And Ethiopians from that southern land
Which lies without the circuit of the stars,
Did not the Bull with curving hoof advanced
O'erstep the limit. From that mountain zone
They come, where rising from a common fount   300
Euphrates flows and Tigris, and did earth
Permit, were joined with either name; but now
While like th' Egyptian flood Euphrates spreads
His fertilising water, Tigris first
Drawn down by earth in covered depths is plunged
And holds a secret course; then born again
Flows on unhindered to the Persian sea.

But warlike Parthia wavered 'twixt the chiefs,
Content to have made them two [2]; while Scythia's hordes
Dipped fresh their darts in poison, whom the stream   310
Of Bactros bounds and vast Hyrcanian woods.
Hence springs that rugged nation swift and fierce,
Descended from the Twins' great charioteer. [3]
Nor failed Sarmatia, nor the tribes that dwell
By richest Phasis, and on Halys' banks,
Which sealed the doom of Croesus' king; nor where
From far Rhipaean ranges Tanais flows,
On either hand a quarter of the world,
Asia and Europe, and in winding course
Carves out a continent; nor where the strait   320

---

[1] That is to say, looking towards the west; meaning that they came from the other side of the equator. (See Book IX., 630.)
[2] See Book I., 117.
[3] A race called Heniochi, said to be descended from the charioteer of Castor and Pollux.

In boiling surge pours to the Pontic deep
Maeotis' waters, rivalling the pride
Of those Herculean pillar-gates that guard
The entrance to an ocean. Thence with hair
In golden fillets, Arimaspians came,
And fierce Massagetae, who quaff the blood
Of the brave steed on which they fight and flee.

Not when great Cyrus on Memnonian realms
His warriors poured; nor when, their weapons piled, [1]
The Persian told the number of his host;   330
Nor when th' avenger [2] of a brother's shame
Loaded the billows with his mighty fleet,
Beneath one chief so many kings made war;
Nor e'er met nations varied thus in garb
And thus in language. To Pompeius' death
Thus Fortune called them: and a world in arms
Witnessed his ruin. From where Afric's god,
Two-horned Ammon, rears his temple, came
All Libya ceaseless, from the wastes that touch
The bounds of Egypt to the shore that meets   340
The Western Ocean. Thus, to award the prize
Of Empire at one blow, Pharsalia brought
'Neath Caesar's conquering hand the banded world.

Now Caesar left the walls of trembling Rome
And swift across the cloudy Alpine tops
He winged his march; but while all others fled
Far from his path, in terror of his name,
Phocaea's [1] manhood with un-Grecian faith

---

[1] "Effusis telis". I have so taken this difficult expression. Herodotus (7, 60)
says the men were numbered in ten thousands by being packed close together
and having a circle drawn round them. After the first ten thousand had been
so measured a fence was put where the circle had been, and the subsequent
ten thousands were driven into the enclosure. It is not unlikely that they piled
their weapons before being so measured, and Lucan's account would then be
made to agree with that of Herodotus. Francken, on the other hand, quotes a
Scholiast, who says that each hundredth man shot off an arrow.
[2] Agamemnon.

Held to their pledged obedience, and dared
To follow right not fate; but first of all   350
With olive boughs of truce before them borne
The chieftain they approach, with peaceful words
In hope to alter his unbending will
And tame his fury. "Search the ancient books
Which chronicle the deeds of Latian fame;
Thou'lt ever find, when foreign foes pressed hard,
Massilia's prowess on the side of Rome.
And now, if triumphs in an unknown world
Thou seekest, Caesar, here our arms and swords
Accept in aid: but if, in impious strife   360
Of civil discord, with a Roman foe
Thou seek'st to join in battle, weeping then
We hold aloof: no stranger hand may touch
Celestial wounds. Should all Olympus' hosts
Have rushed to war, or should the giant brood
Assault the stars, yet men would not presume
Or by their prayers or arms to help the gods:
And, ignorant of the fortunes of the sky,
Taught by the thunderbolts alone, would know
That Jupiter supreme still held the throne.   370
Add that unnumbered nations join the fray:
Nor shrinks the world so much from taint of crime
That civil wars reluctant swords require.
But grant that strangers shun thy destinies
And only Romans fight -- shall not the son
Shrink ere he strike his father? on both sides
Brothers forbid the weapon to be hurled?
The world's end comes when other hands are armed [2]
Than those which custom and the gods allow.
For us, this is our prayer: Leave, Caesar, here   380
Thy dreadful eagles, keep thy hostile signs
Back from our gates, but enter thou in peace

---

[1] Massilia (Marseilles) was founded from Phocaea in Asia Minor about 600
B.C. Lucan (line 393) appears to think that the founders were fugitives from
their city when it was stormed by the Persians sixty years later. See Thucydi-
des I. 13; Grote, "History of Greece", chapter xxii.
[2] A difficult passage, of which this seems to be the meaning least free from
objection.

Massilia's ramparts; let our city rest
Withdrawn from crime, to Magnus and to thee
Safe: and should favouring fate preserve our walls
Inviolate, when both shall wish for peace
Here meet unarmed. Why hither turn'st thou now
Thy rapid march? Nor weight nor power have we
To sway the mighty conflicts of the world.
We boast no victories since our fatherland   390
We left in exile: when Phocaea's fort
Perished in flames, we sought another here;
And here on foreign shores, in narrow bounds
Confined and safe, our boast is sturdy faith;
Nought else. But if our city to blockade
Is now thy mind -- to force the gates, and hurl
Javelin and blazing torch upon our homes --
Do what thou wilt: cut off the source that fills
Our foaming river, force us, prone in thirst,
To dig the earth and lap the scanty pool;   400
Seize on our corn and leave us food abhorred:
Nor shall this people shun, for freedom's sake,
The ills Saguntum bore in Punic siege; [1]
Torn, vainly clinging, from the shrunken breast
The starving babe shall perish in the flames.
Wives at their husbands' hands shall pray their fate,
And brothers' weapons deal a mutual death.
Such be our civil war; not, Caesar, thine."

But Caesar's visage stern betrayed his ire
Which thus broke forth in words: "Vain is the hope   410
Ye rest upon my march: speed though I may
Towards my western goal, time still remains
To blot Massilia out. Rejoice, my troops!
Unsought the war ye longed for meets you now:
The fates concede it. As the tempests lose
Their strength by sturdy forests unopposed,
And as the fire that finds no fuel dies,
Even so to find no foe is Caesar's ill.

---

[1] Murviedro of the present day. Its gallant defence against Hannibal has been
compared to that of Saragossa against the French.

When those who may be conquered will not fight
That is defeat. Degenerate, disarmed   420
Their gates admit me! Not content, forsooth,
With shutting Caesar out they shut him in!
They shun the taint of war! Such prayer for peace
Brings with it chastisement. In Caesar's age
Learn that not peace, but war within his ranks
Alone can make you safe."

          Fearless he turns
His march upon the city, and beholds
Fast barred the gate-ways, while in arms the youths
Stand on the battlements. Hard by the walls   430
A hillock rose, upon the further side
Expanding in a plain of gentle slope,
Fit (as he deemed it) for a camp with ditch
And mound encircling. To a lofty height
The nearest portion of the city rose,
While intervening valleys lay between.
These summits with a mighty trench to bind
The chief resolves, gigantic though the toil.
But first, from furthest boundaries of his camp,
Enclosing streams and meadows, to the sea   440
To draw a rampart, upon either hand
Heaved up with earthy sod; with lofty towers
Crowned; and to shut Massilia from the land.

Then did the Grecian city win renown
Eternal, deathless, for that uncompelled
Nor fearing for herself, but free to act
She made the conqueror pause: and he who seized
All in resistless course found here delay:
And Fortune, hastening to lay the world
Low at her favourite's feet, was forced to stay   450
For these few moments her impatient hand.

Now fell the forests far and wide, despoiled
Of all their giant trunks: for as the mound
On earth and brushwood stood, a timber frame
Held firm the soil, lest pressed beneath its towers
The mass might topple down. There stood a grove

Which from the earliest time no hand of man
Had dared to violate; hidden from the sun [1]
Its chill recesses; matted boughs entwined
Prisoned the air within. No sylvan nymphs   460
Here found a home, nor Pan, but savage rites
And barbarous worship, altars horrible
On massive stones upreared; sacred with blood
Of men was every tree. If faith be given
To ancient myth, no fowl has ever dared
To rest upon those branches, and no beast
Has made his lair beneath: no tempest falls,
Nor lightnings flash upon it from the cloud.
Stagnant the air, unmoving, yet the leaves
Filled with mysterious trembling; dripped the streams   470
From coal-black fountains; effigies of gods
Rude, scarcely fashioned from some fallen trunk
Held the mid space: and, pallid with decay,
Their rotting shapes struck terror. Thus do men
Dread most the god unknown. 'Twas said that caves
Rumbled with earthquakes, that the prostrate yew
Rose up again; that fiery tongues of flame
Gleamed in the forest depths, yet were the trees
Unkindled; and that snakes in frequent folds
Were coiled around the trunks. Men flee the spot   480
Nor dare to worship near: and e'en the priest
Or when bright Phoebus holds the height, or when
Dark night controls the heavens, in anxious dread
Draws near the grove and fears to find its lord.

Spared in the former war, still dense it rose
Where all the hills were bare, and Caesar now
Its fall commanded. But the brawny arms
Which swayed the axes trembled, and the men,
Awed by the sacred grove's dark majesty,
Held back the blow they thought would be returned.   490
This Caesar saw, and swift within his grasp
Uprose a ponderous axe, which downward fell
Cleaving a mighty oak that towered to heaven,

---

[1] See note to Book I., 506.

While thus he spake: "Henceforth let no man dread
To fell this forest: all the crime is mine.
This be your creed." He spake, and all obeyed,
For Caesar's ire weighed down the wrath of Heaven.
Yet ceased they not to fear. Then first the oak,
Dodona's ancient boast; the knotty holm;
The cypress, witness of patrician grief,   500
The buoyant alder, laid their foliage low
Admitting day; though scarcely through the stems
Their fall found passage. At the sight the Gauls
Grieved; but the garrison within the walls
Rejoiced: for thus shall men insult the gods
And find no punishment? Yet fortune oft
Protects the guilty; on the poor alone
The gods can vent their ire. Enough hewn down,
They seize the country wagons; and the hind,
His oxen gone which else had drawn the plough,   510
Mourns for his harvest.

          But the eager chief
Impatient of the combat by the walls
Carries the warfare to the furthest west.

Meanwhile a giant mound, on star-shaped wheels
Concealed, they fashion, crowned with double towers
High as the battlements, by cause unseen
Slow creeping onwards; while amazed the foe,
Beheld, and thought some subterranean gust
Had burst the caverns of the earth and forced   520
The nodding pile aloft, and wondered sore
Their walls should stand unshaken. From its height
Hissed clown the weapons; but the Grecian bolts
With greater force were on the Romans hurled;
Nor by the arm unaided, for the lance
Urged by the catapult resistless rushed
Through arms and shield and flesh, and left a death
Behind, nor stayed its course: and massive stones
Cast by the beams of mighty engines fell;
As from the mountain top some time-worn rock   530
At length by winds dislodged, in all its track
Spreads ruin vast: nor crushed the life alone

Forth from the body, but dispersed the limbs
In fragments undistinguished and in blood.
But as protected by the armour shield
The might of Rome drew nigh beneath the wall
(The front rank with their bucklers interlaced
And held above their helms), the missiles fell
Behind their backs, nor could the toiling Greeks
Deflect their engines, throwing still the bolts   540
Far into space; but from the rampart top
Flung ponderous masses down. Long as the shields
Held firm together, like to hail that falls
Harmless upon a roof, so long the stones
Crushed down innocuous; but as the blows
Rained fierce and ceaseless and the Romans tired,
Some here and there sank fainting. Next the roof
Advanced with earth besprinkled: underneath
The ram conceals his head, which, poised and swung,
They dash with mighty force upon the wall,   550
Covered themselves with mantlets. Though the head
Light on the lower stones, yet as the shock
Falls and refalls, from battlement to base
The rampart soon shall topple. But by balks
And rocky fragments overwhelmed, and flames,
The roof at length gave way; and worn with toil
All spent in vain, the wearied troops withdrew
And sought the shelter of their tents again.

Thus far to hold their battlements was all
The Greeks had hoped; now, venturing attack,   560
With glittering torches for their arms, by night
Fearless they sallied forth: nor lance they bear
Nor deadly bow, nor shaft; for fire alone
Is now their weapon. Through the Roman works
Driven by the wind the conflagration spread:
Nor did the newness of the wood make pause
The fury of the flames, which, fed afresh
By living torches, 'neath a smoky pall
Leaped on in fiery tongues. Not wood alone
But stones gigantic crumbling into dust   570
Dissolved beneath the heat; the mighty mound
Lay prone, yet in its ruin larger seemed.

Next, conquered on the land, upon the main
They try their fortunes. On their simple craft
No painted figure-head adorned the bows
Nor claimed protection from the gods; but rude,
Just as they fell upon their mountain homes,
The trees were knit together, and the deck
Gave steady foot-hold for an ocean fight.

Meantime had Caesar's squadron kept the isles   580
Named Stoechades [1], and Brutus [2] turret ship
Mastered the Rhone. Nor less the Grecian host --
Boys not yet grown to war, and aged men,
Armed for the conflict, with their all at stake.
Nor only did they marshal for the fight
Ships meet for service; but their ancient keels
Brought from the dockyards. When the morning rays
Broke from the waters, and the sky was clear,
And all the winds were still upon the deep,
Smoothed for the battle, swift on either part   590
The fleets essay the open; and the ships
Tremble beneath the oars that urge them on,
By sinewy arms impelled. Upon the wings
That bound the Roman fleet, the larger craft
With triple and quadruple banks of oars
Gird in the lesser: so they front the sea;
While in their rear, shaped as a crescent moon,
Liburnian galleys follow. Over all
Towers Brutus' deck praetorian. Oars on oars
Propel the bulky vessel through the main,   600
Six ranks; the topmost strike the waves afar.
When such a space remained between the fleets
As could be covered by a single stroke,
Innumerable voices rose in air

---

[1] Three islands off the coast near Toulon, now called the Isles d'Hyeres.
[2] This was Decimus Brutus, an able and trusted lieutenant of Caesar, who
made him one of his heirs in the second degree. He, however, joined the con-
spiracy, and it was he who on the day of the murder induced Caesar to go to
the Senate House. Less than two years later, after the siege of Perasia, he was
deserted by his army, taken and put to death.

Drowning with resonant din the beat of oars
And note of trumpet summoning: and all
Sat on the benches and with mighty stroke
Swept o'er the sea and gained the space between.
Then crashed the prows together, and the keels
Rebounded backwards, and unnumbered darts   610
Or darkened all the sky or, in their fall,
The vacant ocean. As the wings grew wide,
Less densely packed the fleet, some Grecian ships
Pressed in between; as when with west and east
The tide contends, this way the waves are driven
And that the sea; so as they plough the deep
In various lines converging, what the prow
Throws up advancing, from the foemen's oars
Falls back repelled. But soon the Grecian fleet
Was handier found in battle, and in flight   620
Pretended, and in shorter curves could round;
More deftly governed by the guiding helm:
While on the Roman side their steadier keels
Gave vantage, as to men who fight on land.
Then Brutus to the pilot of his ship:
"Dost suffer them to range the wider deep,
Contending with the foe in naval skill?
Draw close the war and drive us on the prows
Of these Phocaeans." Him the pilot heard;
And turned his vessel slantwise to the foe.   630
Then was the sea all covered with the war:
Then Grecian ships attacking Brutus found
Their ruin in the stroke, and vanquished lay
Beside his bulwarks; while with grappling hooks
Others laid fast the foe, themselves by oars
Held back the while. And now no outstretched arm
Hurls forth the javelin, but hand to hand
With swords they wage the fight: each from his ship
Leans forward to the stroke, and falls when slain
Upon a foeman's deck. Deep flows the stream   640
Of purple slaughter to the foamy main:
By piles of floating corpses are the sides,
Though grappled, kept asunder. Some, half dead,
Plunge in the ocean, gulping down the brine
Encrimsoned with their blood; some lingering still

Draw their last struggling breath amid the wreck
Of broken navies: weapons which have missed
Find yet their victims, and the falling steel
Fails not in middle deep to deal the wound.
One vessel circled by Phocaean keels   650
Divides her strength, and on the right and left
On either side with equal war contends;
On whose high poop while Tagus fighting gripped
The stern Phocaean, pierced his back and breast
Two fatal weapons; in the midst the steel
Meets, and the blood, uncertain whence to flow,
Stands still, arrested, till with double course
Forth by a sudden gush it drives each dart,
And sends the life abroad through either wound.

Here fated Telon also steered his ship: 660
No pilot's hand upon an angry sea
More deftly ruled a vessel. Well he knew,
Or by the sun or crescent moon, how best
To set his canvas fitted for the breeze
To-morrow's light would bring. His rushing stem
Shattered a Roman vessel: but a dart
Hurled at the moment quivers in his breast.
He falls, and in the fall his dying hand
Diverts the prow. Then Gyareus, in act
To climb the friendly deck, by javelin pierced,   670
Still as he hung, by the retaining steel
Fast to the side was nailed.
                    Twin brethren stand
A fruitful mother's pride; with different fates,
But ne'er distinguished till death's savage hand
Struck once, and ended error: he that lived,
Cause of fresh anguish to their sorrowing souls,
Called ever to the weeping parents back
The image of the lost: who, as the oars
Grecian and Roman mixed their teeth oblique,   680
Grasped with his dexter hand the Roman ship;
When fell a blow that shore his arm away.
So died, upon the side it held, the hand,
Nor loosed its grasp in death. Yet with the wound
His noble courage rose, and maimed he dared

Renew the fray, and stretched across the sea
To grasp the lost -- in vain! another blow
Lopped arm and hand alike. Nor shield nor sword
Henceforth are his. Yet even now he seeks
No sheltering hold, but with his chest advanced   690
Before his brother armed, he claims the fight,
And holding in his breast the darts which else
Had slain his comrades, pierced with countless spears,
He fails in death well earned; yet ere his end
Collects his parting life, and all his strength
Strains to the utmost and with failing limbs
Leaps on the foeman's deck; by weight alone
Injurious; for streaming down with gore
And piled on high with corpses, while her sides
Sounded to ceaseless blows, the fated ship   700
Let in the greedy brine until her ways
Were level with the waters -- then she plunged
In whirling eddies downwards -- and the main
First parted, then closed in upon its prey.

Full many wondrous deaths, with fates diverse,
Upon the sea in that day's fight befell.
Caught by a grappling-hook that missed the side,
Had Lysidas been whelmed in middle deep;
But by his feet his comrades dragged him back,
And rent in twain he hung; nor slowly flowed   710
As from a wound the blood; but all his veins [1]
Were torn asunder and the stream of life
Gushed o'er his limbs till lost amid the deep.
From no man dying has the vital breath
Rushed by so wide a path; the lower trunk
Succumbed to death, but with the lungs and heart
Long strove the fates, and hardly won the whole.

While, bent upon the fight, an eager crew
Were gathered to the margin of their deck
(Leaving the upper side as bare of foes),   720

---

[1] According to some these were the lines which Lucan recited while bleeding to death; according to others, those at Book ix., line 952.

Their ship was overset. Beneath the keel
Which floated upwards, prisoned in the sea,
And powerless by spread of arms to float
The main, they perished. One who haply swam
Amid the battle, chanced upon a death
Strange and unheard of; for two meeting prows
Transfixed his body. At the double stroke
Wide yawned his chest; blood issued from his mouth
With flesh commingled; and the brazen beaks
Resounding clashed together, by the bones   730
Unhindered: now they part and through the gap
Swift pours the sea and drags the corse below.
Next, of a shipwrecked crew, the larger part
Struggling with death upon the waters, reached
A comrade bark; but when with elbows raised do
They seized upon the bulwarks and the ship
Rolled, nor could bear their weight, the ruthless crew
Hacked off their straining arms; then maimed they sank
Below the seething waves, to rise no more.

Now every dart was hurled and every spear,   740
The soldier weaponless; yet their rage found arms:
One hurls an oar; another's brawny arm
Tugs at the twisted stern; or from the seats
The oarsmen driving, swings a bench in air.
The ships are broken for the fight. They seize
The fallen dead and snatch the sword that slew.
Nay, many from their wounds, frenzied for arms,
Pluck forth the deadly steel, and pressing still
Upon their yawning sides, hurl forth the spear
Back to the hostile ranks from which it came;   750
Then ebbs their life blood forth.

                    But deadlier yet
Was that fell force most hostile to the sea;
For, thrown in torches and in sulphurous bolts
Fire all-consuming ran among the ships,
Whose oily timbers soaked in pitch and wax
Inflammable, gave welcome to the flames.
Nor could the waves prevail against the blaze
Which claimed as for its own the fragments borne

Upon the waters. Lo! on burning plank   760
One hardly 'scapes destruction; one to save
His flaming ship, gives entrance to the main.
Of all the forms of death each fears the one
That brings immediate dying: yet quails not
Their heart in shipwreck: from the waves they pluck
The fallen darts and furnishing the ship
Essay the feeble stroke; and should that hope
Still fail their hand, they call the sea to aid
And seizing in their grasp some floating foe
Drag him to mutual death.   770

          But on that day
Phoceus above all others proved his skill.
Well trained was he to dive beneath the main
And search the waters with unfailing eye;
And should an anchor 'gainst the straining rope
Too firmly bite the sands, to wrench it free.
Oft in his fatal grasp he seized a foe
Nor loosed his grip until the life was gone.
Such was his frequent deed; but this his fate:
For rising, victor (as he thought), to air,   780
Full on a keel he struck and found his death.
Some, drowning, seized a hostile oar and checked
The flying vessel; not to die in vain,
Their single care; some on their vessel's side
Hanging, in death, with wounded frame essayed
To check the charging prow.

          Tyrrhenus high
Upon the bulwarks of his ship was struck
By leaden bolt from Balearic sling
Of Lygdamus; straight through his temples passed   790
The fated missile; and in streams of blood
Forced from their seats his trembling eyeballs fell.
Plunged in a darkness as of night, he thought
That life had left him; yet ere long he knew
The living rigour of his limbs; and cried,
"Place me, O friends, as some machine of war
Straight facing towards the foe; then shall my darts
Strike as of old; and thou, Tyrrhenus, spend

Thy latest breath, still left, upon the fight:
So shalt thou play, not wholly dead, the part   800
That fits a soldier, and the spear that strikes
Thy frame, shall miss the living." Thus he spake,
And hurled his javelin, blind, but not in vain;
For Argus, generous youth of noble blood,
Below the middle waist received the spear
And failing drave it home. His aged sire
From furthest portion of the conquered ship
Beheld; than whom in prime of manhood none,
More brave in battle: now no more he fought,
Yet did the memory of his prowess stir   810
Phocaean youths to emulate his fame.
Oft stumbling o'er the benches the old man hastes
To reach his boy, and finds him breathing still.
No tear bedewed his cheek, nor on his breast
One blow he struck, but o'er his eyes there fell
A dark impenetrable veil of mist
That blotted out the day; nor could he more
Discern his luckless Argus. He, who saw
His parent, raising up his drooping head
With parted lips and silent features asks   820
A father's latest kiss, a father's hand
To close his dying eyes. But soon his sire,
Recovering from his swoon, when ruthless grief
Possessed his spirit, "This short space," he cried,
"I lose not, which the cruel gods have given,
But die before thee. Grant thy sorrowing sire
Forgiveness that he fled thy last embrace.
Not yet has passed thy life blood from the wound
Nor yet is death upon thee -- still thou may'st [1]
Outlive thy parent." Thus he spake, and seized   830
The reeking sword and drave it to the hilt,
Then plunged into the deep, with headlong bound,
To anticipate his son: for this he feared
A single form of death should not suffice.

---

[1] It was regarded as the greatest of misfortunes if a child died before his parent.

BOOK III

Now gave the fates their judgment, and in doubt
No longer was the war: the Grecian fleet
In most part sunk; -- some ships by Romans oared
Conveyed the victors home: in headlong flight
Some sought the yards for shelter. On the strand
What tears of parents for their offspring slain,   840
How wept the mothers! 'Mid the pile confused
Ofttimes the wife sought madly for her spouse
And chose for her last kiss some Roman slain;
While wretched fathers by the blazing pyres
Fought for the dead. But Brutus thus at sea
First gained a triumph for great Caesar's arms. [1]

---

[1] It was Brutus who gained the naval victory over the Veneti some seven years before; the first naval fight, that we know of, fought in the Atlantic Ocean.

BOOK IV

CAESAR IN SPAIN. WAR IN THE ADRIATIC SEA. DEATH OF CURIO.

But in the distant regions of the earth
Fierce Caesar warring, though in fight he dealt
No baneful slaughter, hastened on the doom
To swift fulfillment. There on Magnus' side
Afranius and Petreius [1] held command,
Who ruled alternate, and the rampart guard
Obeyed the standard of each chief in turn.
There with the Romans in the camp were joined
Asturians [2] swift, and Vettons lightly armed,
And Celts who, exiled from their ancient home,   10
Had joined "Iberus" to their former name.
Where the rich soil in gentle slope ascends
And forms a modest hill, Ilerda [3] stands,
Founded in ancient days; beside her glides
Not least of western rivers, Sicoris
Of placid current, by a mighty arch

---

[1] Both of these generals were able and distinguished officers. Afranius was slain by Caesar's soldiers after the battle of Thapsus. Petreius, after the same battle, escaped along with Juba; and failing to find a refuge, they challenged each other to fight. Petreius was killed, and Juba, the survivor, put an end to himself.

[2] These are the names of Spanish tribes. The Celtiberi dwelt on the Ebro.

[3] Lerida, on the river Segre, above its junction with the Ebro. Cinga is the modern Cinca, which falls into the Segre (Sicoris).

Of stone o'erspanned, which not the winter floods
Shall overwhelm. Upon a rock hard by
Was Magnus' camp; but Caesar's on a hill,
Rivalling the first; and in the midst a stream.   20
Here boundless plains are spread beyond the range
Of human vision; Cinga girds them in
With greedy waves; forbidden to contend
With tides of ocean; for that larger flood
Who names the land, Iberus, sweeps along
The lesser stream commingled with his own.

Guiltless of war, the first day saw the hosts
In long array confronted; standard rose
Opposing standard, numberless; yet none
Essayed attack, in shame of impious strife.   30
One day they gave their country and her laws.
But Caesar, when from heaven fell the night,
Drew round a hasty trench; his foremost rank
With close array concealing those who wrought.
Then with the morn he bids them seize the hill
Which parted from the camp Ilerda's walls,
And gave them safety. But in fear and shame
On rushed the foe and seized the vantage ground,
First in the onset. From the height they held
Their hopes of conquest; but to Caesar's men   40
Their hearts by courage stirred, and their good swords
Promised the victory. Burdened up the ridge
The soldier climbed, and from the opposing steep
But for his comrade's shield had fallen back;
None had the space to hurl the quivering lance
Upon the foeman: spear and pike made sure
The failing foothold, and the falchion's edge
Hewed out their upward path. But Caesar saw
Ruin impending, and he bade his horse
By circuit to the left, with shielded flank,   50
Hold back the foe. Thus gained his troops retreat,
For none pressed on them; and the victor chiefs,
Forced to withdrawal, gained the day in vain.

Henceforth the fitful changes of the year
Governed the fates and fashioned out the war.

For stubborn frost still lay upon the land,
And northern winds, controlling all the sky,
Prisoned the rain in clouds; the hills were nipped
With snow unmelted, and the lower plains
By frosts that fled before the rising sun;   60
And all the lands that stretched towards the sky
Which whelms the sinking stars, 'neath wintry heavens
Were parched and arid. But when Titan neared
The Ram, who, backward gazing on the stars,
Bore perished Helle, [1] and the hours were held
In juster balance, and the day prevailed,
The earliest faded moon which in the vault
Hung with uncertain horn, from eastern winds
Received a fiery radiance; whose blasts
Forced Boreas back: and breaking on the mists   70
Within his regions, to the Occident
Drave all that shroud Arabia and the land
Of Ganges; all that or by Caurus [2] borne
Bedim the Orient sky, or rising suns
Permit to gather; pitiless flamed the day
Behind them, while in front the wide expanse
Was driven; nor on mid earth sank the clouds
Though weighed with vapour. North and south alike
Were showerless, for on Calpe's rock alone
All moisture gathered; here at last, forbidden   80
To pass that sea by Zephyr's bounds contained,
And by the furthest belt [3] of heaven, they pause,
In masses huge convolved; the widest breadth
Of murky air scarce holds them, which divides
Earth from the heavens; till pressed by weight of sky

---

[1] Phrixus and Helle, the children of Nephele, were to be sacrificed to Zeus:
but Nephele rescued them, and they rode away through the air on the Ram
with the golden fleece. But Helle fell into the sea, which from her was named
the Hellespont. (See Book IX., 1126.) The sun enters Aries about March 20.
The Ram is pictured among the constellations with his head averse.
[2] See Book I., 463.
[3] See Mr. Heitland's introduction, upon the meaning of the word "cardo". The
word "belt" seems fairly to answer to the two great circles or four meridians
which he describes. The word occurs again at line 760; Book V., 80; Book
VII., 452.

In densest volume to the earth they pour
Their cataracts; no lightning could endure
Such storm unquenched: though oft athwart the gloom
Gleamed its pale fire. Meanwhile a watery arch
Scarce touched with colour, in imperfect shape   90
Embraced the sky and drank the ocean waves,
So rendering to the clouds their flood outpoured.

And now were thawed the Pyrenaean snows
Which Titan had not conquered; all the rocks
Were wet with melting ice; accustomed springs
Found not discharge; and from the very banks
Each stream received a torrent. Caesar's arms
Are shipwrecked on the field, his tottering camp
Swims on the rising flood; the trench is filled
With whirling waters; and the plain no more   100
Yields corn or kine; for those who forage seek,
Err from the hidden furrow. Famine knocks
(First herald of o'erwhelming ills to come),
Fierce at the door; and while no foe blockades
The soldier hungers; fortunes buy not now
The meanest measure; yet, alas! is found
The fasting peasant, who, in gain of gold,
Will sell his little all! And now the hills
Are seen no more; and rivers whelmed in one;
Beasts with their homes sweep downwards; and the tide   110
Repels the foaming torrent. Nor did night
Acknowledge Phoebus' rise, for all the sky
Felt her dominion and obscured its face,
And darkness joined with darkness. Thus doth lie
The lowest earth beneath the snowy zone
And never-ending winters, where the sky
Is starless ever, and no growth of herb
Sprouts from the frozen earth; but standing ice
Tempers [1] the stars which in the middle zone
Kindle their flames. Thus, Father of the world,   120
And thou, trident-god who rul'st the sea
Second in place, Neptunus, load the air

---

[1] The idea is that the cold of the poles tempers the heat of the equator.

With clouds continual; forbid the tide,
Once risen, to return: forced by thy waves
Let rivers backward run in different course,
Thy shores no longer reaching; and the earth,
Shaken, make way for floods. Let Rhine o'erflow
And Rhone their banks; let torrents spread afield
Unmeasured waters: melt Rhipaean snows:
Spread lakes upon the land, and seas profound, 130
And snatch the groaning world from civil war.

Thus for a little moment Fortune tried
Her darling son; then smiling to his part
Returned; and gained her pardon for the past
By greater gifts to come. For now the air
Had grown more clear, and Phoebus' warmer rays
Coped with the flood and scattered all the clouds
In fleecy masses; and the reddening east
Proclaimed the coming day; the land resumed
Its ancient marks; no more in middle air 140
The moisture hung, but from about the stars
Sank to the depths; the forest glad upreared
Its foliage; hills again emerged to view
And 'neath the warmth of day the plains grew firm.

When Sicoris kept his banks, the shallop light
Of hoary willow bark they build, which bent
On hides of oxen, bore the weight of man
And swam the torrent. Thus on sluggish Po
Venetians float; and on th' encircling sea [1]
Are borne Britannia's nations; and when Nile 150
Fills all the land, are Memphis' thirsty reeds
Shaped into fragile boats that swim his waves.
The further bank thus gained, they haste to curve
The fallen forest, and to form the arch

---

[1] Fuso: either spacious, outspread; or, poured into the land (referring to the estuaries) as Mr. Haskins prefers; or, poured round the island. Portable leathern skiffs seem to have been in common use in Caesar's time in the English Channel. These were the rowing boats of the Gauls. (Mommsen, vol. iv., 219.)

By which imperious Sicoris shall be spanned.
Yet fearing he might rise in wrath anew,
Not on the nearest marge they placed the beams,
But in mid-field. Thus the presumptuous stream
They tame with chastisement, parting his flood
In devious channels out; and curb his pride.   160

Petreius, when he saw that Caesar's fates
Swept all before them, left Ilerda's steep,
His trust no longer in the Roman world;
And sought for strength amid those distant tribes,
Who, loving death, rush in upon the foe, [1]
And win their conquests at the point of sword.
But in the dawn, when Caesar saw the camp
Stand empty on the hill, "To arms!" he cried:
"Seek not the bridge nor ford: plunge in the stream
And breast the foaming torrent." Then did hope   170
Of coming battle find for them a way
Which they had shunned in flight.

                    Their arms regained,
Their streaming limbs they cherished till the blood
Coursed in their veins; until the shadows fell
Short on the sward, and day was at the height.
Then dashed the horsemen on, and held the foe
'Twixt flight and battle. In the plain arose
Two rocky heights: from each a loftier ridge
Of hills ranged onwards, sheltering in their midst   180
A hollow vale, whose deep and winding paths
Were safe from warfare; which, when Caesar saw:
That if Petreius held, the war must pass
To lands remote by savage tribes possessed;
"Speed on," he cried, "and meet their flight in front;
Fierce be your frown and battle in your glance:
No coward's death be theirs; but as they flee
Plunge in their breasts the sword." They seize the pass
And place their camp. Short was the span between
Th' opposing sentinels; with eager eyes   190

---

[1] Compare Book I., 519.

Undimmed by space, they gazed on brothers, sons,
Or friends and fathers; and within their souls
They grasped the impious horror of the war.
Yet for a little while no voice was heard,
For fear restrained; by waving blade alone
Or gesture, spake they; but their passion grew,
And broke all discipline; and soon they leaped
The hostile rampart; every hand outstretched [1]
Embraced the hand of foeman, palm in palm;
One calls by name his neighhour, one his host,   200
Another with his schoolmate talks again
Of olden studies: he who in the camp
Found not a comrade, was no son of Rome.
Wet are their arms with tears, and sobs break in
Upon their kisses; each, unstained by blood,
Dreads what he might have done. Why beat thy breast?
Why, madman, weep? The guilt is thine alone
To do or to abstain. Dost fear the man
Who takes his title to be feared from thee?
When Caesar's trumpets sound the call to arms   210
Heed not the summons; when thou seest advance
His standards, halt. The civil Fury thus
Shall fold her wings; and in a private robe
Caesar shall love his kinsman.

Holy Peace

That sway'st the world; thou whose eternal bands
Sustain the order of material things,
Come, gentle Concord! [2] these our times do now
For good or evil destiny control
The coming centuries! Ah, cruel fate!   220
Now have the people lost their cloak for crime:
Their hope of pardon. They have known their kin.

---

[1] Compare the passage in Tacitus, "Histories", ii., 45, in which the historian describes how the troops of Otho and Vitellius wept over each other after the battle and deplored the miseries of a civil war. "Victi victoresque in lacrumas effusi, sortem civilium armorum misera laetitia detestantes."

[2] "Saecula nostra" may refer either to Lucan's own time or to the moment arrived at in the poem; or it may, as Francken suggests, have a more general meaning.

BOOK IV

Woe for the respite given by the gods
Making more black the hideous guilt to come!

Now all was peaceful, and in either camp
Sweet converse held the soldiers; on the grass
They place the meal; on altars built of turf
Pour out libations from the mingled cup;
On mutual couch with stories of their fights,
They wile the sleepless hours in talk away;   230
"Where stood the ranks arrayed, from whose right hand
The quivering lance was sped:" and while they boast
Or challenge, deeds of prowess in the war,
Faith was renewed and trust. Thus made the fates
Their doom complete, and all the crimes to be;
Grew with their love.

          For when Petreius knew
The treaties made; himself and all his camp
Sold to the foe; he stirs his guard to work
An impious slaughter: the defenceless foe   240
Flings headlong forth: and parts the fond embrace
By stroke of weapon and in streams of blood.
And thus in words of wrath, to stir the war:
"Of Rome forgetful, to your faith forsworn!
And could ye not with victory gained return,
Restorers of her liberty, to Rome?
Lose then! but losing call not Caesar lord.
While still your swords are yours, with blood to shed
In doubtful battle, while the fates are hid,
Will you like cravens to your master bear   250
Doomed eagles? Will you ask upon your knees
That Caesar deign to treat his slaves alike,
And spare, forsooth, like yours, your leaders' lives? [1]
Nay! never shall our safety be the price
Of base betrayal! Not for boon of life
We wage a civil war. This name of peace

---

[1] "Petenda est"? -- "is it fit that you should beg for the lives of your leaders?"
Mr. Haskins says, "shall you have to beg for them?" But it means that to do
so is the height of disgrace.

81

Drags us to slavery. Ne'er from depths of earth,
Fain to withdraw her wealth, should toiling men
Draw store of iron; ne'er entrench a town;
Ne'er should the war-horse dash into the fray   260
Nor fleet with turret bulwarks breast the main,
If freedom for dishonourable peace
Could thus be bought. The foe are pledged to fight
By their own guilt. But you, who still might hope
For pardon if defeated -- what can match
Your deep dishonour? Shame upon your peace.
Thou callest, Magnus, ignorant of fate,
From all the world thy powers, and dost entreat
Monarchs of distant realms, while haply here
We in our treaties bargain for thy life!"   270

Thus did he stir their minds and rouse anew
The love of impious battle. So when beasts
Grown strange to forests, long confined in dens,
Their fierceness lose, and learn to bear with man;
Once should they taste of blood, their thirsty jaws
Swell at the touch, and all the ancient rage
Comes back upon them till they hardly spare
Their keeper. Thus they rush on every crime:
And blows which dealt at chance, and in the night
Of battle, had brought hatred on the gods,   280
Though blindly struck, their recent vows of love
Made monstrous, horrid. Where they lately spread
The mutual couch and banquet, and embraced
Some new-found friend, now falls the fatal blow
Upon the self-same breast; and though at first
Groaning at the fell chance, they drew the sword;
Hate rises as they strike, the murderous arm
Confirms the doubtful will: with monstrous joy
Through the wild camp they smite their kinsmen down;
And carnage raged unchecked; and each man strove,   290
Proud of his crime, before his leader's face
To prove his shamelessness of guilt.

But thou,
Caesar, though losing of thy best, dost know
The gods do favour thee. Thessalian fields

Gave thee no better fortune, nor the waves
That lave Massilia; nor on Pharos' main
Didst thou so triumph. By this crime alone
Thou from this moment of the better cause
Shalt be the Captain.   300

        Since the troops were stained
With foulest slaughter thus, their leaders shunned
All camps with Caesar's joined, and sought again
Ilerda's lofty walls; but Caesar's horse
Seized on the plain and forced them to the hills
Reluctant. There by steepest trench shut in,
He cuts them from the river, nor permits
Their circling ramparts to enclose a spring.

By this dread path Death trapped his captive prey.
Which when they knew, fierce anger filled their souls,   310
And took the place of fear. They slew the steeds
Now useless grown, and rushed upon their fate;
Hopeless of life and flight. But Caesar cried:
"Hold back your weapons, soldiers, from the foe,
Strike not the breast advancing; let the war
Cost me no blood; he falls not without price
Who with his life-blood challenges the fray.
Scorning their own base lives and hating light,
To Caesar's loss they rush upon their death,
Nor heed our blows. But let this frenzy pass,   320
This madman onset; let the wish for death
Die in their souls." Thus to its embers shrank
The fire within when battle was denied,
And fainter grew their rage until the night
Drew down her starry veil and sank the sun.
Thus keener fights the gladiator whose wound
Is recent, while the blood within the veins
Still gives the sinews motion, ere the skin
Shrinks on the bones: but as the victor stands
His fatal thrust achieved, and points the blade   330
Unfaltering, watching for the end, there creeps
Torpor upon the limbs, the blood congeals
About the gash, more faintly throbs the heart,
And slowly fading, ebbs the life away.

Raving for water now they dig the plains
Seeking for hidden fountains, not with spade
And mattock only searching out the depths,
But with the sword; they hack the stony heights,
In shafts that reach the level of the plain.
No further flees from light the pallid wretch 340
Who tears the bowels of the earth for gold.
Yet neither riven stones revealed a spring,
Nor streamlet whispered from its hidden source;
To water trickled on the gravel bed,
Nor dripped within the cavern. Worn at length
With labour huge, they crawl to light again,
After such toil to fall to thirst and heat
The readier victims: this was all they won.
All food they loathe; and 'gainst their deadly thirst
Call famine to their aid. Damp clods of earth 350
They squeeze upon their mouths with straining hands.
Where'er on foulest mud some stagnant slime
Or moisture lies, though doomed to die they lap
With greedy tongues the draught their lips had loathed
Had life been theirs to choose. Beast-like they drain
The swollen udder, and where milk was not,
They sucked the life-blood forth. From herbs and boughs
Dripping with dew, from tender shoots they pressed,
Say, from the pith of trees, the juice within.

Happy the host that onward marching finds 360
Its savage enemy has fouled the wells
With murderous venom; had'st thou, Caesar, cast
The reeking filth of shambles in the stream,
And henbane dire and all the poisonous herbs
That lurk on Cretan slopes, still had they drunk
The fatal waters, rather than endure
Such lingering agony. Their bowels racked
With torments as of flame; the swollen tongue
And jaws now parched and rigid, and the veins;
Each laboured breath with anguish from the lungs 370
Enfeebled, moistureless, was scarcely drawn,
And scarce again returned; and yet agape,
Their panting mouths sucked in the nightly dew;

They watch for showers from heaven, and in despair
Gaze on the clouds, whence lately poured a flood.
Nor were their tortures less that Meroe
Saw not their sufferings, nor Cancer's zone,
Nor where the Garamantian turns the soil;
But Sicoris and Iberus at their feet,
Two mighty floods, but far beyond their reach,   380
Rolled down in measureless volume to the main.

But now their leaders yield; Afranius,
Vanquished, throws down his arms, and leads his troops,
Now hardly living, to the hostile camp
Before the victor's feet, and sues for peace.
Proud was his bearing, and despite of ills,
His mien majestic, of his triumphs past
Still mindful in disaster -- thus he stood,
Though suppliant for grace, a leader yet;
From fearless heart thus speaking: "Had the fates   390
Thrown me before some base ignoble foe,
Not, Caesar, thee; still had this arm fought on
And snatched my death. Now if I suppliant ask,
'Tis that I value still the boon of life
Given by a worthy hand. No party ties
Roused us to arms against thee; when the war,
This civil war, broke out, it found us chiefs;
And with our former cause we kept the faith,
So long as brave men should. The fates' decree
No longer we withstand. Unto thy will   400
We yield the western tribes: the east is thine
And all the world lies open to thy march.
Be generous! blood nor sword nor wearied arm
Thy conquests bought. Thou hast not to forgive
Aught but thy victory won. Nor ask we much.
Give us repose; to lead in peace the life
Thou shalt bestow; suppose these armed lines
Are corpses prostrate on the field of war
Ne'er were it meet that thy victorious ranks

Should mix with ours, the vanquished. Destiny   410
Has run for us its course: one boon I beg;
Bid not the conquered conquer in thy train."

85

Such were his words, and Caesar's gracious smile
Granted his prayer, remitting rights that war
Gives to the victor. To th' unguarded stream
The soldiers speed: prone on the bank they lie
And lap the flood or foul the crowded waves.
In many a burning throat the sudden draught
Poured in too copious, filled the empty veins
And choked the breath within: yet left unquenched   420
The burning pest which though their frames were full
Craved water for itself. Then, nerved once more,
Their strength returned. Oh, lavish luxury,
Contented never with the frugal meal!
Oh greed that searchest over land and sea
To furnish forth the banquet! Pride that joy'st
In sumptuous tables! learn what life requires,
How little nature needs! No ruddy juice
Pressed from the vintage in some famous year,
Whose consuls are forgotten, served in cups   430
With gold and jewels wrought restores the spark,
The failing spark, of life; but water pure
And simplest fruits of earth. The flood, the field
Suffice for nature. Ah! the weary lot
Of those who war! But these, their amour laid
Low at the victor's feet, with lightened breast,
Secure themselves, no longer dealing death,
Beset by care no more, seek out their homes.
What priceless gift in peace had they secured!
How grieved it now their souls to have poised the dart   440
With arm outstretched; to have felt their raving thirst;
And prayed the gods for victory in vain!
Nay, hard they think the victor's lot, for whom
A thousand risks and battles still remain;
If fortune never is to leave his side,
How often must he triumph! and how oft
Pour out his blood where'er great Caesar leads!
Happy, thrice happy, he who, when the world
Is nodding to its ruin, knows the spot
Where he himself shall, though in ruin, lie!   450
No trumpet call shall break his sleep again:
But in his humble home with faithful spouse

And sons unlettered Fortune leaves him free
From rage of party; for if life he owes
To Caesar, Magnus sometime was his lord.
Thus happy they alone live on apart,
Nor hope nor dread the event of civil war.

Not thus did Fortune upon Caesar smile
In all the parts of earth; [1] but 'gainst his arms
Dared somewhat, where Salona's lengthy waste   460
Opposes Hadria, and Iadar warm
Meets with his waves the breezes of the west.
There brave Curectae dwell, whose island home
Is girded by the main; on whom relied
Antonius; and beleaguered by the foe,
Upon the furthest margin of the shore,
(Safe from all ills but famine) placed his camp.
But for his steeds the earth no forage gave,
Nor golden Ceres harvest; but his troops
Gnawed the dry herbage of the scanty turf   470
Within their rampart lines. But when they knew
That Baslus was on th' opposing shore
With friendly force, by novel mode of flight
They aim to reach him. Not the accustomed keel
They lay, nor build the ship, but shapeless rafts
Of timbers knit together, strong to bear
All ponderous weight; on empty casks beneath
By tightened chains made firm, in double rows
Supported; nor upon the deck were placed
The oarsmen, to the hostile dart exposed,   480
But in a hidden space, by beams concealed.
And thus the eye amazed beheld the mass
Move silent on its path across the sea,
By neither sail nor stalwart arm propelled.

They watch the main until the refluent waves
Ebb from the growing sands; then, on the tide
Receding, launch their vessel; thus she floats

---

[1] The scene is the Dalmatian coast of the Adriatic. Here was Diocletian's palace. (Described in the 13th chapter of Gibbon.)

87

With twin companions: over each uprose
With quivering battlements a lofty tower.
Octavius, guardian of Illyrian seas,   490
Restrained his swifter keels, and left the rafts
Free from attack, in hope of larger spoil
From fresh adventures; for the peaceful sea
May tempt them, and their goal in safety reached,
To dare a second voyage. Round the stag
Thus will the cunning hunter draw a line
Of tainted feathers poisoning the air;
Or spread the mesh, and muzzle in his grasp
The straining jaws of the Molossian hound,
And leash the Spartan pack; nor is the brake   500
Trusted to any dog but such as tracks
The scent with lowered nostrils, and refrains
From giving tongue the while; content to mark
By shaking leash the covert of the prey.

Ere long they manned the rafts in eager wish
To quit the island, when the latest glow
Still parted day from night. But Magnus' troops,
Cilician once, taught by their ancient art,
In fraudulent deceit had left the sea
To view unguarded; but with chains unseen   510
Fast to Illyrian shores, and hanging loose,
They blocked the outlet in the waves beneath.
The leading rafts passed safely, but the third
Hung in mid passage, and by ropes was hauled
Below o'ershadowing rocks. These hollowed out
In ponderous masses overhung the main,
And nodding seemed to fall: shadowed by trees
Dark lay the waves beneath. Hither the tide
Brings wreck and corpse, and, burying with the flow,
Restores them with the ebb: and when the caves   520
Belch forth the ocean, swirling billows fall
In boisterous surges back, as boils the tide
In that famed whirlpool on Sicilian shores.

Here, with Venetian settlers for its load,
Stood motionless the raft. Octavius' ships
Gathered around, while foemen on the land

Filled all the shore. But well the captain knew,
Volteius, how the secret fraud was planned,
And tried in vain with sword and steel to burst
The bands that held them; without hope he fights,   530
Uncertain where to avoid or front the foe.
Caught in this strait they strove as brave men should
Against opposing hosts; nor long the fight,
For fallen darkness brought a truce to arms.

Then to his men disheartened and in fear
Of coming fate Volteius, great of soul,
Thus spake in tones commanding: "Free no more,
Save for this little night, consult ye now
In this last moment, soldiers, how to face
Your final fortunes. No man's life is short   540
Who can take thought for death, nor is your fame
Less than a conqueror's, if with breast advanced
Ye meet your destined doom. None know how long
The life that waits them. Summon your own fate,
And equal is your praise, whether the hand
Quench the last flicker of departing light,
Or shear the hope of years. But choice to die
Is thrust not on the mind -- we cannot flee;
See at our throats, e'en now, our kinsmen's swords.
Then choose for death; desire what fate decrees.   550
At least in war's blind cloud we shall not fall;
Nor when the flying weapons hide the day,
And slaughtered heaps of foemen load the field,
And death is common, and the brave man sinks
Unknown, inglorious. Us within this ship,
Seen of both friends and foes, the gods have placed;
Both land and sea and island cliffs shall bear,
From either shore, their witness to our death,
In which some great and memorable fame
Thou, Fortune, dost prepare. What glorious deeds   560
Of warlike heroism, of noble faith,
Time's annals show! All these shall we surpass.
True, Caesar, that to fall upon our swords
For thee is little; yet beleaguered thus,
With neither sons nor parents at our sides,
Shorn of the glory that we might have earned,

We give thee here the only pledge we may.
Yet let these hostile thousands fear the souls
That rage for battle and that welcome death,
And know us for invincible, and joy   570
That no more rafts were stayed. They'll offer terms
And tempt us with a base unhonoured life.
Would that, to give that death which shall be ours
The greater glory, they may bid us hope
For pardon and for life! lest when our swords
Are reeking with our hearts'-blood, they may say
This was despair of living. Great must be
The prowess of our end, if in the hosts
That fight his battles, Caesar is to mourn
This little handful lost. For me, should fate   580
Grant us retreat, -- myself would scorn to shun
The coming onset. Life I cast away,
The frenzy of the death that comes apace
Controls my being. Those alone whose end
Inspires them, know the happiness of death,
Which the high gods, that men may bear to live,
Keep hid from others." Thus his noble words
Warmed his brave comrades' hearts; and who with fear
And tearful eyes had looked upon the Wain,
Turning his nightly course, now hoped for day,   590
Such precepts deep within them. Nor delayed
The sky to dip the stars below the main;
For Phoebus in the Twins his chariot drave
At noon near Cancer; and the hours of night [1]
Were shortened by the Archer.

                    When day broke,
Lo! on the rocks the Istrians; while the sea
Swarmed with the galleys and their Grecian fleet
All armed for fight: but first the war was stayed
And terms proposed: life to the foe they thought   600
Would seem the sweeter, by delay of death
Thus granted. But the band devoted stood,

---

[1] That is, night was at its shortest.

Proud of their promised end, and life forsworn,
And careless of the battle: no debate
Could shake their high resolve. [1] In numbers few
'Gainst foemen numberless by land and sea,
They wage the desperate fight; then satiate
Turn from the foe. And first demanding death
Volteius bared his throat. "What youth," he cries,
"Dares strike me down, and through his captain's wounds   610
Attest his love for death?" Then through his side
Plunge blades uncounted on the moment drawn.
He praises all: but him who struck the first
Grateful, with dying strength, he does to death.
They rush together, and without a foe
Work all the guilt of battle. Thus of yore,
Rose up the glittering Dircaean band
From seed by Cadmus sown, and fought and died,
Dire omen for the brother kings of Thebes.
And so in Phasis' fields the sons of earth,   620
Born of the sleepless dragon, all inflamed
By magic incantations, with their blood
Deluged the monstrous furrow, while the Queen
Feared at the spells she wrought. Devoted thus
To death, they fall, yet in their death itself
Less valour show than in the fatal wounds
They take and give; for e'en the dying hand
Missed not a blow -- nor did the stroke alone
Inflict the wound, but rushing on the sword
Their throat or breast received it to the hilt;   630
And when by fatal chance or sire with son,
Or brothers met, yet with unfaltering weight
Down flashed the pitiless sword: this proved their love,
To give no second blow. Half living now
They dragged their mangled bodies to the side,
Whence flowed into the sea a crimson stream
Of slaughter. 'Twas their pleasure yet to see
The light they scorned; with haughty looks to scan
The faces of their victors, and to feel

---

[1] On the following passage see Dean Merivale's remarks, "History of the Roman Empire", chapter xvi.

The death approaching. But the raft was now   640
Piled up with dead; which, when the foemen saw,
Wondering at such a chief and such a deed,
They gave them burial. Never through the world
Of any brave achievement was the fame
More widely blazed. Yet meaner men, untaught
By such examples, see not that the hand
Which frees from slavery needs no valiant mind
To guide the stroke. But tyranny is feared
As dealing death; and Freedom's self is galled
By ruthless arms; and knows not that the sword   650
Was given for this, that none need live a slave.
Ah Death! would'st thou but let the coward live
And grant the brave alone the prize to die!

Nor less were Libyan fields ablaze with war.
For Curio rash from Lilybaean [1] coast
Sailed with his fleet, and borne by gentle winds
Betwixt half-ruined Carthage, mighty once,
And Clupea's cliff, upon the well-known shore
His anchors dropped. First from the hoary sea
Remote, where Bagra slowly ploughs the sand,   660
He placed his camp: then sought the further hills
And mazy passages of cavernous rocks,
Antaeus' kingdom called. From ancient days
This name was given; and thus a swain retold
The story handed down from sire to son:
"Not yet exhausted by the giant brood,
Earth still another monster brought to birth,
In Libya's caverns: huger far was he,
More justly far her pride, than Briareus
With all his hundred hands, or Typhon fierce,   670
Or Tityos: 'twas in mercy to the gods
That not in Phlegra's [2] fields Antaeus grew,

---

[1] That is, Sicilian.
[2] For Phlegra, the scene of the battle between the giants and the gods, see Book VII., 170, and Book IX., 774. Ben Jonson ("Sejanus", Act v., scene 10) says of Sejanus: --   "Phlegra, the field where all the sons of earth   Mustered against the gods, did ne'er acknowledge   So proud and huge a monster."

But here in Libya; to her offspring's strength,
Unmeasured, vast, she added yet this boon,
That when in weariness and labour spent
He touched his parent, fresh from her embrace
Renewed in rigour he should rise again.
In yonder cave he dwelt, 'neath yonder rock
He made his feast on lions slain in chase:
There slept he; not on skins of beasts, or leaves,   680
But fed his strength upon the naked earth.
Perished the Libyan hinds and those who came,
Brought here in ships, until he scorned at length
The earth that gave him strength, and on his feet
Invincible and with unaided might
Made all his victims. Last to Afric shores,
Drawn by the rumour of such carnage, came
Magnanimous Alcides, he who freed
Both land and sea of monsters. Down on earth
He threw his mantle of the lion's skin   690
Slain in Cleone; nor Antaeus less
Cast down the hide he wore. With shining oil,
As one who wrestles at Olympia's feast,
The hero rubs his limbs: the giant feared
Lest standing only on his parent earth
His strength might fail; and cast o'er all his bulk
Hot sand in handfuls. Thus with arms entwined
And grappling hands each seizes on his foe;
With hardened muscles straining at the neck
Long time in vain; for firm the sinewy throat   700
Stood column-like, nor yielded; so that each
Wondered to find his peer. Nor at the first
Divine Alcides put forth all his strength,
By lengthy struggle wearing out his foe,
Till chilly drops stood on Antaeas' limbs,
And toppled to its fall the stately throat,
And smitten by the hero's blows, the legs
Began to totter. Breast to breast they strive
To gain the vantage, till the victor's arms
Gird in the giant's yielding back and sides,   710
And squeeze his middle part: next 'twixt the thighs
He puts his feet, and forcing them apart,
Lays low the mighty monster limb by limb.

The dry earth drank his sweat, while in his veins
Warm ran the life-blood, and with strength refreshed,
The muscle swelled and all the joints grew firm,
And with his might restored, he breaks his bonds
And rives the arms of Hercules away.
Amazed the hero stood at such a strength.
Not thus he feared, though then unused to war,   720
That hydra fierce, which smitten in the marsh
Of Inachus, renewed its severed heads.
Again they join in fight, one with the powers
Which earth bestowed, the other with his own:
Nor did the hatred of his step-dame [1] find
In all his conflicts greater room for hope.
She sees bedewed in sweat the neck and limbs
Which once had borne the mountain of the gods
Nor knew the toil: and when Antaeus felt
His foeman's arms close round him once again,   730
He flung his wearying limbs upon the sand
To rise with strength renewed; all that the earth,
Though labouring sore, could breathe into her son
She gave his frame. But Hercules at last
Saw how his parent gave the giant strength.
'Stand thou,' he cried; 'no more upon the ground
Thou liest at thy will -- here must thou stay
Within mine arms constrained; against this breast,
Antaeus, shalt thou fall.' He lifted up
And held by middle girth the giant form,   740
Still struggling for the earth: but she no more
Could give her offspring rigour. Slowly came
The chill of death upon him, and 'twas long
Before the hero, of his victory sure,
Trusted the earth and laid the giant down.
Hence hoar antiquity that loves to prate
And wonders at herself [2], this region called
Antaeus' kingdom. But a greater name
It gained from Scipio, when he recalled
From Roman citadels the Punic chief.   750

---

[1] Juno.
[2] That is, extols ancient deeds.

Here was his camp; here can'st thou see the trace
Of that most famous rampart [1] whence at length
Issued the Eagles of triumphant Rome."

But Curio rejoiced, as though for him
The fortunes of the spot must hold in store
The fates of former chiefs: and on the place
Of happy augury placed his tents ill-starred,
Took from the hills their omens; and with force
Unequal, challenged his barbarian foe.

All Africa that bore the Roman yoke   760
Then lay 'neath Varus. He, though placing first
Trust in his Latian troops, from every side
And furthest regions, summons to his aid
The nations who confessed King Juba's rule.
Not any monarch over wider tracts
Held the dominion. From the western belt [2]
Near Gades, Atlas parts their furthest bounds;
But from the southern, Hammon girds them in
Hard by the whirlpools; and their burning plains
Stretch forth unending 'neath the torrid zone,   770
In breadth its equal, till they reach at length
The shore of ocean upon either hand.
From all these regions tribes unnumbered flock
To Juba's standard: Moors of swarthy hue
As though from Ind; Numidian nomads there
And Nasamon's needy hordes; and those whose darts
Equal the flying arrows of the Mede:
Dark Garamantians leave their fervid home;
And those whose coursers unrestrained by bit
Or saddle, yet obey the rider's hand   780
Which wields the guiding switch: the hunter, too,
Who wanders forth, his home a fragile hut,
And blinds with flowing robe (if spear should fail)
The angry lion, monarch of the steppe.

---

[1] Referring to the battle of Zama.
[2] See line 82.

Not eagerness alone to save the state
Stirred Juba's spirit: private hatred too
Roused him to war. For in the former year,
When Curio[1] all things human and the gods
Polluted, he by tribune law essayed
To ravish Libya from the tyrant's sway,   790
And drive the monarch from his father's throne,
While giving Rome a king. To Juba thus,
Still smarting at the insult, came the war,
A welcome harvest for his crown retained.
These rumours Curio feared: nor had his troops
(Ta'en in Corfinium's hold) [2] in waves of Rhine
Been tested, nor to Caesar in the wars
Had learned devotion: wavering in their faith,
Their second chief they doubt, their first betrayed.

Yet when the general saw the spirit of fear   800
Creep through his camp, and discipline to fail,
And sentinels desert their guard at night,
Thus in his fear he spake: "By daring much
Fear is disguised; let me be first in arms,
And bid my soldiers to the plain descend,
While still my soldiers. Idle days breed doubt.
By fight forestall the plot [3]. Soon as the thirst
Of bloodshed fills the mind, and eager hands
Grip firm the sword, and pressed upon the brow
The helm brings valour to the failing heart --   810
Who cares to measure leaders' merits then?
Who weighs the cause? With whom the soldier stands,
For him he fights; as at the fatal show
No ancient grudge the gladiator's arm
Nerves for the combat, yet as he shall strike
He hates his rival." Thinking thus he leads
His troops in battle order to the plain.
Then victory on his arms deceptive shone

---

[1] Curio was tribune in B.C. 50. His earlier years are stated to have been stained with vice.
[2] See Book II., 537.
[3] Preferring the reading "praeripe", with Francken.

96

Hiding the ills to come: for from the field
Driving the hostile host with sword and spear,   820
He smote them till their camp opposed his way.
But after Varus' rout, unseen till then,
All eager for the glory to be his,
By stealth came Juba: silent was his march;
His only fear lest rumour should forestall
His coming victory. In pretended war
He sends Sabura forth with scanty force
To tempt the enemy, while in hollow vale
He holds the armies of his realm unseen.
Thus doth the sly ichneumon [1] with his tail   830
Waving, allure the serpent of the Nile
Drawn to the moving shadow: he, with head
Turned sideways, watches till the victim glides
Within his reach, then seizes by the throat
Behind the deadly fangs: forth from its seat
Balked of its purpose, through the brimming jaws
Gushes a tide of poison. Fortune smiled
On Juba's stratagem; for Curio
(The hidden forces of the foe unknown)
Sent forth his horse by night without the camp   840
To scour more distant regions. He himself
At earliest peep of dawn bids carry forth
His standards; heeding not his captains' prayer
Urged on his ears: "Beware of Punic fraud,
The craft that taints a Carthaginian war."
Hung over him the doom of coming death
And gave the youth to fate; and civil strife
Dragged down its author.

      On the lofty tops
Where broke the hills abruptly to their fall   850
He ranks his troops and sees the foe afar:

---

[1] Bewick ("Quadrupeds," p. 238) tells the following anecdote of a tame ichneumon which had never seen a serpent, and to which he brought a small one. "Its first emotion seemed to be astonishment mixed with anger; its hair became erect; in an instant it slipped behind the reptile, and with remarkable swiftness and agility leaped upon its head, seized it and crushed it with its teeth."

Who still deceiving, simulated flight,
Till from the height in loose unordered lines
The Roman forces streamed upon the plain,
In thought that Juba fled. Then first was known
The treacherous fraud: for swift Numidian horse
On every side surround them: leader, men --
All see their fate in one dread moment come.
No coward flees, no warrior bravely strides
To meet the battle: nay, the trumpet call   860
Stirs not the charger with resounding hoof
To spurn the rock, nor galling bit compels
To champ in eagerness; nor toss his mane
And prick the ear, nor prancing with his feet
To claim his share of combat. Tired, the neck
Droops downwards: smoking sweat bedews the limbs:
Dry from the squalid mouth protrudes the tongue,
Hoarse, raucous panting issues from their chests;
Their flanks distend: and every curb is dry
With bloody foam; the ruthless sword alone   870
Could move them onward, powerless even then
To charge; but giving to the hostile dart
A nearer victim. But when the Afric horse
First made their onset, loud beneath their hoofs
Rang the wide plain, and rose the dust in air
As by some Thracian whirlwind stirred; and veiled
The heavens in darkness. When on Curio's host
The tempest burst, each footman in the rank
Stood there to meet his fate -- no doubtful end
Hung in the balance: destiny proclaimed   880
Death to them all. No conflict hand to hand
Was granted them, by lances thrown from far
And sidelong sword-thrusts slain: nor wounds alone,
But clouds of weapons falling from the air
By weight of iron o'erwhelmed them. Still drew in
The straightening circle, for the first pressed back
On those behind; did any shun the foe,
Seeking the inner safety of the ring,
He needs must perish by his comrades' swords.
And as the front rank fell, still narrower grew   890
The close crushed phalanx, till to raise their swords
Space was denied. Still close and closer forced

The armed breasts against each other driven
Pressed out the life. Thus not upon a scene
Such as their fortune promised, gazed the foe.
No tide of blood was there to glut their eyes,
No members lopped asunder, though the earth so
Was piled with corpses; for each Roman stood
In death upright against his comrade dead.

Let cruel Carthage rouse her hated ghosts   900
By this fell offering; let the Punic shades,
And bloody Hannibal, from this defeat
Receive atonement: yet 'twas shame, ye gods,
That Libya gained not for herself the day;
And that our Romans on that field should die
To save Pompeius and the Senate's cause.

Now was the dust laid low by streams of blood,
And Curio, knowing that his host was slain.
Chose not to live; and, as a brave man should.
He rushed upon the heap, and fighting fell.   910

In vain with turbid speech hast thou profaned
The pulpit of the forum: waved in vain
From that proud [1] citadel the tribune flag:
And armed the people, and the Senate's rights
Betraying, hast compelled this impious war
Betwixt the rival kinsmen. Low thou liest
Before Pharsalus' fight, and from thine eyes
Is hid the war. 'Tis thus to suffering Rome,
For arms seditious and for civil strife
Ye mighty make atonement with your blood.   920
Happy were Rome and all her sons indeed,
Did but the gods as rigidly protect
As they avenge, her violated laws!
There Curio lies; untombed his noble corpse,
Torn by the vultures of the Libyan wastes.
Yet shall we, since such merit, though unsung,

---

[1] Reading "arce", not "arte". The word "signifer" seems to favour the reading
I have preferred; and Dean Merivale and Hosius adopted it.

Lives by its own imperishable fame,
Give thee thy meed of praise. Rome never bore
Another son, who, had he right pursued,
Had so adorned her laws; but soon the times,   930
Their luxury, corruption, and the curse
Of too abundant wealth, in transverse stream
Swept o'er his wavering mind: and Curio changed,
Turned with his change the scale of human things.
True, mighty Sulla, cruel Marius,
And bloody Cinna, and the long descent
Of Caesar and of Caesar's house became
Lords of our lives. But who had power like him?
All others bought the state: he sold alone. [1]

---

[1] For the character and career of Curio, see Merivale's "History of the Roman Empire", chapter xvi. He was of profligate character, but a friend and pupil of Cicero; at first a rabid partisan of the oligarchy, he had, about the period of his tribuneship (B.C. 50-49), become a supporter of Caesar. How far Gaulish gold was the cause of this conversion we cannot tell. It is in allusion to this change that he was termed the prime mover of the civil war. His arrival in Caesar's camp is described in Book I., line 303. He became Caesar's chief lieutenant in place of the deserter Labienus; and, as described in Book III., was sent to Sardinia and Sicily, whence he expelled the senatorial forces. His final expedition to Africa, defeat and death, form the subject of the latter part of this book. Mommsen describes him as a man of talent, and finds a resemblance between him and Caesar. (Vol. iv., p. 393.)

BOOK V

THE ORACLE. THE MUTINY. THE STORM

Thus had the smiles of Fortune and her frowns
Brought either chief to Macedonian shores
Still equal to his foe. From cooler skies
Sank Atlas' [1] daughters down, and Haemus' slopes
Were white with winter, and the day drew nigh
Devoted to the god who leads the months,
And marking with new names the book of Rome,
When came the Fathers from their distant posts
By both the Consuls to Epirus called [2]
Ere yet the year was dead: a foreign land   10
Obscure received the magistrates of Rome,
And heard their high debate. No warlike camp
This; for the Consul's and the Praetor's axe
Proclaimed the Senate-house; and Magnus sat
One among many, and the state was all.

When all were silent, from his lofty seat
Thus Lentulus began, while stern and sad
The Fathers listened: "If your hearts still beat
With Latian blood, and if within your breasts
Still lives your fathers' vigour, look not now   20
On this strange land that holds us, nor enquire

---

[1] The Pleiades, said to be daughters of Atlas.
[2] These were the Consuls for the expiring year, B.C. 49 -- Caius Marcellus
and L. Lentulus Crus.

Your distance from the captured city: yours
This proud assembly, yours the high command
In all that comes. Be this your first decree,
Whose truth all peoples and all kings confess;
Be this the Senate. Let the frozen wain
Demand your presence, or the torrid zone
Wherein the day and night with equal tread
For ever march; still follows in your steps
The central power of Imperial Rome.   30
When flamed the Capitol with fires of Gaul
When Veii held Camillus, there with him
Was Rome, nor ever though it changed its clime
Your order lost its rights. In Caesar's hands
Are sorrowing houses and deserted homes,
Laws silent for a space, and forums closed
In public fast. His Senate-house beholds
Those Fathers only whom from Rome it drove,
While Rome was full. Of that high order all
Not here, are exiles. [1] Ignorant of war,   40
Its crimes and bloodshed, through long years of peace,
Ye fled its outburst: now in session all
Are here assembled. See ye how the gods
Weigh down Italia's loss by all the world
Thrown in the other scale? Illyria's wave
Rolls deep upon our foes: in Libyan wastes
Is fallen their Curio, the weightier part [2]
Of Caesar's senate! Lift your standards, then,
Spur on your fates and prove your hopes to heaven.
Let Fortune, smiling, give you courage now   50
As, when ye fled, your cause. The Consuls' power

---

[1] That is to say, Caesar's Senate at Rome could boast of those Senators only
whom it had, before Pompeius' flight, declared public enemies. But they
were to be regarded as exiles, having lost their rights, rather than the Senators
in Epirus, who were in full possession of theirs.

[2] Dean Merivale says that probably Caesar's Senate was not less numerous
than his rival's. Duruy says there were senators in Pompeius' camp, out of a
total of between 500 and 600. Mommsen says, "they were veritably emi-
grants. This Roman Coblentz presented a pitiful spectacle of the high
pretensions and paltry performances of the grandees of Rome." (Vol. iv., p.
397.) Almost all the Consulars were with Pompeius.

Fails with the dying year: not so does yours;
By your commandment for the common weal
Decree Pompeius leader." With applause
They heard his words, and placed their country's fates,
Nor less their own, within the chieftain's hands.

Then did they shower on people and on kings
Honours well earned -- Rhodes, Mistress of the Seas,
Was decked with gifts; Athena, old in fame,
Received her praise, and the rude tribes who dwell   60
On cold Taygetus; Massilia's sons
Their own Phocaea's freedom; on the chiefs
Of Thracian tribes, fit honours were bestowed.
They order Libya by their high decree
To serve King Juba's sceptre; and, alas!
On Ptolemaeus, of a faithless race
The faithless sovereign, scandal to the gods,
And shame to Fortune, placed the diadem
Of Pella. Boy! thy sword was only sharp
Against thy people. Ah if that were all!   70
The fatal gift gave, too, Pompeius' life;
Bereft thy sister of her sire's bequest, [1]
Half of the kingdom; Caesar of a crime.
Then all to arms.

       While soldier thus and chief,
In doubtful sort, against their hidden fate
Devised their counsel, Appius [2] alone
Feared for the chances of the war, and sought
Through Phoebus' ancient oracle to break
The silence of the gods and know the end.   80

Between the western belt and that which bounds [3]
The furthest east, midway Parnassus rears

---

[1] By the will of Ptolemy Auletes, Cleopatra had been appointed joint sovereign of Egypt with her young brother. Lucan means that Caesar would have killed Pompeius if young Ptolemy had not done so. She lost her hare of the kingdom, and Caesar was clear of the crime.
[2] Appius was Proconsul, and in command of Achaia, for the Senate.
[3] See Book IV., 82.

His double summit: to the Bromian god
And Paean consecrate, to whom conjoined
The Theban band leads up the Delphic feast
On each third year. This mountain, when the sea
Poured o'er the earth her billows, rose alone,
By one high peak scarce master of the waves,
Parting the crest of waters from the stars.
There, to avenge his mother, from her home   90
Chased by the angered goddess while as yet
She bore him quick within her, Paean came
(When Themis ruled the tripods and the spot) [1]
And with unpractised darts the Python slew.
But when he saw how from the yawning cave
A godlike knowledge breathed, and all the air
Was full of voices murmured from the depths,
He took the shrine and filled the deep recess;
Henceforth to prophesy.

          Which of the gods   100
Has left heaven's light in this dark cave to hide?
What spirit that knows the secrets of the world
And things to come, here condescends to dwell,
Divine, omnipotent? bear the touch of man,
And at his bidding deigns to lift the veil?
Perchance he sings the fates, perchance his song,
Once sung, is fate. Haply some part of Jove
Sent here to rule the earth with mystic power,
Balanced upon the void immense of air,
Sounds through the caves, and in its flight returns   110
To that high home of thunder whence it came.
Caught in a virgin's breast, this deity
Strikes on the human spirit: then a voice
Sounds from her breast, as when the lofty peak
Of Etna boils, forced by compelling flames,
Or as Typheus on Campania's shore
Frets 'neath the pile of huge Inarime. [2]

---

[1] Themis, the goddess of law, was in possession of the Delphic oracle, previ-
ous to Apollo. (Aesch., "Eumenides", line 2.)
[2] The modern isle of Ischia, off the Bay of Naples.

Though free to all that ask, denied to none,
No human passion lurks within the voice
That heralds forth the god; no whispered vow,   120
No evil prayer prevails; none favour gain:
Of things unchangeable the song divine;
Yet loves the just. When men have left their homes
To seek another, it hath turned their steps
Aright, as with the Tyrians; [1] and raised
The hearts of nations to confront their foe,
As prove the waves of Salamis: [2] when earth
Hath been unfruitful, or polluted air
Has plagued mankind, this utterance benign
Hath raised their hopes and pointed to the end.   130
No gift from heaven's high gods so great as this
Our centuries have lost, since Delphi's shrine
Has silent stood, and kings forbade the gods [3]
To speak the future, fearing for their fates.
Nor does the priestess sorrow that the voice
Is heard no longer; and the silent fane
To her is happiness; for whatever breast
Contains the deity, its shattered frame
Surges with frenzy, and the soul divine
Shakes the frail breath that with the god receives,   140
As prize or punishment, untimely death.

These tripods Appius seeks, unmoved for years
These soundless caverned rocks, in quest to learn
Hesperia's destinies. At his command
To loose the sacred gateways and permit
The prophetess to enter to the god,
The keeper calls Phemonoe; [1] whose steps

---

[1] The Tyrians consulted the oracle in consequence of the earthquakes which vexed their country (Book III., line 225), and were told to found colonies.
[2] See Herodotus, Book VII., 140-143. The reference is to the answer given by the oracle to the Athenians that their wooden walls would keep them safe; which Themistocles interpreted as meaning their fleet.
[3] Cicero, on the contrary, suggests that the reason why the oracles ceased was this, that men became less credulous. ("De Div.", ii., 57) Lecky, "History of European Morals from Augustus to Charlemagne", vol. i., p. 368.

105

Round the Castalian fount and in the grove
Were wandering careless; her he bids to pass
The portals. But the priestess feared to tread   150
The awful threshold, and with vain deceits
Sought to dissuade the chieftain from his zeal
To learn the future. "What this hope," she cried,
"Roman, that moves thy breast to know the fates?
Long has Parnassus and its silent cleft
Stifled the god; perhaps the breath divine
Has left its ancient gorge and thro' the world
Wanders in devious paths; or else the fane,
Consumed to ashes by barbarian [2] fire,
Closed up the deep recess and choked the path   160
Of Phoebus; or the ancient Sibyl's books
Disclosed enough of fate, and thus the gods
Decreed to close the oracle; or else
Since wicked steps are banished from the fane,
In this our impious age the god finds none
Whom he may answer." But the maiden's guile
Was known, for though she would deny the gods
Her fears approved them. On her front she binds
A twisted fillet, while a shining wreath
Of Phocian laurels crowns the locks that flow   170
Upon her shoulders. Hesitating yet
The priest compelled her, and she passed within.
But horror filled her of the holiest depths
From which the mystic oracle proceeds;
And resting near the doors, in breast unmoved
She dares invent the god in words confused,
Which proved no mind possessed with fire divine;
By such false chant less injuring the chief
Than faith in Phoebus and the sacred fane.
No burst of words with tremor in their tones,   180
No voice re-echoing through the spacious vault
Proclaimed the deity, no bristling locks
Shook off the laurel chaplet; but the grove

---

[1] This name is one of those given to the Cumaean Sibyl mentioned at line
210. She was said to have been the daughter of Apollo.
[2] Probably by the Gauls under Brennus, B.C. 279.

Unshaken, and the summits of the shrine,
Gave proof she shunned the god. The Roman knew
The tripods yet were idle, and in rage,
"Wretch," he exclaimed, "to us and to the gods,
Whose presence thou pretendest, thou shalt pay
For this thy fraud the punishment; unless
Thou enter the recess, and speak no more,   190
Of this world-war, this tumult of mankind,
Thine own inventions." Then by fear compelled,
At length the priestess sought the furthest depths,
And stayed beside the tripods; and there came
Into her unaccustomed breast the god,
Breathed from the living rock for centuries
Untouched; nor ever with a mightier power
Did Paean's inspiration seize the frame
Of Delphic priestess; his pervading touch
Drove out her former mind, expelled the man,   200
And made her wholly his. In maddened trance
She whirls throughout the cave, her locks erect
With horror, and the fillets of the god
Dashed to the ground; her steps unguided turn
To this side and to that; the tripods fall
O'erturned; within her seethes the mighty fire
Of angry Phoebus; nor with whip alone
He urged her onwards, but with curb restrained;
Nor was it given her by the god to speak
All that she knew; for into one vast mass [1]   210
All time was gathered, and her panting chest
Groaned 'neath the centuries. In order long
All things lay bare: the future yet unveiled
Struggled for light; each fate required a voice;
The compass of the seas, Creation's birth,
Creation's death, the number of the sands,
All these she knew. Thus on a former day
The prophetess upon the Cuman shore, [2]
Disdaining that her frenzy should be slave

---

[1] These lines form the Latin motto prefixed to Shelley's poem, "The Demon of the World".
[2] Referring to the visit of Aeneas to the Sibyl. (Virgil, "Aeneid", vi., 70, &c.)

To other nations, from the boundless threads   220
Chose out with pride of hand the fates of Rome.
E'en so Phemonoe, for a time oppressed
With fates unnumbered, laboured ere she found,
Beneath such mighty destinies concealed,
Thine, Appius, who alone had'st sought the god
In land Castalian; then from foaming lips
First rushed the madness forth, and murmurs loud
Uttered with panting breath and blent with groans;
Till through the spacious vault a voice at length
Broke from the virgin conquered by the god: 230
"From this great struggle thou, O Roman, free
Escap'st the threats of war: alive, in peace,
Thou shalt possess the hollow in the coast
Of vast Euboea." Thus she spake, no more.

Ye mystic tripods, guardians of the fates
And Paean, thou, from whom no day is hid
By heaven's high rulers, Master of the truth,
Why fear'st thou to reveal the deaths of kings,
Rome's murdered princes, and the latest doom
Of her great Empire tottering to its fall,   240
And all the bloodshed of that western land?
Were yet the stars in doubt on Magnus' fate
Not yet decreed, and did the gods yet shrink
From that, the greatest crime? Or wert thou dumb
That Fortune's sword for civil strife might wreak
Just vengeance, and a Brutus' arm once more
Strike down the tyrant?

       From the temple doors
Rushed forth the prophetess in frenzy driven,
Not all her knowledge uttered; and her eyes,   250
Still troubled by the god who reigned within,
Or filled with wild affright, or fired with rage
Gaze on the wide expanse: still works her face
Convulsive; on her cheeks a crimson blush
With ghastly pallor blent, though not of fear.
Her weary heart throbs ever; and as seas
Boom swollen by northern winds, she finds in sighs,
All inarticulate, relief. But while

BOOK V

She hastes from that dread light in which she saw
The fates, to common day, lo! on her path   260
The darkness fell. Then by a Stygian draught
Of the forgetful river, Phoebus snatched
Back from her soul his secrets; and she fell
Yet hardly living.

       Nor did Appius dread
Approaching death, but by dark oracles
Baffled, while yet the Empire of the world
Hung in the balance, sought his promised realm
In Chalcis of Euboea. Yet to escape
All ills of earth, the crash of war -- what god   270
Can give thee such a boon, but death alone?
Far on the solitary shore a grave
Awaits thee, where Carystos' marble crags [1]
Draw in the passage of the sea, and where
The fane of Rhamnus[2] rises to the gods
Who hate the proud, and where the ocean strait
Boils in swift whirlpools, and Euripus draws
Deceitful in his tides, a bane to ships,
Chalcidian vessels to bleak Aulis' shore.

But Caesar carried from the conquered west   280
His eagles to another world of war;
When envying his victorious course the gods
Almost turned back the prosperous tide of fate.
Not on the battle-field borne down by arms
But in his tents, within the rampart lines,
The hoped-for prize of this unholy war
Seemed for a moment gone. That faithful host,
His comrades trusted in a hundred fields,
Or that the falchion sheathed had lost its charm;
Or weary of the mournful bugle call   290
Scarce ever silent; or replete with blood,
Well nigh betrayed their general and sold

---

[1] Appius was seized with fever as soon as he reached the spot; and there he died and was buried, thus fulfilling the oracle.
[2] That is, Nemesis.

For hope of gain their honour and their cause.
No other perilous shock gave surer proof
How trembled 'neath his feet the dizzy height
From which great Caesar looked. A moment since
His high behest drew nations to the field:
Now, maimed of all, he sees that swords once drawn
Are weapons for the soldier, not the chief.
From the stern ranks no doubtful murmur rose;   300
Not silent anger as when one conspires,
His comrades doubting, feared himself in turn;
Alone (he thinks) indignant at the wrongs
Wrought by the despot. In so great a host
Dread found no place. Where thousands share the guilt
Crime goes unpunished. Thus from dauntless throats
They hurled their menace: "Caesar, give us leave
To quit thy crimes; thou seek'st by land and sea
The sword to slay us; let the fields of Gaul
And far Iberia, and the world proclaim   310
How for thy victories our comrades fell.
What boots it us that by an army's blood
The Rhine and Rhone and all the northern lands
Thou hast subdued? Thou giv'st us civil war
For all these battles; such the prize. When fled
The Senate trembling, and when Rome was ours
What homes or temples did we spoil? Our hands
Reek with offence! Aye, but our poverty
Proclaims our innocence! What end shall be
Of arms and armies? What shall be enough   320
If Rome suffice not? and what lies beyond?
Behold these silvered locks, these nerveless hands
And shrunken arms, once stalwart! In thy wars
Gone is the strength of life, gone all its pride!
Dismiss thine aged soldiers to their deaths.
How shameless is our prayer! Not on hard turf
To stretch our dying limbs; nor seek in vain,
When parts the soul, a hand to close our eyes;
Not with the helmet strike the stony clod: [1]
Rather to feel the dear one's last embrace,   330

---

[1] Reading "galeam", with Francken; not "glebam".

And gain a humble but a separate tomb.
Let nature end old age. And dost thou think
We only know not what degree of crime
Will fetch the highest price? What thou canst dare
These years have proved, or nothing; law divine
Nor human ordinance shall hold thine hand.
Thou wert our leader on the banks of Rhine;
Henceforth our equal; for the stain of crime
Makes all men like to like. Add that we serve
A thankless chief: as fortune's gift he takes   340
The fruits of victory our arms have won.
We are his fortunes, and his fates are ours
To fashion as we will. Boast that the gods
Shall do thy bidding! Nay, thy soldiers' will
Shall close the war." With threatening mien and speech
Thus through the camp the troops demand their chief.

When faith and loyalty are fled, and hope
For aught but evil, thus may civil war
In mutiny and discord find its end!
What general had not feared at such revolt?   350
But mighty Caesar trusting on the throw,
As was his wont, his fortune, and o'erjoyed
To front their anger raging at its height
Unflinching comes. No temples of the gods,
Not Jove's high fane on the Tarpeian rock,
Not Rome's high dames nor maidens had he grudged
To their most savage lust: that they should ask
The worst, his wish, and love the spoils of war.
Nor feared he aught save order at the hands
Of that unconquered host. Art thou not shamed   360
That strife should please thee only, now condemned
Even by thy minions? Shall they shrink from blood,
They from the sword recoil? and thou rush on
Heedless of guilt, through right and through unright,
Nor learn that men may lay their arms aside
Yet bear to live? This civil butchery
Escapes thy grasp. Stay thou thy crimes at length;
Nor force thy will on those who will no more.

Upon a turfy mound unmoved he stood

And, since he feared not, worthy to be feared;   370
And thus while anger stirred his soul began:
"Thou that with voice and hand didst rage but now
Against thine absent chief, behold me here;
Here strike thy sword into this naked breast,
To stay the war; and flee, if such thy wish.
This mutiny devoid of daring deed
Betrays your coward souls, betrays the youth
Who tires of victories which gild the arms
Of an unconquered chief, and yearns for flight.
Well, leave me then to battle and to fate!   380
I cast you forth; for every weapon left,
Fortune shall find a man, to wield it well.
Shall Magnus in his flight with such a fleet
Draw nations in his train; and not to me as
My victories bring hosts, to whom shall fall
The prize of war accomplished, who shall reap
Your laurels scorned, and scathless join the train
That leads my chariot to the sacred hill?
While you, despised in age and worn in war,
Gaze on our triumph from the civic crowd.   390
Think you your dastard flight shall give me pause?
If all the rivers that now seek the sea
Were to withdraw their waters, it would fail
By not one inch, no more than by their flow
It rises now. Have then your efforts given
Strength to my cause? Not so: the heavenly gods
Stoop not so low; fate has no time to judge
Your lives and deaths. The fortunes of the world
Follow heroic souls: for the fit few
The many live; and you who terrified   400
With me the northern and Iberian worlds,
Would flee when led by Magnus. Strong in arms
For Caesar's cause was Labienus; [1] now
That vile deserter, with his chief preferred,
Wanders o'er land and sea. Nor were your faith

---

[1] Labienus left Caesar's ranks after the Rubicon was crossed, and joined his
rival. In his mouth Lucan puts the speech made at the oracle of Hammon in
Book IX. He was slain at Munda, B.C. 45.

One whit more firm to me if, neither side
Espoused, you ceased from arms. Who leaves me once,
Though not to fight against me with the foe,
Joins not my ranks again. Surely the gods
Smile on these arms who for so great a war   410
Grant me fresh soldiers. From what heavy load
Fortune relieves me! for the hands which aimed
At all, to which the world did not suffice,
I now disarm, and for myself alone
Reserve the conflict. Quit ye, then, my camp,
'Quirites', [1] Caesar's soldiers now no more,
And leave my standards to the grasp of men!
Yet some who led this mad revolt I hold,
Not as their captain now, but as their judge.
Lie, traitors, prone on earth, stretch out the neck   420
And take th' avenging blow. And thou whose strength
Shall now support me, young and yet untaught,
Behold the doom and learn to strike and die."

Such were his words of ire, and all the host
Drew back and trembled at the voice of him
They would depose, as though their very swords
Would from their scabbards leap at his command
Themselves unwilling; but he only feared
Lest hand and blade to satisfy the doom
Might be denied, till they submitting pledged   430
Their lives and swords alike, beyond his hope.
To strike and suffer [2] holds in surest thrall
The heart inured to guilt; and Caesar kept,
By dreadful compact ratified in blood,
Those whom he feared to lose.

        He bids them march
Upon Brundusium, and recalls the ships

---

[1] That is, civilians; no longer soldiers. This one contemptuous expression is said to have shocked and abashed the army. (Tacitus, "Annals", I., 42.)
[2] Reading "tenet", with Hosius and Francken; not "timet", as Haskins. The prospect of inflicting punishment attracted, while the suffering of it subdued, the mutineers.

From soft Calabria's inlets and the point
Of Leucas, and the Salapinian marsh,
Where sheltered Sipus nestles at the feet   440
Of rich Garganus, jutting from the shore
In huge escarpment that divides the waves
Of Hadria; on each hand, his seaward slopes
Buffeted by the winds; or Auster borne
From sweet Apulia, or the sterner blast
Of Boreas rushing from Dalmatian strands.

But Caesar entered trembling Rome unarmed,
Now taught to serve him in the garb of peace.
Dictator named, to grant their prayers, forsooth:
Consul, in honour of the roll of Rome.   450
Then first of all the names by which we now
Lie to our masters, men found out the use:
For to preserve his right to wield the sword
He mixed the civil axes with his brands;
With eagles, fasces; with an empty word
Clothing his power; and stamped upon the time
A worthy designation; for what name
Could better mark the dread Pharsalian year
Than "Caesar, Consul"? [1] Now the famous field
Pretends its ancient ceremonies: calls   460
The tribes in order and divides the votes
In vain solemnity of empty urns.
Nor do they heed the portents of the sky:
Deaf were the augurs to the thunder roll;
The owl flew on the left; yet were the birds
Propitious sworn. Then was the ancient name
Degraded first; and monthly Consuls, [2]
Shorn of their rank, are chosen to mark the years.
And Trojan Alba's [1] god (since Latium's fall

---

[1] Caesar was named Dictator while at Massilia. Entering Rome, he held the office for eleven days only, but was elected Consul for the incoming year, B.C. 48, along with Servilius Isauricus. (Caesar, "De Bello Civili", iii., 1; Merivale, chapter xvi.)

[2] In the time of the Empire, the degraded Consulship, preserved only as a name, was frequently transferred monthly, or even shorter, intervals from one favourite to another.

Deserving not) beheld the wonted fires   470
Blaze from his altars on the festal night.

Then through Apulia's fallows, that her hinds
Left all untilled, to sluggish weeds a prey
Passed Caesar onward, swifter than the fire
Of heaven, or tigress dam: until he reached
Brundusium's winding ramparts, built of old
By Cretan colonists. There icy winds
Constrained the billows, and his trembling fleet
Feared for the winter storms nor dared the main.
But Caesar's soul burned at the moments lost   480
For speedy battle, nor could brook delay
Within the port, indignant that the sea
Should give safe passage to his routed foe:
And thus he stirred his troops, in seas unskilled,
With words of courage: "When the winter wind
Has seized on sky and ocean, firm its hold;
But the inconstancy of cloudy spring
Permits no certain breezes to prevail
Upon the billows. Straight shall be our course.
No winding nooks of coast, but open seas   490
Struck by the northern wind alone we plough,
And may he bend the spars, and bear us swift
To Grecian cities; else Pompeius' oars,
Smiting the billows from Phaeacian [2] coasts,
May catch our flagging sails. Cast loose the ropes
From our victorious prows. Too long we waste
Tempests that blow to bear us to our goal."

Now sank the sun to rest; the evening star
Shone on the darkening heaven, and the moon
Reigned with her paler light, when all the fleet   500
Freed from retaining cables seized the main.
With slackened sheet the canvas wooed the breeze,

---

[1] Caesar performed the solemn rites of the great Latin festival on the Alban
Mount during his Dictatorship. (Compare Book VII., line 471.)
[2] Dyrrhachium was founded by the Corcyreams, with whom the Homeric
Phaeacians have been identified.

Which rose and fell and fitful died away,
Till motionless the sails, and all the waves
Were still as deepest pool, where never wind
Ripples the surface. Thus in Scythian climes
Cimmerian Bosphorus restrains the deep
Bound fast in frosty fetters; Ister's streams [1]
No more impel the main, and ships constrained
Stand fast in ice; and while in depths below   510
The waves still murmur, loud the charger's hoof
Sounds on the surface, and the travelling wheel
Furrows a track upon the frozen marsh.
Cruel as tempest was the calm that lay
In stagnant pools upon the mournful deep:
Against the course of nature lay outstretched
A rigid ocean: 'twas as if the sea
Forgat its ancient ways and knew no more
The ceaseless tides, nor any breeze of heaven,
Nor quivered at the image of the sun,   520
Mirrored upon its wave. For while the fleet
Hung in mid passage motionless, the foe
Might hurry to attack, with sturdy stroke
Churning the deep; or famine's deadly grip
Might seize the ships becalmed. For dangers new
New vows they find. "May mighty winds arise
And rouse the ocean, and this sluggish plain
Cast off stagnation and be sea once more."
Thus did they pray, but cloudless shone the sky,
Unrippled slept the surface of the main;   530
Until in misty clouds the moon arose
And stirred the depths, and moved the fleet along
Towards the Ceraunian headland; and the waves
And favouring breezes followed on the ships,
Now speeding faster, till (their goal attained)
They cast their anchors on Palaeste's [2] shore.

This land first saw the chiefs in neighbouring camps

---

[1] Apparently making the Danube discharge into the Sea of Azov. See Mr.
Heitland's Introduction, p. 53.
[2] At the foot of the Acroceraunian range.

Confronted, which the streams of Apsus bound
And swifter Genusus; a lengthy course
Is run by neither, but on Apsus' waves   540
Scarce flowing from a marsh, the frequent boat
Finds room to swim; while on the foamy bed
Of Genusus by sun or shower compelled
The melted snows pour seawards. Here were met
(So Fortune ordered it) the mighty pair;
And in its woes the world yet vainly hoped
That brought to nearer touch their crime itself
Might bleed abhorrence: for from either camp
Voices were clearly heard and features seen.
Nor e'er, Pompeius, since that distant day   550
When Caesar's daughter and thy spouse was reft
By pitiless fate away, nor left a pledge,
Did thy loved kinsman (save on sands of Nile)
So nearly look upon thy face again.

But Caesar's mind though frenzied for the fight
Was forced to pause until Antonius brought
The rearward troops; Antonius even now
Rehearsing Leucas' fight. With prayers and threats
Caesar exhorts him. "Why delay the fates,
Thou cause of evil to the suffering world?   560
My speed hath won the major part: from thee
Fortune demands the final stroke alone.
Do Libyan whirlpools with deceitful tides
Uncertain separate us? Is the deep
Untried to which I call? To unknown risks
Art thou commanded? Caesar bids thee come,
Thou sluggard, not to leave him. Long ago
I ran my ships midway through sands and shoals
To harbours held by foes; and dost thou fear
My friendly camp? I mourn the waste of days   570
Which fate allotted us. Upon the waves
And winds I call unceasing: hold not back
Thy willing troops, but let them dare the sea;
Here gladly shall they come to join my camp,
Though risking shipwreck. Not in equal shares
The world has fallen between us: thou alone
Dost hold Italia, but Epirus I

And all the lords of Rome." Twice called and thrice
Antonius lingered still: but Caesar thought
To reap in full the favour of the gods,   580
Not sit supine; and knowing danger yields
To whom heaven favours, he upon the waves
Feared by Antonius' fleets, in shallow boat
Embarked, and daring sought the further shore.

Now gentle night had brought repose from arms;
And sleep, blest guardian of the poor man's couch,
Restored the weary; and the camp was still.
The hour was come that called the second watch
When mighty Caesar, in the silence vast
With cautious tread advanced to such a deed [1]   590
As slaves should dare not. Fortune for his guide,
Alone he passes on, and o'er the guard
Stretched in repose he leaps, in secret wrath
At such a sleep. Pacing the winding beach,
Fast to a sea-worn rock he finds a boat
On ocean's marge afloat. Hard by on shore
Its master dwelt within his humble home.
No solid front it reared, for sterile rush
And marshy reed enwoven formed the walls,
Propped by a shallop with its bending sides   600
Turned upwards. Caesar's hand upon the door
Knocks twice and thrice until the fabric shook.
Amyclas from his couch of soft seaweed
Arising, calls: "What shipwrecked sailor seeks
My humble home? Who hopes for aid from me,
By fates adverse compelled?" He stirs the heap
Upon the hearth, until a tiny spark
Glows in the darkness, and throws wide the door.
Careless of war, he knew that civil strife

---

[1] Caesar himself says nothing of this adventure. But it is mentioned by Dion,
Appian and Plutarch ("Caesar", 38). Dean Merivale thinks the story may
have been invented to introduce the apophthegm used by Caesar to the sailor,
"Fear nothing: you carry Caesar and his fortunes" (lines 662-665). Mommsen
accepts the story, as of an attempt which was only abandoned because no
mariner could be induced to undertake it. Lucan colours it with his wildest
and most exaggerated hyperbole.

Stoops not to cottages. Oh! happy life   610
That poverty affords! great gift of heaven
Too little understood! what mansion wall,
What temple of the gods, would feel no fear
When Caesar called for entrance? Then the chief:
"Enlarge thine hopes and look for better things.
Do but my bidding, and on yonder shore
Place me, and thou shalt cease from one poor boat
To earn thy living; and in years to come
Look for a rich old age: and trust thy fates
To those high gods whose wont it is to bless   620
The poor with sudden plenty." So he spake
E'en at such time in accents of command,
For how could Caesar else? Amyclas said,
"'Twere dangerous to brave the deep to-night.
The sun descended not in ruddy clouds
Or peaceful rays to rest; part of his beams
Presaged a southern gale, the rest proclaimed
A northern tempest; and his middle orb,
Shorn of its strength, permitted human eyes
To gaze upon his grandeur; and the moon   630
Rose not with silver horns upon the night
Nor pure in middle space; her slender points
Not drawn aright, but blushing with the track
Of raging tempests, till her lurid light
Was sadly veiled within the clouds. Again
The forest sounds; the surf upon the shore;
The dolphin's mood, uncertain where to play;
The sea-mew on the land; the heron used
To wade among the shallows, borne aloft
And soaring on his wings -- all these alarm;   640
The raven, too, who plunged his head in spray,
As if to anticipate the coming rain,
And trod the margin with unsteady gait.
But if the cause demands, behold me thine.
Either we reach the bidden shore, or else
Storm and the deep forbid -- we can no more."

Thus said he loosed the boat and raised the sail.
No sooner done than stars were seen to fall
In flaming furrows from the sky: nay, more;

The pole star trembled in its place on high: 650
Black horror marked the surging of the sea;
The main was boiling in long tracts of foam,
Uncertain of the wind, yet seized with storm.
Then spake the captain of the trembling bark:
"See what remorseless ocean has in store!
Whether from east or west the storm may come
Is still uncertain, for as yet confused
The billows tumble. Judged by clouds and sky
A western tempest: by the murmuring deep
A wild south-eastern gale shall sweep the sea.   660
Nor bark nor man shall reach Hesperia's shore
In this wild rage of waters. To return
Back on our course forbidden by the gods,
Is our one refuge, and with labouring boat
To reach the shore ere yet the nearest land
Way be too distant."

              But great Caesar's trust
Was in himself, to make all dangers yield.
And thus he answered: "Scorn the threatening sea,
Spread out thy canvas to the raging wind;   670
If for thy pilot thou refusest heaven,
Me in its stead receive. Alone in thee
One cause of terror just -- thou dost not know
Thy comrade, ne'er deserted by the gods,
Whom fortune blesses e'en without a prayer.
Break through the middle storm and trust in me.
The burden of this fight fails not on us
But on the sky and ocean; and our bark
Shall swim the billows safe in him it bears.
Nor shall the wind rage long: the boat itself   680
Shall calm the waters. Flee the nearest shore,
Steer for the ocean with unswerving hand:
Then in the deep, when to our ship and us
No other port is given, believe thou hast
Calabria's harbours. And dost thou not know
The purpose of such havoc? Fortune seeks
In all this tumult of the sea and sky
A boon for Caesar." Then a hurricane
Swooped on the boat and tore away the sheet:

The fluttering sail fell on the fragile mast: 690
And groaned the joints. From all the universe
Commingled perils rush. In Atlas' seas
First Corus [1] lifts his head, and stirs the depths
To fury, and had forced upon the rocks
Whole seas and oceans; but the chilly north
Drove back the deep that doubted which was lord.
But Scythian Aquilo prevailed, whose blast
Tossed up the main and showed as shallow pools
Each deep abyss; and yet was not the sea
Heaped on the crags, for Corus' billows met   700
The waves of Boreas: such seas had clashed
Even were the winds withdrawn; Eurus enraged
Burst from the cave, and Notus black with rain,
And all the winds from every part of heaven
Strove for their own; and thus the ocean stayed
Within his boundaries. No petty seas
Rapt in the storm are whirled. The Tuscan deep
Invades th' Aegean; in Ionian gulfs
Sounds wandering Hadria. How long the crags
Which that day fell, the Ocean's blows had braved!   710
What lofty peaks did vanquished earth resign!
And yet on yonder coast such mighty waves
Took not their rise; from distant regions came
Those monster billows, driven on their course
By that great current which surrounds the world. [2]
Thus did the King of Heaven, when length of years
Wore out the forces of his thunder, call
His brother's trident to his help, what time
The earth and sea one second kingdom formed
And ocean knew no limit but the sky.   720
Now, too, the sea had risen to the stars
In mighty mass, had not Olympus' chief

---

[1] See Book I., 463.
[2] The ocean current, which, according to Hecataeus, surrounded the world.
But Herodotus of this theory says, "For my part I know of no river called
Ocean, and I think that Homer or one of the earlier poets invented the name
and introduced it into his poetry." (Book II., 23, and Book IV., 36.) In "Oce-
anus" Aeschylus seems to have intended to personify the great surrounding
stream. ("Prom. Vinc.", lines 291, 308.)

Pressed down its waves with clouds: came not from heaven
That night, as others; but the murky air
Was dim with pallor of the realms below; [1]
The sky lay on the deep; within the clouds
The waves received the rain: the lightning flash
Clove through the parted air a path obscured
By mist and darkness: and the heavenly vaults
Re-echoed to the tumult, and the frame   730
That holds the sky was shaken. Nature feared
Chaos returned, as though the elements
Had burst their bonds, and night had come to mix
Th' infernal shades with heaven.

                In such turmoil
Not to have perished was their only hope.
Far as from Leucas point the placid main
Spreads to the horizon, from the billow's crest
They viewed the dashing of th' infuriate sea;
Thence sinking to the middle trough, their mast   740
Scarce topped the watery height on either hand,
Their sails in clouds, their keel upon the ground.
For all the sea was piled into the waves,
And drawn from depths between laid bare the sand.
The master of the boat forgot his art,
For fear o'ercame; he knew not where to yield
Or where to meet the wave: but safety came
From ocean's self at war: one billow forced
The vessel under, but a huger wave
Repelled it upwards, and she rode the storm   750
Through every blast triumphant. Not the shore
Of humble Sason [2], nor Thessalia's coast
Indented, not Ambracia's scanty ports
Dismay the sailors, but the giddy tops
Of high Ceraunia's cliffs.

         But Caesar now,

---

[1] Comp. VI., 615.
[2] Sason is a small island just off the Ceraunian rocks, the point of which is now called Cape Linguetta, and is nearly opposite to Brindisi.

Thinking the peril worthy of his fates:
"Are such the labours of the gods?" exclaimed,
"Bent on my downfall have they sought me thus,
Here in this puny skiff in such a sea?   760
If to the deep the glory of my fall
Is due, and not to war, intrepid still
Whatever death they send shall strike me down.
Let fate cut short the deeds that I would do
And hasten on the end: the past is mine.
The northern nations fell beneath my sword;
My dreaded name compels the foe to flee.
Pompeius yields me place; the people's voice
Gave at my order what the wars denied.
And all the titles which denote the powers   770
Known to the Roman state my name shall bear.
Let none know this but thou who hear'st my prayers,
Fortune, that Caesar summoned to the shades,
Dictator, Consul, full of honours, died
Ere his last prize was won. I ask no pomp
Of pyre or funeral; let my body lie
Mangled beneath the waves: I leave a name
That men shall dread in ages yet to come
And all the earth shall honour." Thus he spake,
When lo! a tenth gigantic billow raised   780
The feeble keel, and where between the rocks
A cleft gave safety, placed it on the shore.
Thus in a moment fortune, kingdoms, lands,
Once more were Caesar's.

           But on his return
When daylight came, he entered not the camp
Silent as when he parted; for his friends
Soon pressed around him, and with weeping eyes
In accents welcome to his ears began:
"Whither in reckless daring hast thou gone,   790
Unpitying Caesar? Were these humble lives
Left here unguarded while thy limbs were given,
Unsought for, to be scattered by the storm?
When on thy breath so many nations hang
For life and safety, and so great a world
Calls thee its master, to have courted death

Proves want of heart. Was none of all thy friends
Deserving held to join his fate with thine?
When thou wast tossed upon the raging deep
We lay in slumber! Shame upon such sleep!   800
And why thyself didst seek Italia's shores?
'Twere cruel (such thy thought) to speak the word
That bade another dare the furious sea.
All men must bear what chance or fate may bring,
The sudden peril and the stroke of death;
But shall the ruler of the world attempt
The raging ocean? With incessant prayers
Why weary heaven? is it indeed enough
To crown the war, that Fortune and the deep
Have cast thee on our shores? And would'st thou use   810
The grace of favouring deities, to gain
Not lordship, not the empire of the world,
But lucky shipwreck!" Night dispersed, and soon
The sun beamed on them, and the wearied deep,
The winds permitting, lulled its waves to rest.
And when Antonius saw a breeze arise
Fresh from a cloudless heaven, to break the sea,
He loosed his ships which, by the pilots' hands
And by the wind in equal order held,
Swept as a marching host across the main.   820
But night unfriendly from the seamen snatched
All governance of sail, parting the ships
In divers paths asunder. Like as cranes
Deserting frozen Strymon for the streams
Of Nile, when winter falls, in casual lines
Of wedge-like figures [1] first ascend the sky;
But when in loftier heaven the southern breeze
Strikes on their pinions tense, in loose array
Dispersed at large, in flight irregular,
They wing their journey onwards. Stronger winds   830
With day returning blew the navy on,
Past Lissus' shelter which they vainly sought,
Till bare to northern blasts, Nymphaeum's port,
But safe in southern, gave the fleet repose,

---

[1] Compare "Paradise Lost", VII., 425.

For favouring winds came on.

When Magnus knew
That Caesar's troops were gathered in their strength
And that the war for quick decision called
Before his camp, Cornelia he resolved
To send to Lesbos' shore, from rage of fight   840
Safe and apart: so lifting from his soul
The weight that burdened it. Thus, lawful Love.
Thus art thou tyrant o'er the mightiest mind!
His spouse was the one cause why Magnus stayed
Nor met his fortunes, though he staked the world
And all the destinies of Rome. The word
He speaks not though resolved; so sweet it seemed,
When on the future pondering, to gain
A pause from Fate! But at the close of night,
When drowsy sleep had fled, Cornelia sought   850
To soothe the anxious bosom of her lord
And win his kisses. Then amazed she saw
His cheek was tearful, and with boding soul
She shrank instinctive from the hidden wound,
Nor dared to rouse him weeping. But he spake:
"Dearer to me than life itself, when life
Is happy (not at moments such as these);
The day of sorrow comes, too long delayed,
Nor long enough! With Caesar at our gates
With all his forces, a secure retreat   860
Shall Lesbos give thee. Try me not with prayers.
This fatal boon I have denied myself.
Thou wilt not long be absent from thy lord.
Disasters hasten, and things highest fall
With speediest ruin. 'Tis enough for thee
To hear of Magnus' peril; and thy love [1]
Deceives thee with the thought that thou canst gaze
Unmoved on civil strife. It shames my soul
On the eve of war to slumber at thy side,
And rise from thy dear breast when trumpets call   870
A woeful world to misery and arms.

---

[1] Reading "Teque tuus decepit amor", as preferred by Hosius.

I fear in civil war to feel no loss
To Magnus. Meantime safer than a king
Lie hid, nor let the fortune of thy lord
Whelm thee with all its weight. If unkind heaven
Our armies rout, still let my choicest part
Survive in thee; if fated is my flight,
Still leave me that whereto I fain would flee."

Hardly at first her senses grasped the words
In their full misery; then her mind amazed   880
Could scarce find utterance for the grief that pressed.
"Nought, Magnus, now is left wherewith to upbraid
The gods and fates of marriage; 'tis not death
That parts our love, nor yet the funeral pyre,
Nor that dread torch which marks the end of all.
I share the ignoble lot of vulgar lives:
My spouse rejects me. Yes, the foe is come!
Break we our bonds and Julia's sire appease! --
Is this thy consort, Magnus, this thy faith
In her fond loving heart? Can danger fright   890
Her and not thee? Long since our mutual fates
Hang by one chain; and dost thou bid me now
The thunder-bolts of ruin to withstand
Without thee? Is it well that I should die
Even while you pray for fortune? And suppose
I flee from evil and with death self-sought
Follow thy footsteps to the realms below --
Am I to live till to that distant isle
Some tardy rumour of thy fall may come?
Add that thou fain by use would'st give me strength   900
To bear such sorrow and my doom. Forgive
Thy wife confessing that she fears the power.
And if my prayers shall bring the victory,
The joyful tale shall come to me the last
In that lone isle of rocks. When all are glad,
My heart shall throb with anguish, and the sail
Which brings the message I shall see with fear,
Not safe e'en then: for Caesar in his flight
Might seize me there, abandoned and alone
To be his hostage. If thou place me there,   910
The spouse of Magnus, shall not all the world

126

Well know the secret Mitylene holds?
This my last prayer: if all is lost but flight,
And thou shalt seek the ocean, to my shores
Turn not thy keel, ill-fated one: for there,
There will they seek thee." Thus she spoke distraught,
Leaped from the couch and rushed upon her fate;
No stop nor stay: she clung not to his neck
Nor threw her arms about him; both forego
The last caress, the last fond pledge of love,   920
And grief rushed in unchecked upon their souls;
Still gazing as they part no final words
Could either utter, and the sweet Farewell
Remained unspoken. This the saddest day
Of all their lives: for other woes that came
More gently struck on hearts inured to grief.
Borne to the shore with failing limbs she fell
And grasped the sands, embracing, till at last
Her maidens placed her senseless in the ship.

Not in such grief she left her country's shores   930
When Caesar's host drew near; for now she leaves,
Though faithful to her lord, his side in flight
And flees her spouse. All that next night she waked;
Then first what means a widowed couch she knew,
Its cold, its solitude. When slumber found
Her eyelids, and forgetfulness her soul,
Seeking with outstretched arms the form beloved,
She grasps but air. Though tossed by restless love,
She leaves a place beside her as for him
Returning. Yet she feared Pompeius lost   940
To her for ever. But the gods ordained
Worse than her fears, and in the hour of woe
Gave her to look upon his face again.

BOOK VI

THE FIGHT NEAR DYRRHACHIUM.
SCAEVA'S EXPLOITS. THE WITCH OF

THESSALIA

Now that the chiefs with minds intent on fight
Had drawn their armies near upon the hills
And all the gods beheld their chosen pair,
Caesar, the Grecian towns despising, scorned
To reap the glory of successful war
Save at his kinsman's cost. In all his prayers
He seeks that moment, fatal to the world,
When shall be cast the die, to win or lose,
And all his fortune hang upon the throw.   10
Thrice he drew out his troops, his eagles thrice,
Demanding battle; thus to increase the woe
Of Latium, prompt as ever: but his foes,
Proof against every art, refused to leave
The rampart of their camp. Then marching swift
By hidden path between the wooded fields
He seeks, and hopes to seize, Dyrrhachium's [1] fort;

---

[1] Dyrrhachium (or Epidamnus) was a Corcyraean colony, but its founder was
of Corinth, the metropolis of Corcyra. It stood some sixty miles north of the
Ceraunian promontory (Book V., 747). About the year 1100 it was stormed
and taken by Robert the Guiscard, after furious battles with the troops of the
Emperor Alexius. Its modern name is Durazzo. It may be observed that, ac-
cording to Caesar's account, he succeeded in getting between Pompey and
Dyrrhachium, B.C. 3, 41, 42.

BOOK VI

But Magnus, speeding by the ocean marge,
First camped on Petra's slopes, a rocky hill
Thus by the natives named. From thence he keeps 20
Watch o'er the fortress of Corinthian birth
Which by its towers alone without a guard
Was safe against a siege. No hand of man
In ancient days built up her lofty wall,
No hammer rang upon her massive stones:
Not all the works of war, nor Time himself
Shall undermine her. Nature's hand has raised
Her adamantine rocks and hedged her in
With bulwarks girded by the foamy main:
And but for one short bridge of narrow earth 30
Dyrrhachium were an island. Steep and fierce,
Dreaded of sailors, are the cliffs that bear
Her walls; and tempests, howling from the west,
Toss up the raging main upon the roofs;
And homes and temples tremble at the shock.

Thirsting for battle and with hopes inflamed
Here Caesar hastes, with distant rampart lines
Seeking unseen to coop his foe within,
Though spread in spacious camp upon the hills.
With eagle eye he measures out the land 40
Meet to be compassed, nor content with turf
Fit for a hasty mound, he bids his troops
Tear from the quarries many a giant rock:
And spoils the dwellings of the Greeks, and drags
Their walls asunder for his own. Thus rose
A mighty barrier which no ram could burst
Nor any ponderous machine of war.
Mountains are cleft, and level through the hills
The work of Caesar strides: wide yawns the moat,
Forts show their towers rising on the heights, 50
And in vast circle forests are enclosed
And groves and spacious lands, and beasts of prey,
As in a line of toils. Pompeius lacked
Nor field nor forage in th' encircled span
Nor room to move his camp; nay, rivers rose
Within, and ran their course and reached the sea;
And Caesar wearied ere he saw the whole,

129

And daylight failed him. Let the ancient tale
Attribute to the labours of the gods
The walls of Ilium: let the fragile bricks   60
Which compass in great Babylon, amaze
The fleeting Parthian. Here a larger space
Than those great cities which Orontes swift
And Tigris' stream enclose, or that which boasts
In Eastern climes, the lordly palaces
Fit for Assyria's kings, is closed by walls
Amid the haste and tumult of a war
Forced to completion. Yet this labour huge
Was spent in vain. So many hands had joined
Or Sestos with Abydos, or had tamed   70
With mighty mole the Hellespontine wave,
Or Corinth from the realm of Pelops' king
Had rent asunder, or had spared each ship
Her voyage round the long Malean cape,
Or had done anything most hard, to change
The world's created surface. Here the war
Was prisoned: blood predestinate to flow
In all the parts of earth; the host foredoomed
To fall in Libya or in Thessaly
Was here: in such small amphitheatre   80
The tide of civil passion rose and fell.

At first Pompeius knew not: so the hind
Who peaceful tills the mid-Sicilian fields
Hears not Pelorous [1] sounding to the storm;
So billows thunder on Rutupian shores [2],
Unheard by distant Caledonia's tribes.
But when he saw the mighty barrier stretch
O'er hill and valley, and enclose the land,
He bade his columns leave their rocky hold
And seize on posts of vantage in the plain;   90
Thus forcing Caesar to extend his troops
On wider lines; and holding for his own
Such space encompassed as divides from Rome

---

[1] C. del Faro, the N.E. point of Sicily.
[2] The shores of Kent.

Aricia, [1] sacred to that goddess chaste
Of old Mycenae; or as Tiber holds
From Rome's high ramparts to the Tuscan sea,
Unless he deviate. No bugle call
Commands an onset, and the darts that fly
Fly though forbidden; but the arm that flings
For proof the lance, at random, here and there   100
Deals impious slaughter. Weighty care compelled
Each leader to withhold his troops from fight;
For there the weary earth of produce failed
Pressed by Pompeius' steeds, whose horny hoofs
Rang in their gallop on the grassy fields
And killed the succulence. They strengthless lay
Upon the mown expanse, nor pile of straw,
Brought from full barns in place of living grass,
Relieved their craving; shook their panting flanks,
And as they wheeled Death struck his victim down.   110
Then foul contagion filled the murky air
Whose poisonous weight pressed on them in a cloud
Pestiferous; as in Nesis' isle [2] the breath
Of Styx rolls upwards from the mist-clad rocks;
Or that fell vapour which the caves exhale
From Typhon [3] raging in the depths below.
Then died the soldiers, for the streams they drank
Held yet more poison than the air: the skin
Was dark and rigid, and the fiery plague
Made hard their vitals, and with pitiless tooth   120
Gnawed at their wasted features, while their eyes
Started from out their sockets, and the head
Drooped for sheer weariness. So the disease
Grew swifter in its strides till scarce was room,
'Twixt life and death, for sickness, and the pest
Slew as it struck its victim, and the dead
Thrust from the tents (such all their burial) lay

---

[1] Aricia was situated on the Via Appia, about sixteen miles from Rome.
There was a temple of Diana close to it, among some woods on a small lake.
Aricia was Horace's first halting place on his journey to Brundisium ("Sat-
ires", i. 5). As to Diana, see Book I., line 501.
[2] An island in the Bay of Puteoli.
[3] Typhon, the hundred-headed giant, was buried under Mount Etna.

Blent with the living. Yet their camp was pitched
Hard by the breezy sea by which might come
All nations' harvests, and the northern wind   130
Not seldom rolled the murky air away.
Their foe, not vexed with pestilential air
Nor stagnant waters, ample range enjoyed
Upon the spacious uplands: yet as though
In leaguer, famine seized them for its prey.
Scarce were the crops half grown when Caesar saw
How prone they seized upon the food of beasts,
And stripped of leaves the bushes and the groves,
And dragged from roots unknown the doubtful herb.
Thus ate they, starving, all that teeth may bite   140
Or fire might soften, or might pass their throats
Dry, parched, abraded; food unknown before
Nor placed on tables: while the leaguered foe
Was blessed with plenty.

                    When Pompeius first
Was pleased to break his bonds and be at large,
No sudden dash he makes on sleeping foe
Unarmed in shade of night; his mighty soul
Scorns such a path to victory. 'Twas his aim,
To lay the turrets low; to mark his track,   150
By ruin spread afar; and with the sword
To hew a path between his slaughtered foes.
Minucius' [1] turret was the chosen spot
Where groves of trees and thickets gave approach
Safe, unbetrayed by dust.

                    Up from the fields
Flashed all at once his eagles into sight
And all his trumpets blared. But ere the sword
Could win the battle, on the hostile ranks
Dread panic fell; prone as in death they lay   160
Where else upright they should withstand the foe;
Nor more availed their valour, and in vain
The cloud of weapons flew, with none to slay.

---

[1] This was Scaeva's name.

Then blazing torches rolling pitchy flame
Are hurled, and shaken nod the lofty towers
And threaten ruin, and the bastions groan
Struck by the frequent engine, and the troops
Of Magnus by triumphant eagles led
Stride o'er the rampart, in their front the world.

Yet now that passage which not Caesar's self   170
Nor thousand valiant squadrons had availed
To rescue from their grasp, one man in arms
Steadfast till death refused them; Scaeva named
This hero soldier: long he served in fight
Waged 'gainst the savage on the banks of Rhone;
And now centurion made, through deeds of blood,
He bore the staff before the marshalled line.
Prone to all wickedness, he little recked
How valourous deeds in civil war may be
Greatest of crimes; and when he saw how turned   180
His comrades from the war and sought in flight
A refuge, [1] "Whence," he cried, "this impious fear
Unknown to Caesar's armies? Do ye turn
Your backs on death, and are ye not ashamed
Not to be found where slaughtered heroes lie?
Is loyalty too weak? Yet love of fight
Might bid you stand. We are the chosen few
Through whom the foe would break. Unbought by blood
This day shall not be theirs. 'Neath Caesar's eye,
True, death would be more happy; but this boon   190
Fortune denies: at least my fall shall be
Praised by Pompeius. Break ye with your breasts
Their weapons; blunt the edges of their swords
With throats unyielding. In the distant lines
The dust is seen already, and the sound
Of tumult and of ruin finds the ear
Of Caesar: strike; the victory is ours:
For he shall come who while his soldiers die
Shall make the fortress his." His voice called forth
The courage that the trumpets failed to rouse   200

---

[1] The vinewood staff was the badge of the centurion's office.

When first they rang: his comrades mustering come
To watch his deeds; and, wondering at the man,
To test if valour thus by foes oppressed,
In narrow space, could hope for aught but death.
But Scaeva standing on the tottering bank
Heaves from the brimming turret on the foe
The corpses of the fallen; the ruined mass
Furnishing weapons to his hands; with beams,
And ponderous stones, nay, with his body threats
His enemies; with poles and stakes he thrusts   210
The breasts advancing; when they grasp the wall
He lops the arm: rocks crush the foeman's skull
And rive the scalp asunder: fiery bolts
Dashed at another set his hair aflame,
Till rolls the greedy blaze about his eyes
With hideous crackle. As the pile of slain
Rose to the summit of the wall he sprang,
Swift as across the nets a hunted pard,
Above the swords upraised, till in mid throng
Of foes he stood, hemmed in by densest ranks   220
And ramparted by war; in front and rear,
Where'er he struck, the victor. Now his sword
Blunted with gore congealed no more could wound,
But brake the stricken limb; while every hand
Flung every quivering dart at him alone;
Nor missed their aim, for rang against his shield
Dart after dart unerring, and his helm
In broken fragments pressed upon his brow;
His vital parts were safeguarded by spears
That bristled in his body. Fortune saw   230
Thus waged a novel combat, for there warred
Against one man an army. Why with darts,
Madmen, assail him and with slender shafts,
'Gainst which his life is proof? Or ponderous stones
This warrior chief shall overwhelm, or bolts
Flung by the twisted thongs of mighty slings.
Let steelshod ram or catapult remove
This champion of the gate. No fragile wall
Stands here for Caesar, blocking with its bulk
Pompeius' way to freedom. Now he trusts   240
His shield no more, lest his sinister hand,

Idle, give life by shame; and on his breast
Bearing a forest of spears, though spent with toil
And worn with onset, falls upon his foe
And braves alone the wounds of all the war.
Thus may an elephant in Afric wastes,
Oppressed by frequent darts, break those that fall
Rebounding from his horny hide, and shake
Those that find lodgment, while his life within
Lies safe, protected, nor doth spear avail   250
To reach the fount of blood. Unnumbered wounds
By arrow dealt, or lance, thus fail to slay
This single warrior. But lo! from far
A Cretan archer's shaft, more sure of aim
Than vows could hope for, strikes on Scaeva's brow
To light within his eye: the hero tugs
Intrepid, bursts the nerves, and tears the shaft
Forth with the eyeball, and with dauntless heel
Treads them to dust. Not otherwise a bear
Pannonian, fiercer for the wound received,   260
Maddened by dart from Libyan thong propelled,
Turns circling on her wound, and still pursues
The weapon fleeing as she whirls around.
Thus, in his rage destroyed, his shapeless face
Stood foul with crimson flow. The victors' shout
Glad to the sky arose; no greater joy
A little blood could give them had they seen
That Caesar's self was wounded. Down he pressed
Deep in his soul the anguish, and, with mien,
No longer bent on fight, submissive cried,   270
"Spare me, ye citizens; remove the war
Far hence: no weapons now can haste my death;
Draw from my breast the darts, but add no more.
Yet raise me up to place me in the camp
Of Magnus, living: this your gift to him;
No brave man's death my title to renown,
But Caesar's flag deserted." So he spake.
Unhappy Aulus thought his words were true,
Nor saw within his hand the pointed sword;
And leaping forth in haste to make his own   280
The prisoner and his arms, in middle throat
Received the lightning blade. By this one death

Rose Scaeva's valour again; and thus he cried,
Such be the punishment of all who thought
Great Scaeva vanquished; if Pompeius seeks
Peace from this reeking sword, low let him lay
At Caesar's feet his standards. Me do ye think
Such as yourselves, and slow to meet the fates?
Your love for Magnus and the Senate's cause
Is less than mine for death." These were his words;   290
And dust in columns proved that Caesar came.
Thus was Pompeius' glory spared the stain
Of flight compelled by Scaeva. He, when ceased
The battle, fell, no more by rage of fight,
Or sight of blood out-pouring from his wounds,
Roused to the combat. Fainting there he lay
Upon the shoulders of his comrades borne,
Who him adoring (as though deity
Dwelt in his bosom) for his matchless deeds,
Plucked forth the gory shafts and took his arms   300
To deck the gods and shield the breast of Mars.
Thrice happy thou with such a name achieved,
Had but the fierce Iberian from thy sword,
Or heavy shielded Teuton, or had fled
The light Cantabrian: with no spoils shalt thou
Adorn the Thunderer's temple, nor upraise
The shout of triumph in the ways of Rome.
For all thy prowess, all thy deeds of pride
Do but prepare her lord.

             Nor on this hand   310
Repulsed, Pompeius idly ceased from war,
Content within his bars; but as the sea
Tireless, which tempests force upon the crag
That breaks it, or which gnaws a mountain side
Some day to fall in ruin on itself;
He sought the turrets nearest to the main,
On double onset bent; nor closely kept
His troops in hand, but on the spacious plain
Spread forth his camp. They joyful leave the tents
And wander at their will. Thus Padus flows   320
In brimming flood, and foaming at his bounds,
Making whole districts quake; and should the bank

Fail 'neath his swollen waters, all his stream
Breaks forth in swirling eddies over fields
Not his before; some lands are lost, the rest
Gain from his bounty.

        Hardly from his tower
Had Caesar seen the fire or known the fight:
And coming found the rampart overthrown,
The dust no longer stirred, the rains cold   330
As from a battle done. The peace that reigned
There and on Magnus' side, as though men slept,
Their victory won, aroused his angry soul.
Quick he prepares, so that he end their joy
Careless of slaughter or defeat, to rush
With threatening columns on Torquatus' post.
But swift as sailor, by his trembling mast
Warned of Circeian tempest, furls his sails,
So swift Torquatus saw, and prompt to wage
The war more closely, he withdrew his men   340
Within a narrower wall.

        Now past the trench
Were Caesar's companies, when from the hills
Pompeius hurled his host upon their ranks
Shut in, and hampered. Not so much o'erwhelmed
As Caesar's soldiers is the hind who dwells
On Etna's slopes, when blows the southern wind,
And all the mountain pours its cauldrons forth
Upon the vale; and huge Enceladus [1]
Writhing beneath his load spouts o'er the plains   350
A blazing torrent.

        Blinded by the dust,
Encircled, vanquished, ere the fight, they fled
In cloud of terror on their rearward foe,
So rushing on their fates. Thus had the war
Shed its last drop of blood and peace ensued,
But Magnus suffered not, and held his troops.

---

[1] This giant, like Typhon, was buried under Mount Etna.

Back from the battle.

Thou, oh Rome, had'st been
Free, happy, mistress of thy laws and rights   360
Were Sulla here. Now shalt thou ever grieve
That in his crowning crime, to have met in fight
A pious kinsman, Caesar's vantage lay.
Oh tragic destiny! Nor Munda's fight
Hispania had wept, nor Libya mourned
Encrimsoned Utica, nor Nilus' stream,
With blood unspeakable polluted, borne
A nobler corse than her Egyptian kings:
Nor Juba [1] lain unburied on the sands,
Nor Scipio with his blood outpoured appeased   370
The ghosts of Carthage; nor the blameless life
Of Cato ended: and Pharsalia's name
Had then been blotted from the book of fate.

But Caesar left the region where his arms
Had found the deities averse, and marched
His shattered columns to Thessalian lands.
Then to Pompeius came (whose mind was bent
To follow Caesar wheresoe'er he fled)
His captains, striving to persuade their chief
To seek Ausonia, his native land,   380
Now freed from foes. "Ne'er will I pass," he said,
"My country's limit, nor revisit Rome
Like Caesar, at the head of banded hosts.
Hesperia when the war began was mine;
Mine, had I chosen in our country's shrines, [2]
In midmost forum of her capital,
To join the battle. So that banished far
Be war from Rome, I'll cross the torrid zone
Or those for ever frozen Scythian shores.

---

[1] Juba and Petreius killed each other after the battle of Thepsus to avoid falling into Caesar's hands. See Book IV., line 5.
[2] So Cicero: "Shall I, who have been called saviour of the city and father of my country, bring into it an army of Getae Armenians and Colchians?" ("Ep. ad Atticum," ix., 10.)

What! shall my victory rob thee of the peace   390
I gave thee by my flight? Rather than thou
Should'st feel the evils of this impious war,
Let Caesar deem thee his." Thus said, his course
He turned towards the rising of the sun,
And following devious paths, through forests wide,
Made for Emathia, the land by fate
Foredoomed to see the issue.

Thessalia on that side where Titan first
Raises the wintry day, by Ossa's rocks
Is prisoned in: but in th' advancing year   400
When higher in the vault his chariot rides
'Tis Pelion that meets the morning rays.
And when beside the Lion's flames he drives
The middle course, Othrys with woody top
Screens his chief ardour. On the hither side
Pindus receives the breezes of the west
And as the evening falls brings darkness in.
There too Olympus, at whose foot who dwells
Nor fears the north nor sees the shining bear.
Between these mountains hemmed, in ancient time   410
The fields were marsh, for Tempe's pass not yet
Was cleft, to give an exit to the streams
That filled the plain: but when Alcides' hand
Smote Ossa from Olympus at a blow, [1]
And Nereus wondered at the sudden flood
Of waters to the main, then on the shore
(Would it had slept for ever 'neath the deep)
Seaborn Achilles' home Pharsalus rose;
And Phylace [2] whence sailed that ship of old
Whose keel first touched upon the beach of Troy;   420
And Dorion mournful for the Muses' ire
On Thamyris [3] vanquished: Trachis; Melibe
Strong in the shafts [1] of Hercules, the price

---

[1] See Book VIII., line 3.
[2] Protesilaus, from this place, first landed at Troy.
[3] Thamyris challenged the Muses to a musical contest, and being vanquished, was by them deprived of sight.

Of that most awful torch; Larissa's hold
Potent of yore; and Argos,[2] famous erst,
O'er which men pass the ploughshare: and the spot
Fabled as Echionian Thebes,[3] where once
Agave bore in exile to the pyre
(Grieving 'twas all she had) the head and neck
Of Pentheus massacred. The lake set free   430
Flowed forth in many rivers: to the west
Aeas,[4] a gentle stream; nor stronger flows
The sire of Isis ravished from his arms;
And Achelous, rival for the hand
Of Oeneus' daughter, rolls his earthy flood[5]
To silt the shore beside the neighbouring isles.
Evenus[6] purpled by the Centaur's blood
Wanders through Calydon: in the Malian Gulf
Thy rapids fall, Spercheius: pure the wave
With which Amphrysos[7] irrigates the meads   440

---

[1] The arrows given to Philoctetes by Hercules as a reward for kindling his
funeral pyre.
[2] This is the Pelasgic, not the historical, Argos.
[3] Book I., line 632; Book VII., line 904. Agave was a daughter of Cadmus,
and mother of Pentheus, king of the Boeotian Thebes. He was opposed to the
mysterious worship of Dionysus, which his mother celebrated, and which he
had watched from a tree. She tore him to pieces, being urged into a frenzy
and mistaking him for a wild beast. She then retired to another Thebes, in
Phthiotis, in triumph, with his head and shoulders. By another legend she did
not leave the Boeotian Thebes. (See Grote, vol. i., p. 220. Edit. 1862.)
[4] Aeas was a river flowing from the boundary of Thessaly through Epirus to
the Ionian Sea. The sire of Isis, or Io, was Inachus; but the river of that name
is usually placed in the Argive territory.
[5] A river rising in Mount Pindus and flowing into the Ionian Sea nearly oppo-
site to Ithaca. At its mouth the sea has been largely silted up.
[6] The god of this river fought with Hercules for the hand of Deianira. After
Hercules had been married to Deianira, and when they were on a journey,
they came to the River Evenus. Here Nessus, a Centaur, acted as ferryman,
and Hercules bade him carry Deianira across. In doing so he insulted her, and
Hercules shot him with an arrow.
[7] Admetus was King of Pherae in Thessaly, and sued for Alcestis, the daugh-
ter of Pelias, who promised her to him if he should come in a chariot drawn
by lions and boars. With the assistance of Apollo, Admetus performed this.
Apollo, for the slaughter of the Cyclops, was condemned to serve a mortal,

Where once Apollo served: Anaurus [1] flows
Breathing no vapour forth; no humid air
Ripples his face: and whatever stream,
Nameless itself, to Ocean gives its waves
Through thee, Peneus: [2] whirled in eddies foams
Apidanus; Enipeus lingers on
Swift only when fresh streams his volume swell:
And thus Asopus takes his ordered course,
Phoenix and Melas; but Eurotas keeps
His stream aloof from that with which he flows,   450
Peneus, gliding on his top as though
Upon the channel. Fable says that, sprung
From darkest pools of Styx, with common floods
He scorns to mingle, mindful of his source,
So that the gods above may fear him still.

Soon as were sped the rivers, Boebian ploughs
Dark with its riches broke the virgin soil;
Then came Lelegians to press the share,
And Dolopes and sons of Oeolus
By whom the glebe was furrowed. Steed-renowned   460
Magnetians dwelt there, and the Minyan race
Who smote the sounding billows with the oar.
There in the cavern from the pregnant cloud
Ixion's sons found birth, the Centaur brood
Half beast, half human: Monychus who broke
The stubborn rocks of Pholoe, Rhoetus fierce
Hurling from Oeta's top gigantic elms

---

and accordingly he tended the flocks of Admetus for nine years. The River
Amphrysos is marked as flowing into the Pagasaean Gulf at a short distance
below Pherae.
[1] Anaurus was a small river passing into the Pagasaean Gulf past Iolcos. In
this river Jason is said to have lost one of his slippers.
[2] The River Peneus flowed into the sea through the pass of Tempe, cloven by
Hercules between Olympus and Ossa (see line 406); and carried with it Aso-
pus, Phoenix, Melas, Enipeus, Apidanus, and Titaresus (or Eurotas). The
Styx is generally placed in Arcadia, but Lucan says that Eurotas rises from
the Stygian pools, and that, mindful of this mysterious source, he refuses to
mingle his streams with that of Peneus, in order that the gods may still fear to
break an oath sworn upon his waters.

Which northern storms could hardly overturn;
Pholus, Alcides' host: Nessus who bore
The Queen across Evenus' [1] waves, to feel   470
The deadly arrow for his shameful deed;
And aged Chiron [2] who with wintry star
Against the huger Scorpion draws his bow.
Here sparkled on the land the warrior seed; [3]
Here leaped the charger from Thessalian rocks [4]
Struck by the trident of the Ocean King,
Omen of dreadful war; here first he learned,
Champing the bit and foaming at the curb,
Yet to obey his lord. From yonder shore
The keel of pine first floated, [5] and bore men   480
To dare the perilous chance of seas unknown:
And here Ionus ruler of the land
First from the furnace molten masses drew
Of iron and brass; here first the hammer fell
To weld them, shapeless; here in glowing stream
Ran silver forth and gold, soon to receive
The minting stamp. 'Twas thus that money came
Whereby men count their riches, cause accursed
Of warfare. Hence came down that Python huge
On Cirrha: hence the laurel wreath which crowns   490
The Pythian victor: here Aloeus' sons
Gigantic rose against the gods, what time
Pelion had almost touched the stars supreme,
And Ossa's loftier peak amid the sky
Opposing, barred the constellations' way.

---

[1] See on line 429.
[2] Chiron, the aged Centaur, instructor of Peleus, Achilles, and others. He was killed by one of the poisoned arrows of Hercules, but placed by Zeus among the stars as the Archer, from which position he appears to be aiming at the Scorpion. His constellation appears in winter.
[3] The teeth of the dragon slain by Cadmus; though this took place in Boeotia.
[4] Poseidon and Athena disputed as to which of them should name the capital of Attica. The gods gave the reward to that one of them who should produce the thing most useful to man; whereupon Athena produced an olive tree, and Poseidon a horse. Homer also places the scene of this event in Thessaly. ("Iliad", xxiii., 247.)
[5] The Argo. Conf. Book III., 223.

When in this fated land the chiefs had placed
Their several camps, foreboding of the end
Now fast approaching, all men's thoughts were turned
Upon the final issue of the war.
And as the hour drew near, the coward minds   500
Trembling beneath the shadow of the fate
Now hanging o'er them, deemed disaster near:
While some took heart; yet doubted what might fall,
In hope and fear alternate. 'Mid the throng
Sextus, unworthy son of worthy sire
Who soon upon the waves that Scylla guards, [1]
Sicilian pirate, exile from his home,
Stained by his deeds of shame the fights he won,
Could bear delay no more; his feeble soul,
Sick of uncertain fate, by fear compelled,   510
Forecast the future: yet consulted not
The shrine of Delos nor the Pythian caves;
Nor was he satisfied to learn the sound
Of Jove's brass cauldron, 'mid Dodona's oaks,
By her primaeval fruits the nurse of men:
Nor sought he sages who by flight of birds,
Or watching with Assyrian care the stars
And fires of heaven, or by victims slain,
May know the fates to come; nor any source
Lawful though secret. For to him was known   520
That which excites the hate of gods above;
Magicians' lore, the savage creed of Dis
And all the shades; and sad with gloomy rites
Mysterious altars. For his frenzied soul
Heaven knew too little. And the spot itself
Kindled his madness, for hard by there dwelt
The brood of Haemon [2] whom no storied witch
Of fiction e'er transcended; all their art
In things most strange and most incredible;
There were Thessalian rocks with deadly herbs   530

---

[1] See Book VII., 1022.
[2] Son of Pelasgus. From him was derived the ancient name of Thessaly, Haemonia.

Thick planted, sensible to magic chants,
Funereal, secret: and the land was full
Of violence to the gods: the Queenly guest [1]
From Colchis gathered here the fatal roots
That were not in her store: hence vain to heaven
Rise impious incantations, all unheard;
For deaf the ears divine: save for one voice
Which penetrates the furthest depths of airs
Compelling e'en th' unwilling deities
To hearken to its accents. Not the care   540
Of the revolving sky or starry pole
Can call them from it ever. Once the sound
Of those dread tones unspeakable has reached
The constellations, then nor Babylon
Nor secret Memphis, though they open wide
The shrines of ancient magic and entreat
The gods, could draw them from the fires that smoke
Upon the altars of far Thessaly.
To hearts of flint those incantations bring
Love, strange, unnatural; the old man's breast   550
Burns with illicit fire. Nor lies the power
In harmful cup nor in the juicy pledge
Of love maternal from the forehead drawn; [2]
Charmed forth by spells alone the mind decays,
By poisonous drugs unharmed. With woven threads
Crossed in mysterious fashion do they bind
Those whom no passion born of beauteous form
Or loving couch unites. All things on earth
Change at their bidding; night usurps the day;
The heavens disobey their wonted laws;   560
At that dread hymn the Universe stands still;
And Jove while urging the revolving wheels
Wonders they move not. Torrents are outpoured
Beneath a burning sun; and thunder roars
Uncaused by Jupiter. From their flowing locks

---

[1] Medea.
[2] It was supposed that there was on the forehead of the new- born foal an excrescence, which was bitten off and eaten by the mother. If she did not do this she had no affection for the foal. (Virgil, "Aeneid", iv., 515.)

Vapours immense shall issue at their call;
When falls the tempest seas shall rise and foam [1]
Moved by their spell; though powerless the breeze
To raise the billows. Ships against the wind
With bellying sails move onward. From the rock   570
Hangs motionless the torrent: rivers run
Uphill; the summer heat no longer swells
Nile in his course; Maeander's stream is straight;
Slow Rhone is quickened by the rush of Saone;
Hills dip their heads and topple to the plain;
Olympus sees his clouds drift overhead;
And sunless Scythia's sempiternal snows
Melt in mid-winter; the inflowing tides
Driven onward by the moon, at that dread chant
Ebb from their course; earth's axes, else unmoved,   580
Have trembled, and the force centripetal
Has tottered, and the earth's compacted frame
Struck by their voice has gaped, [2] till through the void
Men saw the moving sky. All beasts most fierce
And savage fear them, yet with deadly aid
Furnish the witches' arts. Tigers athirst
For blood, and noble lions on them fawn
With bland caresses: serpents at their word
Uncoil their circles, and extended glide
Along the surface of the frosty field;   590
The viper's severed body joins anew;
And dies the snake by human venom slain.

Whence comes this labour on the gods, compelled
To hearken to the magic chant and spells,
Nor daring to despise them? Doth some bond
Control the deities? Is their pleasure so,
Or must they listen? and have silent threats
Prevailed, or piety unseen received

------

[1] "When the boisterous sea,   Without a breath of wind, hath knocked the sky."
        -- Ben Jonson, "Masque of Queens".
[2] The sky was supposed to move round, but to be restrained in its course by the planets. (See Book X., line 244.)

So great a guerdon? Against all the gods
Is this their influence, or on one alone   600
Who to his will constrains the universe,
Himself constrained? Stars most in yonder clime
Shoot headlong from the zenith; and the moon
Gliding serene upon her nightly course
Is shorn of lustre by their poisonous chant,
Dimmed by dark earthly fires, as though our orb
Shadowed her brother's radiance and barred
The light bestowed by heaven; nor freshly shines
Until descending nearer to the earth
She sheds her baneful drops upon the mead.   610

These sinful rites and these her sister's songs
Abhorred Erichtho, fiercest of the race,
Spurned for their piety, and yet viler art
Practised in novel form. To her no home
Beneath a sheltering roof her direful head
Thus to lay down were crime: deserted tombs
Her dwelling-place, from which, darling of hell,
She dragged the dead. Nor life nor gods forbad
But that she knew the secret homes of Styx
And learned to hear the whispered voice of ghosts   620
At dread mysterious meetings. [1] Never sun
Shed his pure light upon that haggard cheek
Pale with the pallor of the shades, nor looked
Upon those locks unkempt that crowned her brow.
In starless nights of tempest crept the hag
Out from her tomb to seize the levin bolt;
Treading the harvest with accursed foot
She burned the fruitful growth, and with her breath
Poisoned the air else pure. No prayer she breathed
Nor supplication to the gods for help   630
Nor knew the pulse of entrails as do men
Who worship. Funeral pyres she loves to light

---

[1] "Coatus audire silentum." To be present at the meetings of the dead and hear their voices. So, in the sixth Aeneid, the dead Greek warriors in feeble tones endeavour to express their fright at the appearance of the Trojan hero (lines 492, 493).

And snatch the incense from the flaming tomb.
The gods at her first utterance grant her prayer
For things unlawful, lest they hear again
Its fearful accents: men whose limbs were quick
With vital power she thrust within the grave
Despite the fates who owed them years to come:
The funeral reversed brought from the tomb
Those who were dead no longer; and the pyre   640
Yields to her shameless clutch still smoking dust
And bones enkindled, and the torch which held
Some grieving sire but now, with fragments mixed
In sable smoke and ceremental cloths
Singed with the redolent fire that burned the dead.
But those who lie within a stony cell
Untouched by fire, whose dried and mummied frames
No longer know corruption, limb by limb
Venting her rage she tears, the bloodless eyes
Drags from their cavities, and mauls the nail   650
Upon the withered hand: she gnaws the noose
By which some wretch has died, and from the tree
Drags down a pendent corpse, its members torn
Asunder to the winds: forth from the palms
Wrenches the iron, and from the unbending bond
Hangs by her teeth, and with her hands collects
The slimy gore which drips upon the limbs.

Where lay a corpse upon the naked earth
On ravening birds and beasts of prey the hag
Kept watch, nor marred by knife or hand her spoil,   660
Till on his victim seized some nightly wolf; [1]
Then dragged the morsel from his thirsty fangs;
Nor fears she murder, if her rites demand
Blood from the living, or some banquet fell
Requires the panting entrail. Pregnant wombs

---

[1] "As if that piece were sweeter which the wolf had bitten." Note to "The Masque of Queens", in which the first hag says: "I have been all day, look-ing after   A raven feeding on a quarter,   And soon as she turned her beak to the south   I snatched this morsel out of her mouth."
      --Ben Jonson, "Masque of Queens". But more probably the meaning is that the wolf's bite gave the flesh magical efficacy.

Yield to her knife the infant to be placed
On flaming altars: and whene'er she needs
Some fierce undaunted ghost, he fails not her
Who has all deaths in use. Her hand has chased
From smiling cheeks the rosy bloom of life;   670
And with sinister hand from dying youth
Has shorn the fatal lock: and holding oft
In foul embraces some departed friend
Severed the head, and through the ghastly lips,
Held by her own apart, some impious tale
Dark with mysterious horror hath conveyed
Down to the Stygian shades.

      When rumour brought
Her name to Sextus, in the depth of night,
While Titan's chariot beneath our earth   680
Wheeled on his middle course, he took his way
Through fields deserted; while a faithful band,
His wonted ministers in deeds of guilt,
Seeking the hag 'mid broken sepulchres,
Beheld her seated on the crags afar
Where Haemus falls towards Pharsalia's plain. [1]
There was she proving for her gods and priests
Words still unknown, and framing numbered chants
Of dire and novel purpose: for she feared
Lest Mars might stray into another world,   690
And spare Thessalian soil the blood ere long
To flow in torrents; and she thus forbade
Philippi's field, polluted with her song,
Thick with her poisonous distilments sown,
To let the war pass by. Such deaths, she hopes,
Soon shall be hers! the blood of all the world
Shed for her use! to her it shall be given
To sever from their trunks the heads of kings,
Plunder the ashes of the noble dead,
Italia's bravest, and in triumph add   700
The mightiest warriors to her host of shades.
And now what spoils from Magnus' tombless corse

---

[1] Confusing Pharsalia with Philippi. (See line 684.)

Her hand may snatch, on which of Caesar's limbs
She soon may pounce, she makes her foul forecast
And eager gloats.

        To whom the coward son
Of Magnus thus: "Thou greatest ornament
Of Haemon's daughters, in whose power it lies
Or to reveal the fates, or from its course
To turn the future, be it mine to know   710
By thy sure utterance to what final end
Fortune now guides the issue. Not the least
Of all the Roman host on yonder plain
Am I, but Magnus' most illustrious son,
Lord of the world or heir to death and doom.
The unknown affrights me: I can firmly face
The certain terror. Bid my destiny
Yield to thy power the dark and hidden end,
And let me fall foreknowing. From the gods
Extort the truth, or, if thou spare the gods,   720
Force it from hell itself. Fling back the gates
That bar th' Elysian fields; let Death confess
Whom from our ranks he seeks. No humble task
I bring, but worthy of Erichtho's skill
Of such a struggle fought for such a prize
To search and tell the issue."

        Then the witch
Pleased that her impious fame was noised abroad
Thus made her answer: "If some lesser fates
Thy wish had been to change, against their wish   730
It had been easy to compel the gods
To its accomplishment. My art has power
When of one man the constellations press
The speedy death, to compass a delay;
And mine it is, though every star decrees
A ripe old age, by mystic herbs to shear
The life midway. But should some purpose set
From the beginning of the universe,
And all the labouring fortunes of mankind,
Be brought in question, then Thessalian art   740
Bows to the power supreme. But if thou be

Content to know the issue pre-ordained,
That shall be swiftly thine; for earth and air
And sea and space and Rhodopaean crags
Shall speak the future. Yet it easiest seems
Where death in these Thessalian fields abounds
To raise a single corpse. From dead men's lips
Scarce cold, in fuller accents falls the voice;
Not from some mummied flame in accents shrill
Uncertain to the ear."   750

         Thus spake the hag
And through redoubled night, a squalid veil
Swathing her pallid features, stole among
Unburied carcases. Fast fled the wolves,
The carrion birds with maw unsatisfied
Relaxed their talons, as with creeping step
She sought her prophet. Firm must be the flesh
As yet, though cold in death, and firm the lungs
Untouched by wound. Now in the balance hung
The fates of slain unnumbered; had she striven   760
Armies to raise and order back to life
Whole ranks of warriors, the laws had failed
Of Erebus; and, summoned up from Styx,
Its ghostly tenants had obeyed her call,
And rising fought once more. At length the witch
Picks out her victim with pierced throat agape
Fit for her purpose. Gripped by pitiless hook
O'er rocks she drags him to the mountain cave
Accursed by her fell rites, that shall restore
The dead man's life.   770

        Close to the hidden brink
The land that girds the precipice of hell
Sinks towards the depths: with ever falling leaves
A wood o'ershadows, and a spreading yew
Casts shade impenetrable. Foul decay
Fills all the space, and in the deep recess
Darkness unbroken, save by chanted spells,
Reigns ever. Not where gape the misty jaws
Of caverned Taenarus, the gloomy bound
Of either world, through which the nether kings   780

Permit the passage of the dead to earth,
So poisonous, mephitic, hangs the air.
Nay, though the witch had power to call the shades
Forth from the depths, 'twas doubtful if the cave
Were not a part of hell. Discordant hues
Flamed on her garb as by a fury worn;
Bare was her visage, and upon her brow
Dread vipers hissed, beneath her streaming locks
In sable coils entwined. But when she saw
The youth's companions trembling, and himself   790
With eyes cast down, with visage as of death,
Thus spake the witch: "Forbid your craven souls
These fears to cherish: soon returning life
This frame shall quicken, and in tones which reach
Even the timorous ear shall speak the man.
If I have power the Stygian lakes to show,
The bank that sounds with fire, the fury band,
And giants lettered, and the hound that shakes
Bristling with heads of snakes his triple head,
What fear is this that cringes at the sight   800
Of timid shivering shades?"

          Then to her prayer.
First through his gaping bosom blood she pours
Still fervent, washing from his wounds the gore.
Then copious poisons from the moon distils
Mixed with all monstrous things which Nature's pangs
Bring to untimely birth; the froth from dogs
Stricken with madness, foaming at the stream;
A lynx's entrails: and the knot that grows
Upon the fell hyaena; flesh of stags   810
Fed upon serpents; and the sucking fish
Which holds the vessel back [1] though eastern winds
Make bend the canvas; dragon's eyes; and stones
That sound beneath the brooding eagle's wings.
Nor Araby's viper, nor the ocean snake
Who in the Red Sea waters guards the shell,

---

[1] One of the miraculous stories to be found in Pliny's "Natural History". See Lecky's "Augustus to Charlemagne", vol. i., p. 370.

Are wanting; nor the slough on Libyan sands
By horned reptile cast; nor ashes fail
Snatched from an altar where the Phoenix died.
And viler poisons many, which herself   820
Has made, she adds, whereto no name is given:
Pestiferous leaves pregnant with magic chants
And blades of grass which in their primal growth
Her cursed mouth had slimed. Last came her voice
More potent than all herbs to charm the gods
Who rule in Lethe. Dissonant murmurs first
And sounds discordant from the tongues of men
She utters, scarce articulate: the bay
Of wolves, and barking as of dogs, were mixed
With that fell chant; the screech of nightly owl   830
Raising her hoarse complaint; the howl of beast
And sibilant hiss of snake -- all these were there;
And more -- the waft of waters on the rock,
The sound of forests and the thunder peal.
Such was her voice; but soon in clearer tones
Reaching to Tartarus, she raised her song:
"Ye awful goddesses, avenging power
Of Hell upon the damned, and Chaos huge
Who striv'st to mix innumerable worlds,
And Pluto, king of earth, whose weary soul   840
Grieves at his godhead; Styx; and plains of bliss
We may not enter: and thou, Proserpine,
Hating thy mother and the skies above,
My patron goddess, last and lowest form [1]
Of Hecate through whom the shades and I
Hold silent converse; warder of the gate
Who castest human offal to the dog:
Ye sisters who shall spin the threads again; [2]
And thou, O boatman of the burning wave,
Now wearied of the shades from hell to me   850
Returning, hear me if with voice I cry
Abhorred, polluted; if the flesh of man

---

[1] The mysterious goddess Hecate was identified with Luna in heaven, Diana
on earth, and Proserpine in the lower regions. The text is doubtful.
[2] That is, for the second life of her victim.

Hath ne'er been absent from my proffered song,
Flesh washed with brains still quivering; if the child
Whose severed head I placed upon the dish
But for this hand had lived -- a listening ear
Lend to my supplication! From the caves
Hid in the innermost recess of hell
I claim no soul long banished from the light.
For one but now departed, lingering still   860
Upon the brink of Orcus, is my prayer.
Grant (for ye may) that listening to the spell
Once more he seek his dust; and let the shade
Of this our soldier perished (if the war
Well at your hands has merited), proclaim
The destiny of Magnus to his son."

Such prayers she uttered; then, her foaming lips
And head uplifting, present saw the ghost.
Hard by he stood, beside the hated corpse
His ancient prison, and loathed to enter in.   870
There was the yawning chest where fell the blow
That was his death; and yet the gift supreme
Of death, his right, (Ah, wretch!) was reft away.
Angered at Death the witch, and at the pause
Conceded by the fates, with living snake
Scourges the moveless corse; and on the dead
She barks through fissures gaping to her song,
Breaking the silence of their gloomy home:
"Tisiphone, Megaera, heed ye not?
Flies not this wretched soul before your whips   880
The void of Erebus? By your very names,
She-dogs of hell, I'll call you to the day,
Not to return; through sepulchres and death
Your gaoler: from funereal urns and tombs
I'll chase you forth. And thou, too, Hecate,
Who to the gods in comely shape and mien,
Not that of Erebus, appearst, henceforth
Wasted and pallid as thou art in hell

At my command shalt come. I'll noise abroad
The banquet that beneath the solid earth   890
Holds thee, thou maid of Enna; by what bond

153

Thou lov'st night's King, by what mysterious stain
Infected, so that Ceres fears from hell
To call her daughter. And for thee, base king,
Titan shall pierce thy caverns with his rays
And sudden day shall smite thee. Do ye hear?
Or shall I summon to mine aid that god
At whose dread name earth trembles; who can look
Unflinching on the Gorgon's head, and drive
The Furies with his scourge, who holds the depths   900
Ye cannot fathom, and above whose haunts
Ye dwell supernal; who by waves of Styx
Forswears himself unpunished?"

                    Then the blood
Grew warm and liquid, and with softening touch
Cherished the stiffened wounds and filled the veins,
Till throbbed once more the slow returning pulse
And every fibre trembled, as with death
Life was commingled. Then, not limb by limb,
With toil and strain, but rising at a bound   910
Leaped from the earth erect the living man.
Fierce glared his eyes uncovered, and the life
Was dim, and still upon his face remained
The pallid hues of hardly parted death.
Amazement seized upon him, to the earth
Brought back again: but from his lips tight drawn
No murmur issued; he had power alone
When questioned to reply. "Speak," quoth the hag,
"As I shall bid thee; great shall be thy gain
If but thou answerest truly, freed for aye   920
From all Haemonian art. Such burial place
Shall now be thine, and on thy funeral pyre
Such fatal woods shall burn, such chant shall sound,
That to thy ghost no more or magic song
Or spell shall reach, and thy Lethaean sleep
Shall never more be broken in a death
From me received anew: for such reward
Think not this second life enforced in vain.
Obscure may be the answers of the gods
By priestess spoken at the holy shrine;   930
But whose braves the oracles of death

154

In search of truth, should gain a sure response.
Then speak, I pray thee. Let the hidden fates
Tell through thy voice the mysteries to come."

Thus spake she, and her words by mystic force
Gave him his answer; but with gloomy mien,
And tears swift flowing, thus he made reply:
"Called from the margin of the silent stream
I saw no fateful sisters spin the threads.
Yet know I this, that 'mid the Roman shades   940
Reigns fiercest discord; and this impious war
Destroys the peace that ruled the fields of death.
Elysian meads and deeps of Tartarus
In paths diverse the Roman chieftains leave
And thus disclose the fates. The blissful ghosts
Bear visages of sorrow. Sire and son
The Decii, who gave themselves to death
In expiation of their country's doom,
And great Camillus, wept; and Sulla's shade
Complained of fortune. Scipio bewailed   950
The scion of his race about to fall
In sands of Libya: Cato, greatest foe
To Carthage, grieves for that indignant soul
Which shall disdain to serve. Brutus alone
In all the happy ranks I smiling saw,
First consul when the kings were thrust from Rome.
The chains were fallen from boastful Catiline.
Him too I saw rejoicing, and the pair
Of Marii, and Cethegus' naked arm. [1]
The Drusi, heroes of the people, joyed,   960
In laws immoderate; and the famous pair [2]
Of greatly daring brothers: guilty bands
By bars eternal shut within the doors
That close the prison of hell, applaud the fates,
Claiming the plains Elysian: and the King
Throws wide his pallid halls, makes hard the points

---

[1] See Book II., 609.
[2] The Gracchi, the younger of whom aimed at being a perpetual tribune, and
was in some sort a forerunner of the Emperors.

Of craggy rocks, and forges iron chains,
The victor's punishment. But take with thee
This comfort, youth, that there a calm abode,
And peaceful, waits thy father and his house.   970
Nor let the glory of a little span
Disturb thy boding heart: the hour shall come
When all the chiefs shall meet. Shrink not from death,
But glowing in the greatness of your souls,
E'en from your humble sepulchres descend,
And tread beneath your feet, in pride of place,
The wandering phantoms of the gods of Rome. [1]
Which of the chiefs by Tiber's yellow stream,
And which by Nile shall rest (the leaders' fate)
This fight decides, no more. Nor seek to know   980
From me thy fortunes: for the fates in time
Shall give thee all thy due; and thy great sire, [2]
A surer prophet, in Sicilian fields
Shall speak thy future -- doubting even he
What regions of the world thou should'st avoid
And what should'st seek. O miserable race!
Europe and Asia and Libya's plains, [3]
Which saw your conquests, now shall hold alike
Your burial-place -- nor has the earth for you
A happier land than this."   990

            His task performed,
He stands in mournful guise, with silent look
Asking for death again; yet could not die
Till mystic herb and magic chant prevailed.
For nature's law, once used, had power no more
To slay the corpse and set the spirit free.
With plenteous wood she builds the funeral pyre
To which the dead man comes: then as the flames
Seized on his form outstretched, the youth and witch

---

[1] That is, the Caesars, who will be in Tartarus.
[2] Referring probably to an episode intended to be introduced in a later book,
in which the shade of Pompeius was to foretell his fate to Sextus.
[3] Cnaeus was killed in Spain after the battle of Munda; Sextus at Miletus;
Pompeius himself, of course, in Egypt.

BOOK VI

Together sought the camp; and as the dawn   1000
Now streaked the heavens, by the hag's command
The day was stayed till Sextus reached his tent,
And mist and darkness veiled his safe return.

BOOK VII

THE BATTLE

Ne'er to the summons of the Eternal laws
More slowly Titan rose, [1] nor drave his steeds,
Forced by the sky revolving, [2] up the heaven,
With gloomier presage; wishing to endure
The pangs of ravished light, and dark eclipse;
And drew the mists up, not to feed his flames, [3]
But lest his light upon Thessalian earth
Might fall undimmed.

        Pompeius on that morn,
To him the latest day of happy life,   10
In troubled sleep an empty dream conceived.
For in the watches of the night he heard
Innumerable Romans shout his name
Within his theatre; the benches vied
To raise his fame and place him with the gods;
As once in youth, when victory was won
O'er conquered tribes where swift Iberus flows, [4]

---

[1] "It is, methinks, a morning full of fate!   It riseth slowly, as her sullen car
Had all the weight of sleep and death hung at it!"   ...   And her sick head
is bound about with clouds   As if she threatened night ere noon of day."
        -- Ben Jonson, "Catiline", i., 1.
[2] See Book VI., 577.
[3] As to the sun finding fuel in the clouds, see Book I., line 471.
[4] Pompeius triumphed first in 81 B.C. for his victories in Sicily and Africa, at
the age of twenty-four. Sulla at first objected, but finally yielded and said,

And where Sertorius' armies fought and fled,
The west subdued, with no less majesty
Than if the purple toga graced the car,   20
He sat triumphant in his pure white gown
A Roman knight, and heard the Senate's cheer.
Perhaps, as ills drew near, his anxious soul,
Shunning the future wooed the happy past;
Or, as is wont, prophetic slumber showed
That which was not to be, by doubtful forms
Misleading; or as envious Fate forbade
Return to Italy, this glimpse of Rome
Kind Fortune gave. Break not his latest sleep,
Ye sentinels; let not the trumpet call   30
Strike on his ear: for on the morrow's night
Shapes of the battle lost, of death and war
Shall crowd his rest with terrors. Whence shalt thou
The poor man's happiness of sleep regain?
Happy if even in dreams thy Rome could see
Once more her captain! Would the gods had given
To thee and to thy country one day yet
To reap the latest fruit of such a love:
Though sure of fate to come! Thou marchest on
As though by heaven ordained in Rome to die;   40
She, conscious ever of her prayers for thee
Heard by the gods, deemed not the fates decreed
Such evil destiny, that she should lose
The last sad solace of her Magnus' tomb.
Then young and old had blent their tears for thee,
And child unbidden; women torn their hair
And struck their bosoms as for Brutus dead.
But now no public woe shall greet thy death
As erst thy praise was heard: but men shall grieve
In silent sorrow, though the victor's voice   50
Amid the clash of arms proclaims thy fall;
Though incense smoke before the Thunderer's shrine,
And shouts of welcome bid great Caesar hail.

"Let him triumph then in God's name." The triumph for the defeat of Sertorius was not till 71 B.C., in which year Pompeius was elected Consul along with Crassus. (Compare Book IX., 709.)

The stars had fled before the growing morn,
When eager voices (as the fates drew on
The world to ruin) round Pompeius' tent
Demand the battle signal. What! by those
So soon to perish, shall the sign be asked,
Their own, their country's doom? Ah! fatal rage
That hastens on the hour; no other sun   60
Upon this living host shall rise again.
"Pompeius fears!" they cry. "He's slow to act;
Too 'kind to Caesar; and he fondly rules
A world of subject peoples; but with peace
Such rule were ended." Eastern kings no less,
And peoples, eager for their distant homes,
Already murmured at the lengthy war.

Thus hath it pleased the gods, when woe impends
On guilty men, to make them seem its cause.
We court disaster, crave the fatal sword.   70
Of Magnus' camp Pharsalia was the prayer;
For Tullius, of all the sons of Rome
Chief orator, beneath whose civil rule
Fierce Catiline at the peace-compelling axe
Trembled and fled, arose, to Magnus' ear
Bearing the voice of all. To him was war
Grown hateful, and he longed once more to hear
The Senate's plaudits; and with eloquent lips
He lent persuasion to the weaker cause.
"Fortune, Pompeius, for her gifts to thee   80
Asks this one boon, that thou should'st use her now.
Here at thy feet thy leading captains lie;
And here thy monarchs, and a suppliant world
Entreats thee prostrate for thy kinsman's fall.
So long shall Caesar plunge the world in war?
Swift was thy tread when these proud nations fell;
How deep their shame, and justly, should delay
Now mar thy conquests! Where thy trust in Fate,
Thy fervour where? Ingrate! Dost dread the gods,
Or think they favour not the Senate's cause?   90
Thy troops unbidden shall the standards seize
And conquer; thou in shame be forced to win.

BOOK VII

If at the Senate's orders and for us
The war is waged, then give to us the right
To choose the battle-field. Why dost thou keep
From Caesar's throat the swords of all the world?
The weapon quivers in the eager hand:
Scarce one awaits the signal. Strike at once,
Or without thee the trumpets sound the fray.
Art thou the Senate's comrade or her lord?   100
We wait your answer."

       But Pompeius groaned;
His mind was adverse, but he felt the fates
Opposed his wish, and knew the hand divine.
"Since all desire it, and the fates prevail,
So let it be; your leader now no more,
I share the labours of the battle-field.
Let Fortune roll the nations of the earth
In one red ruin; myriads of mankind
See their last sun to-day. Yet, Rome, I swear,   110
This day of blood was forced upon thy son.
Without a wound, the prizes of the war
Might have been thine, and he who broke the peace
In peace forgotten. Whence this lust for crime?
Shall bloodless victories in civil war
Be shunned, not sought? We've ravished from our foe
All boundless seas, and land; his starving troops
Have snatched earth's crop half-grown, in vain attempt
Their hunger to appease; they prayed for death,
Sought for the sword-thrust, and within our ranks   120
Were fain to mix their life-blood with your own.
Much of the war is done: the conscript youth
Whose heart beats high, who burns to join the fray
(Though men fight hard in terror of defeat),
The shock of onset need no longer fear.
Bravest is he who promptly meets the ill
When fate commands it and the moment comes,
Yet brooks delay, in prudence; and shall we,
Our happy state enjoying, risk it all?
Trust to the sword the fortunes of the world?   130
Not victory, but battle, ye demand.
Do thou, O Fortune, of the Roman state

161

Who mad'st Pompeius guardian, from his hands
Take back the charge grown weightier, and thyself
Commit its safety to the chance of war.
Nor blame nor glory shall be mine to-day.
Thy prayers unjustly, Caesar, have prevailed:
We fight! What wickedness, what woes on men,
Destruction on what realms this dawn shall bring!
Crimson with Roman blood yon stream shall run.   140
Would that (without the ruin of our cause)
The first fell bolt hurled on this cursed day
Might strike me lifeless! Else, this battle brings
A name of pity or a name of hate.
The loser bears the burden of defeat;
The victor wins, but conquest is a crime."
Thus to the soldiers, burning for the fray,
He yields, forbidding, and throws down the reins.
So may a sailor give the winds control
Upon his barque, which, driven by the seas,   150
Bears him an idle burden. Now the camp
Hums with impatience, and the brave man's heart
With beats tumultuous throbs against his breast;
And all the host had standing in their looks [1]
The paleness of the death that was to come.
On that day's fight 'twas manifest that Rome
And all the future destinies of man
Hung trembling; and by weightier dread possessed,
They knew not danger. Who would fear for self
Should ocean rise and whelm the mountain tops,   160
And sun and sky descend upon the earth
In universal chaos? Every mind
Is bent upon Pompeius, and on Rome.
They trust no sword until its deadly point
Glows on the sharpening stone; no lance will serve
Till straightened for the fray; each bow is strung
Anew, and arrows chosen for their work
Fill all the quivers; horsemen try the curb
And fit the bridle rein and whet the spur.
If toils divine with human may compare,   170

---

[1] These two lines are taken from Ben Jonson's "Catiline", act v., scene 6.

BOOK VII

'Twas thus, when Phlegra bore the giant crew, [1]
In Etna's furnace glowed the sword of Mars,
Neptunus' trident felt the flame once more;
And great Apollo after Python slain
Sharpened his darts afresh: on Pallas' shield
Was spread anew the dread Medusa's hair;
And broad Sicilia trembled at the blows
Of Vulcan forging thunderbolts for Jove.

Yet Fortune failed not, as they sought the field,
In various presage of the ills to come;   180
All heaven opposed their march: portentous fire
In columns filled the plain, and torches blazed:
And thirsty whirlwinds mixed with meteor bolts
Smote on them as they strode, whose sulphurous flames
Perplexed the vision. Crests were struck from helms;
The melted sword-blade flowed upon the hilt:
The spear ran liquid, and the hurtful steel
Smoked with a sulphur that had come from heaven.
Nay, more, the standards, hid by swarms of bees
Innumerable, weighed the bearer down,   190
Scarce lifted from the earth; bedewed with tears;
No more of Rome the standards, [2] or her state.
And from the altar fled the frantic bull
To fields afar; nor was a victim found
To grace the sacrifice of coming doom.

But thou, Caesar, to what gods of ill
Didst thou appeal? What furies didst thou call,
What powers of madness and what Stygian Kings
Whelmed in th' abyss of hell? Didst favour gain
By sacrifice in this thine impious war?   200
Strange sights were seen; or caused by hands divine
Or due to fearful fancy. Haemus' top
Plunged headlong in the valley, Pindus met
With high Olympus, while at Ossa's feet

---

[1] The volcanic district of Campania, scene of the fabled battle of the giants.
(See Book IV., 666.)
[2] Henceforth to be the standards of the Emperor.

Pharsalia: Dramatic Episodes of the Civil Wars

Red ran Baebeis, [1] and Pharsalia's field
Gave warlike voices forth in depth of night.
Now darkness came upon their wondering gaze,
Now daylight pale and wan, their helmets wreathed
In pallid mist; the spirits of their sires
Hovered in air, and shades of kindred dead   210
Passed flitting through the gloom. Yet to the host
Conscious of guilty prayers which sought to shed
The blood of sires and brothers, earth and air
Distraught, and horrors seething in their hearts
Gave happy omen of the end to come.

Was't strange that peoples whom their latest day
Of happy life awaited (if their minds
Foreknew the doom) should tremble with affright?
Romans who dwelt by far Araxes' stream,
And Tyrian Gades, [2] in whatever clime,   220
'Neath every sky, struck by mysterious dread
Were plunged in sorrow -- yet rebuked the tear,
For yet they knew not of the fatal day.
Thus on Euganean hills [3] where sulphurous fumes
Disclose the rise of Aponus [4] from earth,
And where Timavus broadens in the meads,
An augur spake: "This day the fight is fought,
The arms of Caesar and Pompeius meet

---

[1] A lake at the foot of Mount Ossa. Pindus, Ossa, Olympus, and, above all, Haemus (the Balkans) were at a long distance from Pharsalia. Comp. Book VI., 677.

[2] Gades (Cadiz) is stated to have been founded by the Phoenicians about 1000 B.C.

[3] This alludes to the story told by Plutarch ("Caesar", 47) that, at Patavium, Caius Cornelius, a man reputed for skill in divination, and a friend of Livy the historian, was sitting to watch the birds that day. "And first of all (as Livius says) he discovered the time of the battle, and he said to those present that the affair was now deciding and the men were going into action. Looking again, and observing the signs, he sprang up with enthusiasm and called out, 'You conquer, Caesar.'" (Long's translation.)

[4] The Fontes Aponi were warm springs near Padua. An altar, inscribed to Apollo Aponus, was found at Ribchester, and is now at St. John's College, Cambridge. (Wright, "Celt, Roman, and Saxon", p. 320.)

To end the impious conflict." Or he saw
The bolts of Jupiter, predicting ill;   230
Or else the sky discordant o'er the space
Of heaven, from pole to pole; or else perchance
The sun was sad and misty in the height
And told the battle by his wasted beams.
By Nature's fiat that Thessalian day
Passed not as others; if the gifted sense
Of reading portents had been given to all,
All men had known Pharsalia. Gods of heaven!
How do ye mark the great ones of the earth!
The world gives tokens of their weal or woe;   240
The sky records their fates: in distant climes
To future races shall their tale be told,
Or by the fame alone of mighty deeds
Had in remembrance, or by this my care
Borne through the centuries: and men shall read
In hope and fear the story of the war
And breathless pray, as though it were to come,
For that long since accomplished; and for thee
Thus far, Pompeius, shall that prayer be given.

Reflected from their arms, th' opposing sun   250
Filled all the slope with radiance as they marched
In ordered ranks to that ill-fated fight,
And stood arranged for battle. On the left
Thou, Lentulus, had'st charge; two legions there,
The fourth, and bravest of them all, the first:
While on the right, Domitius, ever stanch,
Though fates be adverse, stood: in middle line
The hardy soldiers from Cilician lands,
In Scipio's care; their chief in Libyan days,
To-day their comrade. By Enipeus' pools   260
And by the rivulets, the mountain troops
Of Cappadocia, and loose of rein
Thy squadrons, Pontus: on the firmer ground
Galatia's tetrarchs and the greater kings;
And all the purple-robed, the slaves of Rome.
Numidian hordes were there from Afric shores,
There Creta's host and Ituraeans found
Full space to wing their arrows; there the tribes

165

From brave Iberia clashed their shields, and there
Gaul stood arrayed against her ancient foe.   270
Let all the nations be the victor's prize,
None grace in future a triumphal car;
This fight demands the slaughter of a world.

Caesar that day to send his troops for spoil
Had left his tent, when on the further hill
Behold! his foe descending to the plain.
The moment asked for by a thousand prayers
Is come, which puts his fortune on the risk
Of imminent war, to win or lose it all.
For burning with desire of kingly power   280
His eager soul ill brooked the small delay
This civil war compelled: each instant lost
Robbed from his due! But when at length he knew
The last great conflict come, the fight supreme,
Whose prize the leadership of all the world:
And felt the ruin nodding to its fall:
Swiftest to strike, yet for a little space
His rage for battle failed; the spirit bold
To pledge itself the issue, wavered now:
For Magnus' fortunes gave no room for hope,   290
Though Caesar's none for fear. Deep in his soul
Such doubt was hidden, as with mien and speech
That augured victory, thus the chief began:
"Ye conquerors of a world, my hope in all,
Prayed for so oft, the dawn of fight is come.
No more entreat the gods: with sword in hand
Seize on our fates; and Caesar in your deeds
This day is great or little. This the day
For which I hold since Rubicon was passed
Your promise given: for this we flew to arms: [1]   300
For this deferred the triumphs we had won,
And which the foe refused: this gives you back
Your homes and kindred, and the peaceful farm,
Your prize for years of service in the field.
And by the fates' command this day shall prove

---

[1] See Book I., 411, and following lines.

Whose quarrel juster: for defeat is guilt
To him on whom it falls. If in my cause
With fire and sword ye did your country wrong,
Strike for acquittal! Should another judge
This war, not Caesar, none were blameless found.   310
Not for my sake this battle, but for you,
To give you, soldiers, liberty and law
'Gainst all the world. Wishful myself for life
Apart from public cares, and for the gown
That robes the private citizen, I refuse
To yield from office till the law allows
Your right in all things. On my shoulders rest
All blame; all power be yours. Nor deep the blood
Between yourselves and conquest. Grecian schools
Of exercise and wrestling [1] send us here   320
Their chosen darlings to await your swords;
And scarcely armed for war, a dissonant crowd
Barbaric, that will start to hear our trump,
Nay, their own clamour. Not in civil strife
Your blows shall fall -- the battle of to-day
Sweeps from the earth the enemies of Rome.
Dash through these cowards and their vaunted kings:
One stroke of sword and all the world is yours.
Make plain to all men that the crowds who decked
Pompeius' hundred pageants scarce were fit   330
For one poor triumph. Shall Armenia care
Who leads her masters, or barbarians shed
One drop of blood to make Pompeius chief
O'er our Italia? Rome, 'tis Rome they hate
And all her children; yet they hate the most
Those whom they know. My fate is in the hands
Of you, mine own true soldiers, proved in all
The wars we fought in Gallia. When the sword
Of each of you shall strike, I know the hand:

---

[1] For the contempt here expressed for the Greek gymnastic schools, see also
Tacitus, "Annals", 14, 21. It is well known that Nero instituted games called
Neronia which were borrowed from the Greeks; and that many of the Roman
citizens despised them as foreign and profligate. Merivale, chapter liii., cites
this passage.

The javelin's flight to me betrays the arm   340
That launched it hurtling: and to-day once more
I see the faces stern, the threatening eyes,
Unfailing proofs of victory to come.
E'en now the battle rushes on my sight;
Kings trodden down and scattered senators
Fill all th' ensanguined plain, and peoples float
Unnumbered on the crimson tide of death.
Enough of words -- I but delay the fates;
And you who burn to dash into the fray,
Forgive the pause. I tremble with the hopes [1]   350
Thus finding utterance. I ne'er have seen
The mighty gods so near; this little field
Alone dividing us; their hands are full
Of my predestined honours: for 'tis I
Who when this war is done shall have the power
O'er all that peoples, all that kings enjoy
To shower it where I will. But has the pole
Been moved, or in its nightly course some star
Turned backwards, that such mighty deeds should pass
Here on Thessalian earth? To-day we reap   360
Of all our wars the harvest or the doom.
Think of the cross that threats us, and the chain,
Limbs hacked asunder, Caesar's head displayed
Upon the rostra; and that narrow field
Piled up with slaughter: for this hostile chief
Is savage Sulla's pupil. 'Tis for you,
If conquered, that I grieve: my lot apart
Is cast long since. This sword, should one of you
Turn from the battle ere the foe be fled,
Shall rob the life of Caesar. O ye gods,   370
Drawn down from heaven by the throes of Rome,
May he be conqueror who shall not draw
Against the vanquished an inhuman sword,

---

[1] Thus paraphrased by Dean Stanley: "I tremble not with terror, but with
hope,   As the great day reveals its coming scope;   Never in earlier days,
our hearts to cheer,   Have such bright gifts of Heaven been brought so near,
Nor ever has been kept the aspiring soul   By space so narrow from so grand
a goal." Inaugural address at St. Andrews. 1873, on the "Study of Greatness".

Nor count it as a crime if men of Rome
Preferred another's standard to his own.
Pompeius' sword drank deep Italian blood
When cabined in yon space the brave man's arm
No more found room to strike. But you, I pray,
Touch not the foe who turns him from the fight,
A fellow citizen, a foe no more.   380
But while the gleaming weapons threaten still,
Let no fond memories unnerve the arm, [1]
No pious thought of father or of kin;
But full in face of brother or of sire,
Drive home the blade. Unless the slain be known
Your foes account his slaughter as a crime;
Spare not our camp, but lay the rampart low
And fill the fosse with ruin; not a man
But holds his post within the ranks to-day.
And yonder tents, deserted by the foe,   390
Shall give us shelter when the rout is done."

Scarce had he paused; they snatch the hasty meal,
And seize their armour and with swift acclaim
Welcome the chief's predictions of the day,
Tread low their camp when rushing to the fight;
And take their post: nor word nor order given,
In fate they put their trust. Nor, had'st thou placed
All Caesars there, all striving for the throne
Of Rome their city, had their serried ranks
With speedier tread dashed down upon the foe.   400

But when Pompeius saw the hostile troops
Move forth in order and demand the fight,
And knew the gods' approval of the day,
He stood astonied, while a deadly chill
Struck to his heart -- omen itself of woe,
That such a chief should at the call to arms,
Thus dread the issue: but with fear repressed,
Borne on his noble steed along the line
Of all his forces, thus he spake: "The day

---

[1] That such were Caesar's orders is also attested by Appian.

Your bravery demands, that final end   410
Of civil war ye asked for, is at hand.
Put forth your strength, your all; the sword to-day
Does its last work. One crowded hour is charged
With nations' destinies. Whoe'er of you
Longs for his land and home, his wife and child,
Seek them with sword. Here in mid battle-field,
The gods place all at stake. Our better right
Bids us expect their favour; they shall dip
Your brands in Caesar's blood, and thus shall give
Another sanction to the laws of Rome,   420
Our cause of battle. If for him were meant
An empire o'er the world, had they not put
An end to Magnus' life? That I am chief
Of all these mingled peoples and of Rome
Disproves an angry heaven. See here combined
All means of victory. Noble men have sought
Unasked the risks of war. Our soldiers boast
Ancestral statues. If to us were given
A Curius, if Camillus were returned,
Or patriot Decius to devote his life,   430
Here would they take their stand. From furthest east
All nations gathered, cities as the sand
Unnumbered, give their aid: a world complete
Serves 'neath our standards. North and south and all
Who have their being 'neath the starry vault,
Here meet in arms conjoined: And shall we not
Crush with our closing wings this paltry foe?
Few shall find room to strike; the rest with voice
Must be content to aid: for Caesar's ranks
Suffice not for us. Think from Rome's high walls   440
The matrons watch you with their hair unbound;
Think that the Senate hoar, too old for arms,
With snowy locks outspread; and Rome herself,
The world's high mistress, fearing now, alas!
A despot -- all exhort you to the fight.
Think that the people that is and that shall be
Joins in the prayer -- in freedom to be born,
In freedom die, their wish. If 'mid these vows
Be still found place for mine, with wife and child,
So far as Imperator may, I bend   450

Before you suppliant -- unless this fight
Be won, behold me exile, your disgrace,
My kinsman's scorn. From this, 'tis yours to save.
Then save! Nor in the latest stage of life,
Let Magnus be a slave."

            Then burned their souls
At these his words, indignant at the thought,
And Rome rose up within them, and to die
Was welcome.

          Thus alike with hearts aflame   460
Moved either host to battle, one in fear
And one in hope of empire. These hands shall do
Such work as not the rolling centuries
Not all mankind though free from sword and war
Shall e'er make good. Nations that were to live
This fight shall crush, and peoples pre-ordained
To make the history of the coming world
Shall come not to the birth. The Latin names
Shall sound as fables in the ears of men,
And ruins loaded with the dust of years   470
Shall hardly mark her cities. Alba's hill,
Home of our gods, no human foot shall tread,
Save of some Senator at the ancient feast
By Numa's orders founded -- he compelled
Serves his high office. [1] Void and desolate
Are Veii, Cora and Laurentum's hold;
Yet not the tooth of envious time destroyed
These storied monuments -- 'twas civil war
That rased their citadels. Where now hath fled
The teeming life that once Italia knew?   480
Not all the earth can furnish her with men:
Untenanted her dwellings and her fields:
Slaves till her soil: one city holds us all:
Crumbling to ruin, the ancestral roof
Finds none on whom to fall; and Rome herself,
Void of her citizens, draws within her gates

---

[1] See Book V., 463.

The dregs of all the world. That none might wage
A civil war again, thus deeply drank
Pharsalia's fight the life-blood of her sons.
Dark in the calendar of Rome for aye,   490
The days when Allia and Cannae fell:
And shall Pharsalus' morn, darkest of all,
Stand on the page unmarked? Alas, the fates!
Not plague nor pestilence nor famine's rage,
Not cities given to the flames, nor towns
Trembling at shock of earthquake shall weigh down
Such heroes lost, when Fortune's ruthless hand
Lops at one blow the gift of centuries,
Leaders and men embattled. How great art thou,
Rome, in thy fall! Stretched to the widest bounds   500
War upon war laid nations at thy feet
Till flaming Titan nigh to either pole
Beheld thine empire; and the furthest east
Was almost thine, till day and night and sky
For thee revolved, and all the stars could see
Throughout their course was Roman. But the fates
In one dread day of slaughter and despair
Turned back the centuries and spoke thy doom.
And now the Indian fears the axe no more
Once emblem of thy power, now no more   510
The girded Consul curbs the Getan horde,
Or in Sarmatian furrows guides the share: [1]
Still Parthia boasts her triumphs unavenged:
Foul is the public life; and Freedom, fled
To furthest Earth beyond the Tigris' stream,
And Rhine's broad river, wandering at her will
'Mid Teuton hordes and Scythian, though by sword
Sought, yet returns not. Would that from the day
When Romulus, aided by the vulture's flight,
Ill-omened, raised within that hateful grove   520
Rome's earliest walls, down to the crimsoned field
In dire Thessalia fought, she ne'er had known

---

[1] That is, marked out the new colony with a plough-share. This was regarded as a religious ceremony, and therefore performed by the Consul with his toga worn in ancient fashion.

BOOK VII

Italia's peoples! Did the Bruti strike
In vain for liberty? Why laws and rights
Sanctioned by all the annals designate
With consular titles? Happier far the Medes
And blest Arabia, and the Eastern lands
Held by a kindlier fate in despot rule!
That nation serves the worst which serves with shame.
No guardian gods watch over us from heaven: 530
Jove ^{1} is no king; let ages whirl along
In blind confusion: from his throne supreme
Shall he behold such carnage and restrain
His thunderbolts? On Mimas shall he hurl
His fires, on Rhodope and Oeta's woods
Unmeriting such chastisement, and leave
This life to Cassius' hand? On Argos fell
At grim Thyestes' feast ^{2} untimely night
By him thus hastened; shall Thessalia's land
Receive full daylight, wielding kindred swords   540
In fathers' hands and brothers'? Careless of men
Are all the gods. Yet for this day of doom
Such vengeance have we reaped as deities
May give to mortals; for these wars shall raise
Our parted Caesars to the gods; and Rome
Shall deck their effigies with thunderbolts,
And stars and rays, and in the very fanes
Swear by the shades of men.

        With swift advance
They seize the space that yet delays the fates   550
Till short the span dividing. Then they gaze
For one short moment where may fall the spear,
What hand may deal their death, what monstrous task
Soon shall be theirs; and all in arms they see,
In reach of stroke, their brothers and their sires
With front opposing; yet to yield their ground
It pleased them not. But all the host was dumb
With horror; cold upon each loving heart,

---

^{1} "Hath Jove no thunder?" -- Ben Jonson, "Catiline", iii., 2.
^{2} Compare Book I., line 600.

Awe-struck, the life-blood pressed; and all men held
With arms outstretched their javelins for a time,   560
Poised yet unthrown. Now may th' avenging gods
Allot thee, Crastinus, [1] not such a death
As all men else do suffer! In the tomb
May'st thou have feeling and remembrance still!
For thine the hand that first flung forth the dart,
Which stained with Roman blood Thessalia's earth.
Madman! To speed thy lance when Caesar's self
Still held his hand! Then from the clarions broke
The strident summons, and the trumpets blared
Responsive signal. Upward to the vault   570
The sound re-echoes where nor clouds may reach
Nor thunder penetrate; and Haemus' slopes [2]
Reverberate to Pelion the din;
Pindus re-echoes; Oeta's lofty rocks
Groan, and Pangaean cliffs, till at their rage
Borne back from all the earth they shook for fear.

Unnumbered darts they hurl, with prayers diverse;
Some hope to wound: others, in secret, yearn
For hands still innocent. Chance rules supreme,
And wayward Fortune upon whom she wills   580
Makes fall the guilt. Yet for the hatred bred
By civil war suffices spear nor lance,
Urged on their flight afar: the hand must grip
The sword and drive it to the foeman's heart.
But while Pompeius' ranks, shield wedged to shield,
Were ranged in dense array, and scarce had space
To draw the blade, came rushing at the charge
Full on the central column Caesar's host,
Mad for the battle. Man nor arms could stay
The crash of onset, and the furious sword   590

---

[1] This act of Crastinus is recorded by Plutarch ("Pompeius", 71), and by Caesar, "Civil War", Book III., 91. Caesar called him by name and said: "Well, Crastinus, shall we win today?" "We shall win with glory, Caesar," he replied in a loud voice, "and to-day you will praise me, living or dead." -- Durny, "History of Rome", vol. iii., 312. He was placed in a special tomb after the battle.
[2] See on line 203.

Clove through the stubborn panoply to the flesh,
There only stayed. One army struck -- their foes
Struck not in answer; Magnus' swords were cold,
But Caesar's reeked with slaughter and with guilt.
Nor Fortune lingered, but decreed the doom
Which swept the ruins of a world away.

Soon as withdrawn from all the spacious plain,
Pompeius' horse was ranged upon the flanks;
Passed through the outer files, the lighter armed
Of all the nations joined the central strife,   600
With divers weapons armed, but all for blood
Of Rome athirst: then blazing torches flew,
Arrows and stones. and ponderous balls of lead
Molten by speed of passage through the air.
There Ituraean archers and the Mede
Winged forth their countless shafts till all the sky
Grew dark with missiles hurled; and from the night
Brooding above, Death struck his victims down,
Guiltless such blow, while all the crime was heaped
Upon the Roman spear. In line oblique   610
Behind the standards Caesar in reserve
Had placed some companies of foot, in fear
The foremost ranks might waver. These at his word,
No trumpet sounding, break upon the ranks
Of Magnus' horsemen where they rode at large
Flanking the battle. They, unshamed of fear
And careless of the fray, when first a steed
Pierced through by javelin spurned with sounding hoof
The temples of his rider, turned the rein,
And through their comrades spurring from the field   620
In panic, proved that not with warring Rome
Barbarians may grapple. Then arose
Immeasurable carnage: here the sword,
There stood the victim, and the victor's arm
Wearied of slaughter. Oh, that to thy plains,
Pharsalia, might suffice the crimson stream
From hosts barbarian, nor other blood
Pollute thy fountains' sources! these alone
Shall clothe thy pastures with the bones of men!
Or if thy fields must run with Roman blood   630

Then spare the nations who in times to come
Must be her peoples!

Now the terror spread
Through all the army, and the favouring fates
Decreed for Caesar's triumph: and the war
Ceased in the wider plain, though still ablaze
Where stood the chosen of Pompeius' force,
Upholding yet the fight. Not here allies
Begged from some distant king to wield the sword:
Here were the Roman sons, the sires of Rome,   640
Here the last frenzy and the last despair:
Here, Caesar, was thy crime: and here shall stay
My Muse repelled: no poesy of mine
Shall tell the horrors of the final strife,
Nor for the coming ages paint the deeds
Which civil war permits. Be all obscured
In deepest darkness! Spare the useless tear
And vain lament, and let the deeds that fell
In that last fight of Rome remain unsung.

But Caesar adding fury to the breasts   650
Already flaming with the rage of war,
That each might bear his portion of the guilt
Which stained the host, unflinching through the ranks
Passed at his will. He looked upon the brands,
These reddened only at the point, and those
Streaming with blood and gory, to the hilt:
He marks the hand which trembling grasped the sword,
Or held it idle, and the cheek that grew
Pale at the blow, and that which at his words
Glowed with the joy of battle: midst the dead   660
He treads the plain and on each gaping wound
Presses his hand to keep the life within.
Thus Caesar passed: and where his footsteps fell
As when Bellona shakes her crimson lash,
Or Mavors scourges on the Thracian mares [1]

---

[1] That is, lashes on his team terrified by the Gorgon shield in the ranks of the enemy.

When shunning the dread face on Pallas' shield,
He drives his chariot, there arose a night
Dark with huge slaughter and with crime, and groans
As of a voice immense, and sound of alms
As fell the wearer, and of sword on sword   670
Crashed into fragments. With a ready hand
Caesar supplies the weapon and bids strike
Full at the visage; and with lance reversed
Urges the flagging ranks and stirs the fight.
Where flows the nation's blood, where beats the heart,
Knowing, he bids them spare the common herd,
But seek the senators -- thus Rome he strikes,
Thus the last hold of Freedom. In the fray,
Then fell the nobles with their mighty names
Of ancient prowess; there Metellus' sons,   680
Corvini, Lepidi, Torquati too,
Not once nor twice the conquerors of kings,
First of all men, Pompeius' name except,
Lay dead upon the field.

          But, Brutus, where,
Where was thy sword? [1] "Veiled by a common helm
Unknown thou wanderest. Thy country's pride,
Hope of the Senate, thou (for none besides);
Thou latest scion of that race of pride,
Whose fearless deeds the centuries record,   690
Tempt not the battle, nor provoke the doom!
Awaits thee on Philippi's fated field
Thy Thessaly. Not here shalt thou prevail
'Gainst Caesar's life. Not yet hath he surpassed
The height of power and deserved a death
Noble at Brutus' hands -- then let him live,
Thy fated victim!

---

[1] Plutarch states that Brutus after the battle escaped and made his way to Larissa, whence he wrote to Caesar. Caesar, pleased that he was alive, asked him to come to him; and it was on Brutus' opinion that Caesar determined to hurry to Egypt as the most probable refuge of Pompeius. Caesar entrusted Brutus with the command of Cisalpine Gaul when he was in Africa.

There upon the field
Lay all the honour of Rome; no common stream
Mixed with the purple tide. And yet of all   700
Who noble fell, one only now I sing,
Thee, brave Domitius. [1] Whene'er the day
Was adverse to the fortunes of thy chief
Thine was the arm which vainly stayed the fight.
Vanquished so oft by Caesar, now 'twas thine
Yet free to perish. By a thousand wounds
Came welcome death, nor had thy conqueror power
Again to pardon. Caesar stood and saw
The dark blood welling forth and death at hand,
And thus in words of scorn: "And dost thou lie,   710
Domitius, there? And did Pompeius name
Thee his successor, thee? Why leavest thou then
His standards helpless?" But the parting life
Still faintly throbbed within Domitius' breast,
Thus finding utterance: "Yet thou hast not won
Thy hateful prize, for doubtful are the fates;
Nor thou the master, Caesar; free as yet,
With great Pompeius for my leader still,
Warring no more, I seek the silent shades,
Yet with this hope in death, that thou subdued   720
To Magnus and to me in grievous guise
May'st pay atonement." So he spake: no more;
Then closed his eyes in death.

'Twere shame to shed,
When thus a world was perishing, the tear
Meet for each fate, or sing the wound that reft
Each life away. Through forehead and through throat
The pitiless weapon clove its deadly path,
Or forced the entrails forth: one fell to earth
Prone at the stroke; one stood though shorn of limb;   730

---

[1] "He perished, after a career of furious partisanship, disgraced with cruelty
and treachery, on the field of Pharsalia" (Merivale, "Hist. Romans under the
Empire", chapter lii.). Unless this man had been an ancestor of Nero it is im-
possible to suppose that Lucan would have thus singled him out. But he
appears to have been the only leader who fell. (Compare Book II, lines 534-
590, for his conduct at Corfinium.)

Glanced from this breast unharmed the quivering spear;
That it transfixed to earth. Here from the veins
Spouted the life-blood, till the foeman's arms
Were crimsoned. One his brother slew, nor dared
To spoil the corse, till severed from the neck
He flung the head afar. Another dashed
Full in his father's teeth the fatal sword,
By murderous frenzy striving to disprove
His kinship with the slain. Yet for each death
We find no separate dirge, nor weep for men   740
When peoples fell. Thus, Rome, thy doom was wrought
At dread Pharsalus. Not, as in other fields,
By soldiers slain, or captains; here were swept
Whole nations to the death; Assyria here,
Achaia, Pontus; and the blood of Rome
Gushing in torrents forth, forbade the rest
To stagnate on the plain. Nor life was reft,
Nor safety only then; but reeled the world
And all her manifold peoples at the blow
In that day's battle dealt; nor only then   750
Felt, but in all the times that were to come.
Those swords gave servitude to every age
That shall be slavish; by our sires was shaped
For us our destiny, the despot yoke.
Yet have we trembled not, nor feared to bare
Our throats to slaughter, nor to face the foe:
We bear the penalty for others' shame.
Such be our doom; yet, Fortune, sharing not
In that last battle, 'twas our right to strike
One blow for freedom ere we served our lord.   760

Now saw Pompeius, grieving, that the gods
Had left his side, and knew the fates of Rome
Passed from his governance; yet all the blood
That filled the field scarce brought him to confess
His fortunes fled. A little hill he sought
Whence to descry the battle raging still
Upon the plain, which when he nearer stood
The warring ranks concealed. Thence did the chief
Gaze on unnumbered swords that flashed in air
And sought his ruin; and the tide of blood   770

In which his host had perished. Yet not as those
Who, prostrate fallen, would drag nations down
To share their evil fate, Pompeius did.
Still were the gods thought worthy of his prayers
To give him solace, in that after him
Might live his Romans. "Spare, ye gods," he said,
"Nor lay whole peoples low; my fall attained,
The world and Rome may stand. And if ye need
More bloodshed, here on me, my wife, and sons
Wreak out your vengeance -- pledges to the fates   780
Such have we given. Too little for the war
Is our destruction? Doth the carnage fail,
The world escaping? Magnus' fortunes lost,
Why doom all else beside him?" Thus he cried,
And passed amid his standards, and recalled
His vanquished host that rushed on fate declared.
Not for his sake such carnage should be wrought.
So thought Pompeius; nor the foeman's sword
He feared, nor death; but lest upon his fall
To quit their chief his soldiers might refuse,   790
And o'er his prostrate corpse a world in arms
Might find its ruin: or perchance he wished
From Caesar's eager eyes to veil his death.
In vain, unhappy! for the fates decree
He shall behold, shorn from the bleeding trunk,
Again thy visage. And thou, too, his spouse,
Beloved Cornelia, didst cause his flight;
Thy longed-for features; yet he shall not die
When thou art present. [1]

       Then upon his steed,   800
Though fearing not the weapons at his back,
Pompeius fled, his mighty soul prepared
To meet his destinies. No groan nor tear,
But solemn grief as for the fates of Rome,
Was in his visage, and with mien unchanged

---

[1] This appears to be the only possible meaning of the text. But in truth, although Cornelia was not by her husband's side at his murder, she was present at the scene.

He saw Pharsalia's woes, above the frowns
Or smiles of Fortune; in triumphant days
And in his fall, her master. The burden laid
Of thine impending fate, thou partest free
To muse upon the happy days of yore.   810
Hope now has fled; but in the fleeting past
How wast thou great! Seek thou the wars no more,
And call the gods to witness that for thee
Henceforth dies no man. In the fights to come
On Afric's mournful shore, by Pharos' stream
And fateful Munda; in the final scene
Of dire Pharsalia's battle, not thy name
Doth stir the war and urge the foeman's arm,
But those great rivals biding with us yet,
Caesar and Liberty; and not for thee   820
But for itself the dying Senate fought,
When thou had'st fled the combat.

                    Find'st thou not
Some solace thus in parting from the fight
Nor seeing all the horrors of its close?
Look back upon the dead that load the plain,
The rivers turbid with a crimson stream;
Then pity thou thy victor. How shall he
Enter the city, who on such a field
Finds happiness? Trust thou in Fortune yet,   830
Her favourite ever; and whate'er, alone
In lands unknown, an exile, be thy lot,
Whate'er thy sufferings 'neath the Pharian king,
'Twere worse to conquer. Then forbid the tear,
Cease, sounds of woe, and lamentation cease,
And let the world adore thee in defeat,
As in thy triumphs. With unfaltering gaze,
Look on the suppliant kings, thy subjects still;
Search out the realms and cities which they hold,
Thy gift, Pompeius; and a fitting place   840
Choose for thy death.

                    First witness of thy fall,
And of thy noble bearing in defeat,
Larissa. Weeping, yet with gifts of price

181

Fit for a victor, from her teeming gates
Poured forth her citizens, their homes and fanes
Flung open; wishing it had been their lot
With thee to share disaster. Of thy name
Still much survives, unto thy former self
Alone inferior, still could'st thou to arms   850
All nations call and challenge fate again.
But thus he spake: "To cities nor to men
Avails the conquered aught; then pledge your faith
To him who has the victory." Caesar trod
Pharsalia's slaughter, while his daughter's spouse
Thus gave him kingdoms; but Pompeius fled
'Mid sobs and groans and blaming of the gods
For this their fierce commandment; and he fled
Full of the fruits and knowledge of the love
The peoples bore him, which he knew not his   860
In times of happiness.

When Italian blood
Flowed deep enough upon the fatal field,
Caesar bade halt, and gave their lives to those
Whose death had been no gain. But that their camp
Might not recall the foe, nor calm of night
Banish their fears, he bids his cohorts dash,
While Fortune glowed and terror filled the plain,
Straight on the ramparts of the conquered foe.
Light was the task to urge them to the spoil;   870
"Soldiers," he said, "the victory is ours,
Full and triumphant: there doth lie the prize
Which you have won, not Caesar; at your feet
Behold the booty of the hostile camp.
Snatched from Hesperian nations ruddy gold,
And all the riches of the Orient world,
Are piled within the tents. The wealth of kings
And of Pompeius here awaits its lords.
Haste, soldiers, and outstrip the flying foe;
E'en now the vanquished of Pharsalia's field   880
Anticipate your spoils." No more he said,
But drave them, blind with frenzy for the gold,
To spurn the bodies of their fallen sires,
And trample chiefs in dashing on their prey.

182

What rampart had restrained them as they rushed
To seize the prize for wickedness and war
And learn the price of guilt? And though they found
In ponderous masses heaped for need of war
The trophies of a world, yet were their minds
Unsatisfied, that asked for all. Whate'er   890
Iberian mines or Tagus bring to day,
Or Arimaspians from golden sands
May gather, had they seized; still had they thought
Their guilt too cheaply sold. When pledged to them
Was the Tarpeian rock, for victory won,
And all the spoils of Rome, by Caesar's word,
Shall camps suffice them?

        Then plebeian limbs
On senators' turf took rest, on kingly couch
The meanest soldier; and the murderer lay   900
Where yesternight his brother or his sire.
In raving dreams within their waking brains
Yet raged the battle, and the guilty hand
Still wrought its deeds of blood, and restless sought
The absent sword-hilt. Thou had'st said that groans
Issued from all the plain, that parted souls
Had breathed a life into the guilty soil,
That earthly darkness teemed with gibbering ghosts
And Stygian terrors. Victory foully won
Thus claimed its punishment. The slumbering sense   910
Already heard the hiss of vengeful flames
As from the depths of Acheron. One saw
Deep in the trances of the night his sire
And one his brother slain. But all the dead
In long array were visioned to the eyes
Of Caesar dreaming. Not in other guise
Orestes saw the Furies ere he fled
To purge his sin within the Scythian bounds;
Nor in more fierce convulsions raged the soul
Of Pentheus raving; nor Agave's [1] mind   920
When she had known her son. Before his gaze

---

[1] See Book VI., 420.

Flashed all the javelins which Pharsalia saw,
Or that avenging day when drew their blades
The Roman senators; and on his couch,
Infernal monsters from the depths of hell
Scourged him in slumber. Thus his guilty mind
Brought retribution. Ere his rival died
The terrors that enfold the Stygian stream
And black Avernus, and the ghostly slain
Broke on his sleep.   930

        Yet when the golden sun
Unveiled the butchery of Pharsalia's field [1]
He shrank not from its horror, nor withdrew
His feasting gaze. There rolled the streams in flood
With crimson carnage; there a seething heap
Rose shrouding all the plain, now in decay
Slow settling down; there numbered he the host
Of Magnus slain; and for the morn's repast
That spot he chose whence he might watch the dead,
And feast his eyes upon Emathia's field   940
Concealed by corpses; of the bloody sight
Insatiate, he forbad the funeral pyre,
And cast Emathia in the face of heaven.
Nor by the Punic victor was he taught,
Who at the close of Cannae's fatal fight
Laid in the earth the Roman consul dead,
To find fit burial for his fallen foes;
For these were all his countrymen, nor yet
His ire by blood appeased. Yet ask we not
For separate pyres or sepulchres apart   950
Wherein to lay the ashes of the fallen:
Burn in one holocaust the nations slain;
Or should it please thy soul to torture more
Thy kinsman, pile on high from Oeta's slopes

---

[1] The whole of this passage is foreign to Caesar's character, and unfounded in fact. Pompeians perished on the field, and were taken prisoners. When Caesar passed over the field he is recorded to have said in pity, "They would have it so; after all my exploits I should have been condemned to death had I not thrown myself upon the protection of my soldiers." -- Plutarch, "Caesar"; Durny, "History of Rome", vol. iii., p. 311.

BOOK VII

And Pindus' top the woods: thus shall he see
While fugitive on the deep the blaze that marks
Thessalia. Yet by this idle rage
Nought dost thou profit; for these corporal frames
Bearing innate from birth the certain germs
Of dissolution, whether by decay   960
Or fire consumed, shall fall into the lap
Of all-embracing nature. Thus if now
Thou should'st deny the pyre, still in that flame
When all shall crumble, ¹ earth and rolling seas
And stars commingled with the bones of men,
These too shall perish. Where thy soul shall go
These shall companion thee; no higher flight
In airy realms is thine, nor smoother couch
Beneath the Stygian darkness; for the dead
No fortune favours, and our Mother Earth   970
All that is born from her receives again,
And he whose bones no tomb or urn protects
Yet sleeps beneath the canopy of heaven.
And thou, proud conqueror, who would'st deny
The rites of burial to thousands slain,
Why flee thy field of triumph? Why desert
This reeking plain? Drink, Caesar, of the streams,
Drink if thou can'st, and should it be thy wish
Breathe the Thessalian air; but from thy grasp
The earth is ravished, and th' unburied host,   980
Routing their victor, hold Pharsalia's field.

Then to the ghastly harvest of the war
Came all the beasts of earth whose facile sense
Of odour tracks the bodies of the slain.
Sped from his northern home the Thracian wolf;
Bears left their dens and lions from afar
Scenting the carnage; dogs obscene and foul
Their homes deserted: all the air was full
Of gathering fowl, who in their flight had long
Pursued the armies. Cranes ¹ who yearly change   990

---

¹ Alluding to the general conflagration in which (by the Stoic doctrines) all
the universe would one day perish.

185

The frosts of Thracia for the banks of Nile,
This year delayed their voyage. As ne'er before
The air grew dark with vultures' hovering wings,
Innumerable, for every grove and wood
Sent forth its denizens; on every tree
Dripped from their crimsoned beaks a gory dew.
Oft on the conquerors and their impious arms
Or purple rain of blood, or mouldering flesh
Fell from the lofty heaven; or limbs of men
From weary talons dropped. Yet even so   1000
The peoples passed not all into the maw
Of ravening beast or fowl; the inmost flesh
Scarce did they touch, nor limbs -- thus lay the dead
Scorned by the spoiler; and the Roman host
By sun and length of days, and rain from heaven,
At length was mingled with Emathia's plain.

Ill-starred Thessalia! By what hateful crime
Didst thou offend that thus on thee alone
Was laid such carnage? By what length of years
Shalt thou be cleansed from the curse of war?   1010
When shall the harvest of thy fields arise
Free from their purple stain? And when the share
Cease to upturn the slaughtered hosts of Rome?
First shall the battle onset sound again,
Again shall flow upon thy fated earth
A crimson torrent. Thus may be o'erthrown
Our sires' memorials; those erected last,
Or those which pierced by ancient roots have spread
Through broken stones their sacred urns abroad.
Thus shall the ploughman of Haemonia gaze   1020
On more abundant ashes, and the rake
Pass o'er more frequent bones. Wert, Thracia, thou.
Our only battlefield, no sailor's hand
Upon thy shore should make his cable fast;
No spade should turn, the husbandman should flee
Thy fields, the resting-place of Roman dead;
No lowing kine should graze, nor shepherd dare

---

[1] Wrongly supposed by Lucan to feed on carrion.

To leave his fleecy charge to browse at will
On fields made fertile by our mouldering dust;
All bare and unexplored thy soil should lie,   1030
As past man's footsteps, parched by cruel suns,
Or palled by snows unmelting! But, ye gods,
Give us to hate the lands which bear the guilt;
Let not all earth be cursed, though not all
Be blameless found.

          'Twas thus that Munda's fight
And blood of Mutina, and Leucas' cape,
And sad Pachynus, [1] made Philippi pure.

---

[1] Alluding to the naval war waged by Sextus Pompeius after Caesar's death.
He took possession of Sicily, and had command of the seas, but was ultimate-
ly defeated by the fleet of Octavius under Agrippa in B.C. 36. Pachynus was
the S.E. promontory of the island, but is used in the sense of Sicily, for this
battle took place on the north coast.

BOOK VIII

DEATH OF POMPEIUS.

Now through Alcides'[1] pass and Tempe's groves
Pompeius, aiming for Haemonian glens
And forests lone, urged on his wearied steed
Scarce heeding now the spur; by devious tracks
Seeking to veil the footsteps of his flight:
The rustle of the foliage, and the noise
Of following comrades filled his anxious soul
With terrors, as he fancied at his side
Some ambushed enemy. Fallen from the height
Of former fortunes, still the chieftain knew   10
His life not worthless; mindful of the fates:
And 'gainst the price he set on Caesar's head,
He measures Caesar's value of his own.

Yet, as he rode, the features of the chief
Made known his ruin. Many as they sought
The camp Pharsalian, ere yet was spread
News of the battle, met the chief, amazed,
And wondered at the whirl of human things:
Nor held disaster sure, though Magnus' self
Told of his ruin. Every witness seen   20
Brought peril on his flight: 'twere better far
Safe in a name obscure, through all the world
To wander; but his ancient fame forbad.

---

[1] Comp. Book VI., line 407.

Too long had great Pompeius from the height
Of human greatness, envied of mankind,
Looked on all others; nor for him henceforth
Could life be lowly. The honours of his youth
Too early thrust upon him, and the deeds
Which brought him triumph in the Sullan days,
His conquering navy and the Pontic war,   30
Made heavier now the burden of defeat,
And crushed his pondering soul. So length of days
Drags down the haughty spirit, and life prolonged
When power has perished. Fortune's latest hour,
Be the last hour of life! Nor let the wretch
Live on disgraced by memories of fame!
But for the boon of death, who'd dare the sea
Of prosperous chance?

        Upon the ocean marge
By red Peneus blushing from the fray,   40
Borne in a sloop, to lightest wind and wave
Scarce equal, he, whose countless oars yet smote
Upon Coreyra's isle and Leucas point,
Lord of Cilicia and Liburnian lands,
Crept trembling to the sea. He bids them steer
For the sequestered shores of Lesbos isle;
For there wert thou, sharer of all his griefs,
Cornelia! Sadder far thy life apart
Than wert thou present in Thessalia's fields.
Racked is thy heart with presages of ill;   50
Pharsalia fills thy dreams; and when the shades
Give place to coming dawn, with hasty step
Thou tread'st some cliff sea-beaten, and with eyes
Gazing afar art first to mark the sail
Of each approaching bark: yet dar'st not ask
Aught of thy husband's fate.

        Behold the boat
Whose bending canvas bears her to the shore:
She brings (unknown as yet) thy chiefest dread,
Rumour of evil, herald of defeat,   60
Magnus, thy conquered spouse. Fear then no more,

But give to grief thy moments. From the ship
He leaps to land; she marks the cruel doom
Wrought by the gods upon him: pale and wan
His weary features, by the hoary locks
Shaded; the dust of travel on his garb.
Dark on her soul a night of anguish fell;
Her trembling limbs no longer bore her frame:
Scarce throbbed her heart, and prone on earth she lay
Deceived in hope of death. The boat made fast,   70
Pompeius treading the lone waste of sand
Drew near; whom when Cornelia's maidens saw,
They stayed their weeping, yet with sighs subdued,
Reproached the fates; and tried in vain to raise
Their mistress' form, till Magnus to his breast
Drew her with cherishing arms; and at the touch
Of soothing hands the life-blood to her veins
Returned once more, and she could bear to look
Upon his features. He forbad despair,
Chiding her grief. "Not at the earliest blow   80
By Fortune dealt, inheritress of fame
Bequeathed by noble fathers, should thy strength
Thus fail and yield: renown shall yet be thine,
To last through ages; not of laws decreed
Nor conquests won; a gentler path to thee
As to thy sex, is given; thy husband's woe.
Let thine affection struggle with the fates,
And in his misery love thy lord the more.
I bring thee greater glory, for that gone
Is all the pomp of power and all the crowd   90
Of faithful senators and suppliant kings;
Now first Pompeius for himself alone
Tis thine to love. Curb this unbounded grief,
While yet I breathe, unseemly. O'er my tomb
Weep out thy full, the final pledge of faith.
Thou hast no loss, nor has the war destroyed
Aught save my fortune. If for that thy grief
That was thy love."

      Roused by her husband's words,
Yet scarcely could she raise her trembling limbs,   100
Thus speaking through her sobs: "Would I had sought

190

Detested Caesar's couch, ill-omened wife
Of spouse unhappy; at my nuptials twice
A Fury has been bridesmaid, and the ghosts
Of slaughtered Crassi, with avenging shades
Brought by my wedlock to the doomed camp
The Parthian massacre. Twice my star has cursed
The world, and peoples have been hurled to death
In one red moment; and the gods through me
Have left the better cause. O, hero mine,   110
mightiest husband, wedded to a wife
Unworthy! 'Twas through her that Fortune gained
The right to strike thee. Wherefore did I wed
To bring thee misery? Mine, mine the guilt,
Mine be the penalty. And that the wave
May bear thee gently onwards, and the kings
May keep their faith to thee, and all the earth
Be ready to thy rule, me from thy side
Cast to the billows. Rather had I died
To bring thee victory; thy disasters thus,   120
Thus expiate. And, cruel Julia, thee,
Who by this war hast vengeance on our vows,
From thine abode I call: atonement find
In this thy rival's death, and spare at least
Thy Magnus." Then upon his breast she fell,
While all the concourse wept -- e'en Magnus' self,
Who saw Thessalia's field without a tear.

But now upon the shore a numerous band
From Mitylene thus approached the chief:
"If 'tis our greatest glory to have kept   130
The pledge with us by such a husband placed,
Do thou one night within these friendly walls
We pray thee, stay; thus honouring the homes
Long since devoted, Magnus, to thy cause.
This spot in days to come the guest from Rome
For thee shall honour. Nowhere shalt thou find
A surer refuge in defeat. All else
May court the victor's favour; we long since
Have earned his chastisement. And though our isle
Rides on the deep, girt by the ocean wave,   140
No ships has Caesar: and to us shall come,

191

Be sure, thy captains, to our trusted shore,
The war renewing. Take, for all is thine,
The treasures of our temples and the gold,
Take all our youth by land or on the sea
To do thy bidding: Lesbos only asks
This from the chief who sought her in his pride,
Not in his fall to leave her." Pleased in soul
At such a love, and joyed that in the world
Some faith still lingered, thus Pompeius said: 150
"Earth has for me no dearer land than this.
Did I not trust it with so sweet a pledge
And find it faithful? Here was Rome for me,
Country and household gods. This shore I sought
Home of my wife, this Lesbos, which for her
Had merited remorseless Caesar's ire:
Nor was afraid to trust you with the means
To gain his mercy. But enough -- through me
Your guilt was caused -- I part, throughout the world
To prove my fate. Farewell thou happiest land!   160
Famous for ever, whether taught by thee
Some other kings and peoples may be pleased
To give me shelter; or should'st thou alone
Be faithful. And now seek I in what lands
Right may be found or wrong. My latest prayer
Receive, O deity, if still with me
Thou bidest, thus. May it be mine again,
Conquered, with hostile Caesar on my tracks
To find a Lesbos where to enter in
And whence to part, unhindered."   170

                    In the boat
He placed his spouse: while from the shore arose
Such lamentation, and such hands were raised
In ire against the gods, that thou had'st deemed
All left their kin for exile, and their homes.
And though for Magnus grieving in his fall
Yet for Cornelia chiefly did they mourn
Long since their gentle guest. For her had wept
The Lesbian matrons had she left to join
A victor husband: for she won their love,   180
By kindly modesty and gracious mien,

Ere yet her lord was conquered, while as yet
Their fortunes stood.

           Now slowly to the deep
Sank fiery Titan; but not yet to those
He sought (if such there be), was shown his orb,
Though veiled from those he quitted. Magnus' mind,
Anxious with waking cares, sought through the kings
His subjects, and the cities leagued with Rome
In faith, and through the pathless tracts that lie   190
Beyond the southern bounds: until the toil
Of sorrowing thought upon the past, and dread
Of that which might be, made him cast afar
His wavering doubts, and from the captain seek
Some counsel on the heavens; how by the sky
He marked his track upon the deep; what star
Guided the path to Syria, and what points
Found in the Wain would pilot him aright
To shores of Libya. But thus replied
The well-skilled watcher of the silent skies: 200
"Not by the constellations moving ever
Across the heavens do we guide our barks;
For that were perilous; but by that star [1]
Which never sinks nor dips below the wave,
Girt by the glittering groups men call the Bears.
When stands the pole-star clear before the mast,
Then to the Bosphorus look we, and the main
Which carves the coast of Scythia. But the more
Bootes dips, and nearer to the sea
Is Cynosura seen, so much the ship   210
Towards Syria tends, till bright Canopus [2] shines,
In southern skies content to hold his course;
With him upon the left past Pharos borne
Straight for the Syrtes shalt thou plough the deep.
But whither now dost bid me shape the yards
And set the canvas?"

---

[1] Comp. Book III., line 256.
[2] Canopus is a star in Argo, invisible in Italy. (Haskins.)

Magnus, doubting still;
"This only be thy care: from Thracia steer
The vessel onward; shun with all thy skill
Italia's distant shore: and for the rest   220
Trust to the winds for guidance. When I sought,
Pledged with the Lesbians, my spouse beloved,
My course was sure: now, Fortune, where thou wilt
Give me a refuge." These his answering words.

The pilot, as they hung from level yards
Shifted the sails; and hauling to the stern
One sheet, he slacked the other, to the left
Steering, where Samian rocks and Chian marred
The stillness of the waters; while the sea
Sent up in answer to the changing keel   230
A different murmur. Not so deftly turns
Curbing his steeds, his wain the Charioteer,
While glows his dexter wheel, and with the left
He almost touches, yet avoids the goal.

Now Titan veiled the stars and showed the shore;
When, following Magnus, came a scattered band
Saved from the Thracian storm. From Lesbos' port
His son; [1] next, captains who preserved their faith;
For at his side, though vanquished in the field,
Cast down by fate, in exile, still there stood,   240
Lords of the earth and all her Orient realms,
The Kings, his ministers.

             To the furthest lands
He bids [2] Deiotarus: "O faithful friend,
Since in Emathia's battle-field was lost
The world, so far as Roman, it remains
To test the faith of peoples of the East
Who drink of Tigris and Euphrates' stream,
Secure as yet from Caesar. Be it thine

---

[1] Sextus.
[2] Tetrarch of Galatia. He was always friendly to Rome, and in the civil war sided with Pompeius. He was at Pharsalia.

Far as the rising of the sun to trace   250
The fates that favour Magnus: to the courts
Of Median palaces, to Scythian steppes;
And to the son of haughty Arsaces,
To bear my message, 'Hold ye to the faith,
Pledged by your priests and by the Thunderer's name
Of Latium sworn? Then fill your quivers full,
Draw to its fullest span th' Armenian bow;
And, Getan archers, wing the fatal shaft.
And you, ye Parthians, if when I sought
The Caspian gates, and on th' Alaunian tribes [1]   260
Fierce, ever-warring, pressed, I suffered you
In Persian tracts to wander, nor compelled
To seek for shelter Babylonian walls;
If beyond Cyrus' kingdom [2] and the bounds
Of wide Chaldaea, where from Nysa's top
Pours down Hydaspes, and the Ganges flood
Foams to the ocean, nearer far I stood
Than Persia's bounds to Phoebus' rising fires;
If by my sufferance, Parthians, you alone
Decked not my triumphs, but in equal state   270
Sole of all Eastern princes, face to face
Met Magnus in his pride, nor only once
Through me were saved; (for after that dread day
Who but Pompeius soothed the kindling fires
Of Latium's anger?) -- by my service paid
Come forth to victory: burst the ancient bounds
By Macedon's hero set: in Magnus' cause
March, Parthians, to Rome's conquest. Rome herself
Prays to be conquered.'"

        Hard the task imposed;   280
Yet doffed his robe, and swift obeyed, the king
Wrapped in a servant's mantle. If a Prince
For safety play the boor, then happier, sure,

---

[1] A Scythian people.
[2] Pompeius seems to have induced the Roman public to believe that he had
led his armies to such extreme distances, but he never in fact did so. --
Mommsen, vol. iv. p. 147.

The peasant's lot than lordship of the world.

The king thus parted, past Icaria's rocks
Pompeius' vessel skirts the foamy crags
Of little Samos: Colophon's tranquil sea
And Ephesus lay behind him, and the air
Breathed freely on him from the Coan shore.
Cuidos he shunned, and, famous for its sun,   290
Rhodos, and steering for the middle deep
Escaped the windings of Telmessus' bay;
Till rose Pamphylian coasts before the bark,
And first the fallen chieftain dared to find
In small Phaseils shelter; for therein
Scarce was the husbandman, and empty homes
Forbad to fear. Next Taurus' heights he saw
And Dipsus falling from his lofty sides:
So sailed he onward.

          Did Pompeius hope,   300
Thus severed by the billows from the foe,
To make his safety sure? His little boat
Flies unmolested past Cilician shores;
But to their exiled lord in chiefest part
The senate of Rome was drawn. Celendrae there
Received their fleet, where fair Selinus' stream
In spacious bay gives refuge from the main;
And to the gathered chiefs in mournful words
At length Pompeius thus resolved his thoughts:
"O faithful comrades mine in war and flight!   310
To me, my country! Though this barren shore
Our place of meeting, and no gathered host
Surrounds us, yet upon our changed estate
I seek your counsel. Rouse ye as of yore
With hearts of courage! Magnus on the field
Not all is perished, nor do fates forbid
But that I rise afresh with living hope
Of future victories, and spurn defeat.
From Libyan ruins did not Marius rise
Again recorded Consul on the page   320
Full of his honours? shall a lighter blow
Keep Magnus down, whose thousand chiefs and ships

Still plough the billows; by defeat his strength
Not whelmed but scattered? And the fame alone
Of our great deeds of glory in the past
Shall now protect us, and the world unchanged
Still love its hero.

"Weigh upon the scales
Ye chiefs, which best may help the needs of Rome,
In faith and armies; or the Parthian realm   330
Egypt or Libya. For myself, ye chiefs,
I veil no secret thoughts, but thus advise.
Place no reliance on the Pharian king;
His age forbids: nor on the cunning Moor,
Who vain of Punic ancestors, and vain
Of Carthaginian memories and descent [1]
Supposed from Hannibal, and swollen with pride
At Varus' supplication, sees in thought
Rome lie beneath him. Wherefore, comrades, seek
At speed, the Eastern world. Those mighty realms   340
Disjoins from us Euphrates, and the gates
Called Caspian; on another sky than ours
There day and night revolve; another sea
Of different hue is severed from our own. [2]
Rule is their wish, nought else: and in their plains
Taller the war-horse, stronger twangs the bow;
There fails nor youth nor age to wing the shaft
Fatal in flight. Their archers first subdued
The lance of Macedon and Baetra's [3] walls,
Home of the Mede; and haughty Babylon   350
With all her storied towers: nor shall they dread
The Roman onset; trusting to the shafts
By which the host of fated Crassus fell.
Nor trust they only to the javelin blade
Untipped with poison: from the rancorous edge

---

[1] Juba was of supposed collateral descent from Hannibal. (Haskins, quoting "The Scholiast.")
[2] Confusing the Red Sea with the Persian Gulf.
[3] Balkh of modern times. Bactria was one of the kingdoms established by the successors of Alexander the Great. It was, however, subdued by the Parthians about the middle of the third century B.C.

The slightest wound deals death.

"Would that my lot
Forced me not thus to trust that savage race
Of Arsaces! [1] Yet now their emulous fate
Contends with Roman destinies: the gods   360
Smile favouring on their nation. Thence I'll pour
On Caesar peoples from another earth
And all the Orient ravished from its home.
But should the East and barbarous treaties fail,
Fate, bear our shipwrecked fortunes past the bounds
Of earth, as known to men. The kings I made
I supplicate not, but in death shall take
To other spheres this solace: chief of all;
His hands, my kinsman's, never shed my blood
Nor soothed me dying. Yet as my mind in turn   370
The varying fortunes of my life recalls,
How was I glorious in that Eastern world!
How great my name by far Maeotis marsh
And where swift Tanais flows! No other land
Has so resounded with my conquests won,
So sent me home triumphant. Rome, do thou
Approve my enterprise! What happier chance
Could favouring gods afford thee? Parthian hosts
Shall fight the civil wars of Rome, and share
Her ills, and fall enfeebled. When the arms   380
Of Caesar meet with Parthian in the fray,
Then must kind Fortune vindicate my lot
Or Crassus be avenged."

But murmurs rose,
And Magnus speaking knew his words condemned.
Then Lentulas [1] answered, with indignant soul,

---

[1] Dion could not believe it possible that Pompeius ever contemplated taking refuge in Parthia, but Plutarch states it as a fact; and says that it was Theophanes of Lesbos who dissuaded him from doing so. ("Pompeius", 76). Mommsen (vol. iv., pp. 421-423) discusses the subject, and says that from Parthia only could Pompeius have attempted to seek support, and that such an attempt, putting the objections to it aside, would probably have failed. Lucan's sympathies were probably with Lentulus.

Foremost to rouse their valour, thus in words
Worthy a Consul: "Have Thessalian woes
Broken thy spirit so? One day's defeat
Condemned the world to ruin? Is the cause   390
Lost in one battle and beyond recall?
Find we no cure for wounds? Does Fortune drive
Thee, Magnus, to the Parthians' feet alone?
And dost thou, fugitive, spurn the lands and skies
Known heretofore, and seek for other poles
And constellations, and Chaldaean gods,
And rites barbarian, servant of the realm Of
Parthia? But why then took we arms
For love of liberty? If thou canst slave
Thou hast deceived the world! Shall Parthia see   400
Thee at whose name, ruler of mighty Rome,
She trembled, at whose feet she captive saw
Hyrcanian kings and Indian princes kneel,
Now humbly suppliant, victim of the fates;
And at thy prayer her puny strength extol
In mad contention with the Western world?
Nor think, Pompeius, thou shalt plead thy cause
In that proud tongue unknown to Parthian ears
Of which thy fame is worthy; sobs and tears
He shall demand of thee. And has our shame   410
Brought us to this, that some barbarian foe
Shall venge Hesperia's wrongs ere Rome her own?
Thou wert our leader for the civil war:
Mid Scythia's peoples dost thou bruit abroad
Wounds and disasters which are ours alone?
Rome until now, though subject to the yoke
Of civic despots, yet within her walls
Has brooked no foreign lord. And art thou pleased
From all the world to summon to her gates
These savage peoples, while the standards lost   420
By far Euphrates when the Crassi fell
Shall lead thy columns? Shall the only king

---

[1] Probably Lucius Lentulus Crus, who had been Consul, for B.C. 49, along with Caius Marcellus. (See Book V., 9.) He was murdered in Egypt by Ptolemy's ministers.

Who failed Emathia, while the fates yet hid
Their favouring voices, brave the victor's power,
And join with thine his fortune? Nay, not so
This nation trusts itself. Each race that claims
A northern birth, unconquered in the fray
Claims but the warrior's death; but as the sky
Slopes towards the eastern tracts and gentler climes
So are the nations. There in flowing robes   430
And garments delicate are men arrayed.
True that the Parthian in Sarmatia's plains,
Where Tigris spreads across the level meads,
Contends invincible; for flight is his
Unbounded; but should uplands bar his path
He scales them not; nor through the night of war
Shall his weak bow uncertain in its aim
Repel the foeman; nor his strength of arm
The torrent stem; nor all a summer's day
In dust and blood bear up against the foe.   440
They fill no hostile trench, nor in their hands
Shall battering engine or machine of war
Dash down the rampart; and whate'er avails
To stop their arrows, battles like a wall. [1]
Wide sweep their horsemen, fleeting in attack
And light in onset, and their troops shall yield
A camp, not take it: poisoned are their shafts;
Nor do they dare a combat hand to hand;
But as the winds may suffer, from afar
They draw their bows at venture. Brave men love   450
The sword which, wielded by a stalwart arm,
Drives home the blow and makes the battle sure.
Not such their weapons; and the first assault
Shall force the flying Mede with coward hand
And empty quiver from the field. His faith
In poisoned blades is placed; but trustest thou
Those who without such aid refuse the war?
For such alliance wilt thou risk a death,
With all the world between thee and thy home?
Shall some barbarian earth or lowly grave   460

---

[1] That is, be as easily defended.

Enclose thee perishing? E'en that were shame
While Crassus seeks a sepulchre in vain.
Thy lot is happy; death, unfeared by men,
Is thy worst doom, Pompeius; but no death
Awaits Cornelia -- such a fate for her
This king shall not reserve; for know not we
The hateful secrets of barbarian love,
Which, blind as that of beasts, the marriage bed
Pollutes with wives unnumbered? Nor the laws
By nature made respect they, nor of kin.   470
In ancient days the fable of the crime
By tyrant Oedipus unwitting wrought,
Brought hate upon his city; but how oft
Sits on the throne of Arsaces a prince
Of birth incestuous? This gracious dame
Born of Metellus, noblest blood of Rome,
Shall share the couch of the barbarian king
With thousand others: yet in savage joy,
Proud of her former husbands, he may grant
Some larger share of favour; and the fates   480
May seem to smile on Parthia; for the spouse
Of Crassus, captive, shall to him be brought
As spoil of former conquest. If the wound
Dealt in that fell defeat in eastern lands
Still stirs thy heart, then double is the shame
First to have waged the war upon ourselves,
Then ask the foe for succour. For what blame
Can rest on thee or Caesar, worse than this
That in the clash of conflict ye forgot
For Crassus' slaughtered troops the vengeance due?   490
First should united Rome upon the Mede
Have poured her captains, and the troops who guard
The northern frontier from the Dacian hordes;
And all her legions should have left the Rhine
Free to the Teuton, till the Parthian dead
Were piled in heaps upon the sands that hide
Our heroes slain; and haughty Babylon
Lay at her victor's feet. To this foul peace
We pray an end; and if Thessalia's day
Has closed our warfare, let the conqueror march   500
Straight on our Parthian foe. Then should this heart,

201

Then only, leap at Caesar's triumph won.
Go thou and pass Araxes' chilly stream
On this thine errand; and the fleeting ghost
Pierced by the Scythian shaft shall greet thee thus:
'Art thou not he to whom our wandering shades
Looked for their vengeance in the guise of war?
And dost thou sue for peace?' There shalt thou meet
Memorials of the dead. Red is yon wall
Where passed their headless trunks: Euphrates here   510
Engulfed them slain, or Tigris' winding stream
Cast on the shore to perish. Gaze on this,
And thou canst supplicate at Caesar's feet
In mid Thessalia seated. Nay, thy glance
Turn on the Roman world, and if thou fear'st
King Juba faithless and the southern realms,
Then seek we Pharos. Egypt on the west
Girt by the trackless Syrtes forces back
By sevenfold stream the ocean; rich in glebe
And gold and merchandise; and proud of Nile   521   520
Asks for no rain from heaven. Now holds this boy
Her sceptre, owed to thee; his guardian thou:
And who shall fear this shadow of a name?
Hope not from monarchs old, whose shame is fled,
Or laws or troth or honour of the gods:
New kings bring mildest sway." [1]

His words prevailed
Upon his hearers. With what freedom speaks,
When states are trembling, patriot despair!
Pompeius' voice was quelled.   530

They hoist their sails
For Cyprus shaped, whose altars more than all
The goddess loves who from the Paphian wave
Sprang, mindful of her birth, if such be truth,
And gods have origin. Past the craggy isle

---

[1] Thus rendered by Sir Thomas May, of the Long Parliament: "Men used
to sceptres are ashamed of nought: The mildest governement a kingdome
finds   Under new kings."

Pompeius sailing, left at length astern
Its southern cape, and struck across the main
With winds transverse and tides; nor reached the mount
Grateful to sailors for its nightly gleam:
But to the bounds of Egypt hardly won   540
With battling canvas, where divided Nile
Pours through the shallows his Pelusian stream. [1]
Now was the season when the heavenly scale
Most nearly balances the varying hours,
Once only equal; for the wintry day
Repays to night her losses of the spring;
And Magnus learning that th' Egyptian king
Lay by Mount Casius, ere the sun was set
Or flagged his canvas, thither steered his ship.

Already had a horseman from the shore   550
In rapid gallop to the trembling court
Brought news their guest was come. Short was the time
For counsel given; but in haste were met
All who advised the base Pellaean king,
Monsters, inhuman; there Achoreus sat
Less harsh in failing years, in Memphis born
Of empty rites, and guardian of the rise [2]
Of fertilising Nile. While he was priest
Not only once had Apis [3] lived the space
Marked by the crescent on his sacred brow.   560
First was his voice, for Magnus raised and troth
And for the pledges of the king deceased:
But, skilled in counsel meet for shameless minds
And tyrant hearts, Pothinus, dared to claim
Judgment of death on Magnus. "Laws and right
Make many guilty, Ptolemmus king.

---

[1] That is, he reached the most eastern mouth of the Nile instead of the western.
[2] At Memphis was the well in which the rise and fall of the water acted as a Nilometer (Mr. Haskins's note).
[3] Comp. Herodotus, Book iii. 27. Apis was a god who appeared at intervals in the shape of a calf with a white mark on his brow. His appearance was the occasion of general rejoicing. Cambyses slew the Apis which came in his time, and for this cause became mad, as the Egyptians said.

And faith thus lauded [1] brings its punishment
When it supports the fallen. To the fates
Yield thee, and to the gods; the wretched shun
But seek the happy. As the stars from earth   570
Differ, and fire from ocean, so from right
Expedience. [2] The tyrant's shorn of strength
Who ponders justice; and regard for right
Bring's ruin on a throne. For lawless power
The best defence is crime, and cruel deeds
Find safety but in doing. He that aims
At piety must flee the regal hall;
Virtue's the bane of rule; he lives in dread
Who shrinks from cruelty. Nor let this chief
Unpunished scorn thy youth, who thinks that thou   580
Not even the conquered from our shore can'st bar.
Nor to a stranger, if thou would'st not reign,
Resign thy sceptre, for the ties of blood
Speak for thy banished sister. Let her rule
O'er Nile and Pharos: we shall at the least
Preserve our Egypt from the Latian arms.
What Magnus owned not ere the war was done,
No more shall Caesar. Driven from all the world,
Trusting no more to Fortune, now he seeks
Some foreign nation which may share his fate.   590
Shades of the slaughtered in the civil war
Compel him: nor from Caesar's arms alone
But from the Senate also does he fly,
Whose blood outpoured has gorged Thessalian fowl;
Monarchs he fears whose all he hath destroyed,
And nations piled in one ensanguined heap,
By him deserted. Victim of the blow
Thessalia dealt, refused in every land,
He asks for help from ours not yet betrayed.

---

[1] That is, by Achoreus, who had just spoken.
[2] Compare Ben Jonson's "Sejanus", Act ii., Scene 2: --   The prince who
shames a tyrant's name to bear   Shall never dare do anything, but fear;
All the command of sceptres quite doth perish   If it begin religious
thoughts to cherish;   Whole empires fall, swayed by these nice respects,
It is the licence of dark deeds protects   E'en states most hated, when no
laws resist   The sword, but that it acteth what it list."

But none than Egypt with this chief from Rome   600
Has juster quarrel; who has sought with arms
To stain our Pharos, distant from the strife
And peaceful ever, and to make our realm
Suspected by his victor. Why alone
Should this our country please thee in thy fall?
Why bringst thou here the burden of thy fates,
Pharsalia's curse? In Caesar's eyes long since
We have offence which by the sword alone
Can find its condonation, in that we
By thy persuasion from the Senate gained   610
This our dominion. By our prayers we helped
If not by arms thy cause. This sword, which fate
Bids us make ready, not for thee I hold
Prepared, but for the vanquished; and on thee
(Would it had been on Caesar) falls the stroke;
For we are borne. as all things, to his side.
And dost thou doubt, since thou art in my power,
Thou art my victim? By what trust in us
Cam'st thou, unhappy? Scarce our people tills
The fields, though softened by the refluent Nile: 620
Know well our strength, and know we can no more.
Rome 'neath the ruin of Pompeius lies:
Shalt thou, king, uphold him? Shalt thou dare
To stir Pharsalia's ashes and to call
War to thy kingdom? Ere the fight was fought
We joined not either army -- shall we now
Make Magnus friend whom all the world deserts?
And fling a challenge to the conquering chief
And all his proud successes? Fair is help
Lent in disaster, yet reserved for those   630
Whom fortune favours. Faith her friends selects
Not from the wretched."

      They decree the crime:
Proud is the boyish tyrant that so soon
His slaves permit him to so great a deed
To give his favouring voice; and for the work
They choose Achillas.

      Where the treacherous shore

Runs out in sand below the Casian mount
And where the shallow waters of the sea   640
Attest the Syrtes near, in little boat
Achillas and his partners in the crime
With swords embark. Ye gods! and shall the Nile
And barbarous Memphis and th' effeminate crew
That throngs Pelusian Canopus raise
Its thoughts to such an enterprise? Do thus
Our fates press on the world? Is Rome thus fallen
That in our civil frays the Phaxian sword
Finds place, or Egypt? O, may civil war
Be thus far faithful that the hand which strikes   650
Be of our kindred; and the foreign fiend
Held worlds apart! Pompeius, great in soul,
Noble in spirit, had deserved a death
From Caesar's self. And, king, hast thou no fear
At such a ruin of so great a name?
And dost thou dare when heaven's high thunder rolls,
Thou, puny boy, to mingle with its tones
Thine impure utterance? Had he not won
A world by arms, and thrice in triumph scaled
The sacred Capitol, and vanquished kings,   660
And championed the Roman Senate's cause;
He, kinsman of the victor? 'Twas enough
To cause forbearance in a Pharian king,
That he was Roman. Wherefore with thy sword
Dost stab our breasts? Thou know'st not, impious boy,
How stand thy fortunes; now no more by right
Hast thou the sceptre of the land of Nile;
For prostrate, vanquished in the civil wars
Is he who gave it.

       Furling now his sails,   670
Magnus with oars approached th' accursed land,
When in their little boat the murderous crew
Drew nigh, and feigning from th' Egyptian court
A ready welcome, blamed the double tides
Broken by shallows, and their scanty beach
Unfit for fleets; and bade him to their craft
Leaving his loftier ship. Had not the fates'
Eternal and unalterable laws

Called for their victim and decreed his end
Now near at hand, his comrades' warning voice   680
Yet might have stayed his course: for if the court
To Magnus, who bestowed the Pharian crown,
In truth were open, should not king and fleet
In pomp have come to greet him? But he yields:
The fates compel. Welcome to him was death
Rather than fear. But, rushing to the side,
His spouse would follow, for she dared not stay,
Fearing the guile. Then he, "Abide, my wife,
And son, I pray you; from the shore afar
Await my fortunes; mine shall be the life   690
To test their honour." But Cornelia still
Withstood his bidding, and with arms outspread
Frenzied she cried: "And whither without me,
Cruel, departest? Thou forbad'st me share
Thy risks Thessalian; dost again command
That I should part from thee? No happy star
Breaks on our sorrow. If from every land
Thou dost debar me, why didst turn aside
In flight to Lesbos? On the waves alone
Am I thy fit companion?" Thus in vain,   700
Leaning upon the bulwark, dazed with dread;
Nor could she turn her straining gaze aside,
Nor see her parting husband. All the fleet
Stood silent, anxious, waiting for the end:
Not that they feared the murder which befell,
But lest their leader might with humble prayer
Kneel to the king he made.

         As Magnus passed,
A Roman soldier from the Pharian boat,
Septimius, salutes him. Gods of heaven!   710
There stood he, minion to a barbarous king,
Nor bearing still the javelin of Rome;
But vile in all his arms; giant in form
Fierce, brutal, thirsting as a beast may thirst
For carnage. Didst thou, Fortune, for the sake
Of nations, spare to dread Pharsalus field
This savage monster's blows? Or dost thou place
Throughout the world, for thy mysterious ends,

Some ministering swords for civil war?
Thus, to the shame of victors and of gods,   720
This story shall be told in days to come:
A Roman swordsman, once within thy ranks,
Slave to the orders of a puny prince,
Severed Pompeius' neck. And what shall be
Septimius' fame hereafter? By what name
This deed be called, if Brutus wrought a crime?

Now came the end, the latest hour of all:
Rapt to the boat was Magnus, of himself
No longer master, and the miscreant crew
Unsheathed their swords; which when the chieftain saw   730
He swathed his visage, for he scorned unveiled
To yield his life to fortune; closed his eyes
And held his breath within him, lest some word,
Or sob escaped, might mar the deathless fame
His deeds had won. And when within his side
Achillas plunged his blade, nor sound nor cry
He gave, but calm consented to the blow
And proved himself in dying; in his breast
These thoughts revolving: "In the years to come
Men shall make mention of our Roman toils,   740
Gaze on this boat, ponder the Pharian faith;
And think upon thy fame and all the years
While fortune smiled: but for the ills of life
How thou could'st bear them, this men shall not know
Save by thy death. Then weigh thou not the shame
That waits on thine undoing. Whose strikes,
The blow is Caesar's. Men may tear this frame
And cast it mangled to the winds of heaven;
Yet have I prospered, nor can all the gods
Call back my triumphs. Life may bring defeat,   750
But death no misery. If my spouse and son
Behold me murdered, silently the more
I suffer: admiration at my death
Shall prove their love." Thus did Pompeius die,
Guarding his thoughts.

                    But now Cornelia filled
The air with lamentations at the sight;

"O, husband, whom my wicked self hath slain!
That lonely isle apart thy bane hath been
And stayed thy coming. Caesar to the Nile   760
Has won before us; for what other hand
May do such work? But whosoe'er thou art
Sent from the gods with power, for Caesar's ire,
Or thine own sake, to slay, thou dost not know
Where lies the heart of Magnus. Haste and do!
Such were his prayer -- no other punishment
Befits the conquered. Yet let him ere his end
See mine, Cornelia's. On me the blame
Of all these wars, who sole of Roman wives
Followed my spouse afield nor feared the fates;   770
And in disaster, when the kings refused,
Received and cherished him. Did I deserve
Thus to be left of thee, and didst thou seek
To spare me? And when rushing on thine end
Was I to live? Without the monarch's help
Death shall be mine, either by headlong leap
Beneath the waters; or some sailor's hand
Shall bind around this neck the fatal cord;
Or else some comrade, worthy of his chief,
Drive to my heart his blade for Magnus' sake,   780
And claim the service done to Ceasar's arms.
What! does your cruelty withhold my fate?
Ah! still he lives, nor is it mine as yet
To win this freedom; they forbid me death,
Kept for the victor's triumph." Thus she spake,
While friendly hands upheld her fainting form;
And sped the trembling vessel from the shore.

Men say that Magnus, when the deadly blows
Fell thick upon him, lost nor form divine,
Nor venerated mien; and as they gazed   790
Upon his lacerated head they marked
Still on his features anger with the gods.
Nor death could change his visage -- for in act
Of striking, fierce Septimius' murderous hand
(Thus making worse his crime) severed the folds
That swathed the face, and seized the noble head
And drooping neck ere yet was fled the life:

Then placed upon the bench; and with his blade
Slow at its hideous task, and blows unskilled
Hacked through the flesh and brake the knotted bone: 800
For yet man had not learned by swoop of sword
Deftly to lop the neck. Achillas claimed
The gory head dissevered. What! shalt thou
A Roman soldier, while thy blade yet reeks
From Magnus' slaughter, play the second part
To this base varlet of the Pharian king?
Nor bear thyself the bleeding trophy home?
Then, that the impious boy (ah! shameful fate)
Might know the features of the hero slain,
Seized by the locks, the dread of kings, which waved   810
Upon his stately front, on Pharian pike
The head was lifted; while almost the life
Gave to the tongue its accents, and the eyes
Were yet scarce glazed: that head at whose command
Was peace or war, that tongue whose eloquent tones
Would move assemblies, and that noble brow
On which were showered the rewards of Rome.
Nor to the tyrant did the sight suffice
To prove the murder done. The perishing flesh,
The tissues, and the brain he bids remove   820
By art nefarious: the shrivelled skin
Draws tight upon the bone; and poisonous juice
Gives to the face its lineaments in death.

Last of thy race, thou base degenerate boy,
About to perish [1] soon, and yield the throne
To thine incestuous sister; while the Prince
From Macedon here in consecrated vault
Now rests, and ashes of the kings are closed
In mighty pyramids, and lofty tombs
Of thine unworthy fathers mark the graves;   830
Shall Magnus' body hither and thither borne
Be battered, headless, by the ocean wave?
Too much it troubled thee to guard the corse

----

[1] He was drowned in attempting to escape in the battle on the Nile in the fol-
lowing autumn.

Unmutilated, for his kinsman's eye
To witness! Such the faith which Fortune kept
With prosperous Pompeius to the end.
'Twas not for him in evil days some ray
Of light to hope for. Shattered from the height
Of power in one short moment to his death!
Years of unbroken victories balanced down   840
By one day's carnage! In his happy time
Heaven did not harass him, nor did she spare
In misery. Long Fortune held the hand
That dashed him down. Now beaten by the sands,
Torn upon rocks, the sport of ocean's waves
Poured through its wounds, his headless carcase lies,
Save by the lacerated trunk unknown.

Yet ere the victor touched the Pharian sands
Some scanty rites to Magnus Fortune gave,
Lest he should want all burial. Pale with fear   850
Came Cordus, hasting from his hiding place;
Quaestor, he joined Pompeius on thy shore,
Idalian Cyprus, bringing in his train
A cloud of evils. Through the darkening shades
Love for the dead compelled his trembling steps,
Hard by the marin of the deep to search
And drag to land his master. Through the clouds
The moon shone sadly, and her rays were dim;
But by its hue upon the hoary main
He knew the body. In a fast embrace   860
He holds it, wrestling with the greedy sea,
And deftly watching for a refluent wave
Gains help to bring his burden to the land.
Then clinging to the loved remains, the wounds
Washed with his tears, thus to the gods he speaks,
And misty stars obscure: "Here, Fortune, lies
Pompeius, thine: no costly incense rare
Or pomp of funeral he dares to ask;
Nor that the smoke rise heavenward from his pyre
With eastern odours rich; nor that the necks   870
Of pious Romans bear him to the tomb,
Their parent; while the forums shall resound
With dirges; nor that triumphs won of yore

211

Be borne before him; nor for sorrowing hosts
To cast their weapons forth. Some little shell
He begs as for the meanest, laid in which
His mutilated corse may reach the flame.
Grudge not his misery the pile of wood
Lit by this menial hand. Is't not enough
That his Cornelia with dishevelled hair   880
Weeps not beside him at his obsequies,
Nor with a last embrace shall place the torch
Beneath her husband dead, but on the deep
Hard by still wanders?"

     Burning from afar
He sees the pyre of some ignoble youth
Deserted of his own, with none to guard:
And quickly drawing from beneath the limbs
Some glowing logs, "Whoe'er thou art," he said
"Neglected shade, uncared for, dear to none,   890
Yet happier than Pompeius in thy death,
Pardon I ask that this my stranger hand
Should violate thy tomb. Yet if to shades
Be sense or memory, gladly shalt thou yield
This from thy pyre to Magnus. 'Twere thy shame,
Blessed with due burial, if his remains
Were homeless." Speaking thus, the wood aflame
Back to the headless trunk at speed he bore,
Which hanging on the margin of the deep,
Almost the sea had won. In sandy trench   900
The gathered fragments of a broken boat,
Trembling, he placed around the noble limbs.
No pile above the corpse nor under lay,
Nor was the fire beneath. Then as he crouched
Beside the blaze, "O, greatest chief," he cried,
Majestic champion of Hesperia's name,
If to be tossed unburied on the deep
Rather than these poor rites thy shade prefer,
From these mine offices thy mighty soul
Withdraw, Pompeius. Injuries dealt by fate   910
Command this duty, lest some bird or beast
Or ocean monster, or fierce Caesar's wrath
Should venture aught upon thee. Take the fire;

All that thou canst; by Roman hand at least
Enkindled. And should Fortune grant return
To loved Hesperia's land, not here shall rest
Thy sacred ashes; but within an urn
Cornelia, from this humble hand received,
Shall place them. Here upon a meagre stone
We draw the characters to mark thy tomb.   920
These letters reading may some kindly friend
Bring back thine head, dissevered, and may grant
Full funeral honours to thine earthly frame."

Then did he cherish the enfeebled fire
Till Magnus' body mingled with its flames.
But now the harbinger of coming dawn
Had paled the constellations: he in fear
Seeks for his hiding place. Whom dost thou dread,
Madman, what punishment for such a crime,
For which thy fame by rumour trumpet-tongued   930
Has been sent down to ages? Praise is thine
For this thy work, at impious Caesar's hands;
Sure of a pardon, go; confess thy task,
And beg the head dissevered. But his work
Was still unfinished, and with pious hand
(Fearing some foe) he seizes on the bones
Now half consumed, and sinews; and the wave
Pours in upon them, and in shallow trench
Commits them to the earth; and lest some breeze
Might bear away the ashes, or by chance   940
Some sailor's anchor might disturb the tomb,
A stone he places, and with stick half burned
Traces the sacred name: HERE MAGNUS LIES.

And art thou, Fortune, pleased that such a spot
Should be his tomb which even Caesar's self
Had chosen, rather than permit his corse
To rest unburied? Why, with thoughtless hand
Confine his shade within the narrow bounds
Of this poor sepulchre? Where the furthest sand
Hangs on the margin of the baffled deep   950
Cabined he lies; yet where the Roman name
Is known, and Empire, such in truth shall be

The boundless measure of his resting-place.
Blot out this stone, this proof against the gods!
Oeta finds room for Hercules alone,
And Nysa's mountain for the Bromian god; [1]
Not all the lands of Egypt should suffice
For Magnus dead: and shall one Pharian stone
Mark his remains? Yet should no turf disclose
His title, peoples of the earth would fear   960
To spurn his ashes, and the sands of Nile
No foot would tread. But if the stone deserves
So great a name, then add his mighty deeds:
Write Lepidus conquered and the Alpine war,
And fierce Sertorius by his aiding arm
O'erthrown; the chariots which as knight he drove; [2]
Cilician pirates driven from the main,
And Commerce safe to nations; Eastern kings
Defeated and the barbarous Northern tribes;
Write that from arms he ever sought the robe;   970
Write that content upon the Capitol
Thrice only triumphed he, nor asked his due.
What mausoleum were for such a chief
A fitting monument? This paltry stone
Records no syllable of the lengthy tale
Of honours: and the name which men have read
Upon the sacred temples of the gods,
And lofty arches built of hostile spoils,
On desolate sands here marks his lowly grave
With characters uncouth, such as the glance   980
Of passing traveller or Roman guest
Might pass unnoticed.

                    Thou Egyptian land
By destiny foredoomed to bear a part
In civil warfare, not unreasoning sang
High Cumae's prophetess, when she forbad [1]

---

[1] Dionysus. But this god, though brought up by the nymphs of Mount Nysa, was not supposed to have been buried there.
[2] See Book VII., line 20.

The stream Pelusian to the Roman arms,
And all the banks which in the summer-tide
Are covered by his flood. What grievous fate
Shall I call down upon thee? May the Nile   990
Turn back his water to his source, thy fields
Want for the winter rain, and all the land
Crumble to desert wastes! We in our fanes
Have known thine Isis and thy hideous gods,
Half hounds, half human, and the drum that bids
To sorrow, and Osiris, whom thy dirge [2]
Proclaims for man. Thou, Egypt, in thy sand
Our dead containest. Nor, though her temples now
Serve a proud master, yet has Rome required
Pompeius' ashes: in a foreign land   1000
Still lies her chief. But though men feared at first
The victor's vengeance, now at length receive
Thy Magnus' bones, if still the restless wave
Hath not prevailed upon that hated shore.
Shall men have fear of tombs and dread to move
The dust of those who should be with the gods?
O, may my country place the crime on me,
If crime it be, to violate such a tomb
Of such a hero, and to bear his dust
Home to Ausonia. Happy, happy he   1010
Who bears such holy office in his trust! [3]

---

[1] This warning of the Sibyl is also alluded to by Cicero in a letter to P. Lentulus, Proconsul of Cilicia. (Mr. Haskins' note. See also Mommsen, vol. iv., p. 305.) It seems to have been discovered in the Sibylline books at the time when it was desired to prevent Pompeius from interfering in the affairs of Egypt, in B.C. 57.

[2] That is, by their weeping for Iris departure they treated him as a mortal and not as a god. Osiris was the soul of Apis (see on line 537), and when that animal grew old and unfit for the residence of Osiris the latter was thought to quit it. Then began the weeping. which continued until a new Apis appeared, selected, of course, by Osiris for his dwelling-place. Then they called out "We have found him, let us rejoice." For a discussion on the Egyptian conception of Osiris, and Iris place in the theogony of that nation, see Hegel's "Lectures on the Philosophy of History": Chapter on Egypt.

[3] It may be noted that the Emperor Hadrian raised a monument on the spot to the memory of Pompeius some sixty years after this was written (Durny's

Haply when famine rages in the land
Or burning southern winds, or fires abound
And earthquake shocks, and Rome shall pray an end
From angry heaven -- by the gods' command,
In council given, shalt thou be transferred
To thine own city, and the priest shall bear
Thy sacred ashes to their last abode.

Who now may seek beneath the raging Crab
Or hot Syene's waste, or Thebes athirst   1020
Under the rainy Pleiades, to gaze
On Nile's broad stream; or whose may exchange
On the Red Sea or in Arabian ports
Some Eastern merchandise, shall turn in awe
To view the venerable stone that marks
Thy grave, Pompeius; and shall worship more
Thy dust commingled with the arid sand,
Thy shade though exiled, than the fane upreared [1]
On Casius' mount to Jove! In temples shrined
And gold, thy memory were viler deemed: 1030
Fortune lies with thee in thy lowly tomb
And makes thee rival of Olympus' king.
More awful is that stone by Libyan seas
Lashed, than are Conquerors' altars. There in earth
A deity rests to whom all men shall bow
More than to gods Tarpeian: and his name
Shall shine the brighter in the days to come
For that no marble tomb about him stands
Nor lofty monument. That little dust
Time shall soon scatter and the tomb shall fall   1040
And all the proofs shall perish of his death.
And happier days shall come when men shall gaze
Upon the stone, nor yet believe the tale:
And Egypt's fable, that she holds the grave
Of great Pompeius, be believed no more

'History of Rome,' iii., 319). Plutarch states that Cornelia had the remains
taken to Rome and interred in a mausoleum. Lucan, it may be supposed,
knew nothing of this.
[1] There was a temple to Jupiter on "Mount Casius old".

Than Crete's which boasts the sepulchre of Jove. [1]

---

[1] The legend that Jove was buried in Crete is also mentioned by Cicero: "De Natura Deorum", iii., 21.

BOOK IX

CATO

Yet in those ashes on the Pharian shore,
In that small heap of dust, was not confined
So great a shade; but from the limbs half burnt
And narrow cell sprang forth [1] and sought the sky
Where dwells the Thunderer. Black the space of air
Upreaching to the poles that bear on high
The constellations in their nightly round;
There 'twixt the orbit of the moon and earth
Abide those lofty spirits, half divine,
Who by their blameless lives and fire of soul   10
Are fit to tolerate the pure expanse
That bounds the lower ether: there shall dwell,
Where nor the monument encased in gold,
Nor richest incense, shall suffice to bring
The buried dead, in union with the spheres,
Pompeius' spirit. When with heavenly light
His soul was filled, first on the wandering stars
And fixed orbs he bent his wondering gaze;
Then saw what darkness veils our earthly day
And scorned the insults heaped upon his corse.   20
Next o'er Emathian plains he winged his flight,

---

[1] This was the Stoic theory. The perfect of men passed after death into a re-
gion between our atmosphere and the heavens, where they remained until the
day of general conflagration, (see Book VII. line 949), with their senses am-
plified and rendered akin to divine.

BOOK IX

And ruthless Caesar's standards, and the fleet
Tossed on the deep: in Brutus' blameless breast
Tarried awhile, and roused his angered soul
To reap the vengeance; last possessed the mind
Of haughty Cato.

      He while yet the scales
Were poised and balanced, nor the war had given
The world its master, hating both the chiefs,
Had followed Magnus for the Senate's cause   30
And for his country: since Pharsalia's field
Ran red with carnage, now was all his heart
Bound to Pompeius. Rome in him received
Her guardian; a people's trembling limbs
He cherished with new hope and weapons gave
Back to the craven hands that cast them forth.
Nor yet for empire did he wage the war
Nor fearing slavery: nor in arms achieved
Aught for himself: freedom, since Magnus fell,
The aim of all his host. And lest the foe   40
In rapid course triumphant should collect
His scattered bands, he sought Corcyra's gulfs
Concealed, and thence in ships unnumbered bore
The fragments of the ruin wrought in Thrace.
Who in such mighty armament had thought
A routed army sailed upon the main
Thronging the sea with keels? Round Malea's cape
And Taenarus open to the shades below
And fair Cythera's isle, th' advancing fleet
Sweeps o'er the yielding wave, by northern breeze   50
Borne past the Cretan shores. But Phycus dared
Refuse her harbour, and th' avenging hand
Left her in ruins. Thus with gentle airs
They glide along the main and reach the shore
From Palinurus [1] named; for not alone
On seas Italian, Pilot of the deep,
Hast thou thy monument; and Libya too
Claims that her waters pleased thy soul of yore.

---

[1] A promontory in Africa was so called, as well as that in Italy.

219

Then in the distance on the main arose
The shining canvas of a stranger fleet,   60
Or friend or foe they knew not. Yet they dread
In every keel the presence of that chief
Their fear-compelling conqueror. But in truth
That navy tears and sorrow bore, and woes
To make e'en Cato weep.

          For when in vain
Cornelia prayed her stepson and the crew
To stay their flight, lest haply from the shore
Back to the sea might float the headless corse;
And when the flame arising marked the place   70
Of that unhallowed rite, "Fortune, didst thou
Judge me unfit," she cried, "to light the pyre
To cast myself upon the hero dead,
The lock to sever, and compose the limbs
Tossed by the cruel billows of the deep,
To shed a flood of tears upon his wounds,
And from the flickering flame to bear away
And place within the temples of the gods
All that I could, his dust? That pyre bestows
No honour, haply by some Pharian hand   80
Piled up in insult to his mighty shade.
Happy the Crassi lying on the waste
Unburied. To the greater shame of heaven
Pompeius has such funeral. And shall this
For ever be my lot? her husbands slain
Cornelia ne'er enclose within the tomb,
Nor shed the tear beside the urn that holds
The ashes of the loved? Yet for my grief
What boots or monument or ordered pomp?
Dost thou not, impious, upon thy heart   90
Pompeius' image, and upon thy soul
Bear ineffaceable? Dust closed in urns
Is for the wife who would survive her lord
Not such as thee, Cornelia! And yet
Yon scanty light that glimmers from afar
Upon the Pharian shore, somewhat of thee
Recalls, Pompeius! Now the flame sinks down
And smoke drifts up across the eastern sky

Bearing thine ashes, and the rising wind
Sighs hateful in the sail. To me no more   100
Dearer than this whatever land may yield
Pompeius' victory, nor the frequent car
That carried him in triumph to the hill;
Gone is that happy husband from my thoughts;
Here did I lose the hero whom I knew;
Here let me stay; his presence shall endear
The sands of Nile where fell the fatal blow.
Thou, Sextus, brave the chances of the war
And bear Pompeius' standard through the world.
For thus thy father spake within mine ear: 110
'When sounds my fatal hour let both my sons
Urge on the war; nor let some Caesar find
Room for an empire, while shall live on earth
Still one in whom Pompeius' blood shall run.
This your appointed task; all cities strong
In freedom of their own, all kingdoms urge
To join the combat; for Pompeius calls.
Nor shall a chieftain of that famous name
Ride on the seas and fail to find a fleet.
Urged by his sire's unconquerable will   120
And mindful of his rights, mine heir shall rouse
All nations to the conflict. One alone,
(Should he contend for freedom) may ye serve;
Cato, none else!' Thus have I kept the faith;
Thy plot [1] prevailed upon me, and I lived
Thy mandate to discharge. Now through the void
Of space, and shades of Hell, if such there be,
I follow; yet how distant be my doom
I know not: first my spirit must endure
The punishment of life, which saw thine end   130
And could survive it; sighs shall break my heart,
Tears shall dissolve it: sword nor noose I need
Nor headlong plunge. 'Twere shameful since thy death,
Were aught but grief required to cause my own."

---

[1] Meaning that her husband gave her this commission in order to prevent her from committing suicide.

She seeks the cabin, veiled, in funeral garb,
In tears to find her solace, and to love
Grief in her husband's room; no prayers were hers
For life, as were the sailors'; nor their shout
Roused by the height of peril, moved her soul,
Nor angered waves: but sorrowing there she lay,   140
Resigned to death and welcoming the storm.

First reached they Cyprus on the foamy brine;
Then as the eastern breeze more gently held
The favouring deep, they touched the Libyan shore
Where stood the camp of Cato. Sad as one
Who deep in fear presages ills to come,
Cnaeus beheld his brother and his band
Of patriot comrades. Swift into the wave
He leaps and cries, "Where, brother, is our sire?
Still stands our country mistress of the world,   150
Or are we fallen, Rome with Magnus' death
Rapt to the shades?" Thus he: but Sextus said

"Oh happy thou who by report alone
Hear'st of the deed that chanced on yonder shore!
These eyes that saw, my brother, share the guilt.
Not Caesar wrought the murder of our sire,
Nor any captain worthy in the fray.
He fell beneath the orders of a king
Shameful and base, while trusting to the gods
Who shield the guest; a king who in that land   160
By his concession ruled: (this the reward
For favours erst bestowed). Within my sight
Pierced through with wounds our noble father fell:
Yet deeming not the petty prince of Nile
So fell a deed would dare, to Egypt's strand
I thought great Caesar come. But worse than all,
Worse than the wounds which gaped upon his frame
Struck me with horror to the inmost heart,
Our murdered father's head, shorn from the trunk
And borne aloft on javelin; this sight,   170
As rumour said, the cruel victor asked
To feast his eyes, and prove the bloody deed.
For whether ravenous birds and Pharian dogs

Have torn his corse asunder, or a fire
Consumed it, which with stealthy flame arose
Upon the shore, I know not. For the parts
Devoured by destiny I only blame
The gods: I weep the part preserved by men."

Thus Sextus spake: and Cnaeus at the words
Flamed into fury for his father's shame.   180
"Sailors, launch forth our navies, by your oars
Forced through the deep though wind and sea oppose:
Captains, lead on: for civil strife ne'er gave
So great a prize; to lay in earth the limbs
Of Magnus, and avenge him with the blood
Of that unmanly tyrant. Shall I spare
Great Alexander's fort, nor sack the shrine
And plunge his body in the tideless marsh?
Nor drag Amasis from the Pyramids,
And all their ancient Kings, to swim the Nile?   190
Torn from his tomb, that god of all mankind
Isis, unburied, shall avenge thy shade;
And veiled Osiris shall I hurl abroad
In mutilated fragments; and the form
Of sacred Apis; [1] and with these their gods
Shall light a furnace, that shall burn the head
They held in insult. Thus their land shall pay
The fullest penalty for the shameful deed.
No husbandman shall live to till the fields
Nor reap the benefit of brimming Nile.   200
Thou only, Father, gods and men alike
Fallen and perished, shalt possess the land."

Such were the words he spake; and soon the fleet
Had dared the angry deep: but Cato's voice
While praising, calmed the youthful chieftain's rage.

Meanwhile, when Magnus' fate was known, the air
Sounded with lamentations which the shore
Re-echoed; never through the ages past,

---

[1] See Book VIII., line 547.

By history recorded, was it known
That thus a people mourned their ruler's death.   210
Yet more when worn with tears, her pallid cheek
Veiled by her loosened tresses, from the ship
Cornelia came, they wept and beat the breast.
The friendly land once gained, her husband's garb,
His arms and spoils, embroidered deep in gold,
Thrice worn of old upon the sacred hill [1]
She placed upon the flame. Such were for her
The ashes of her spouse: and such the love
Which glowed in every heart, that soon the shore
Blazed with his obsequies. Thus at winter-tide   220
By frequent fires th' Apulian herdsman seeks
To render to the fields their verdant growth;
Till blaze Garganus' uplands and the meads
Of Vultur, and the pasture of the herds
By warm Matinum.

       Yet Pompeius' shade
Nought else so gratified, not all the blame
The people dared to heap upon the gods,
For him their hero slain, as these few words
From Cato's noble breast instinct with truth: 230
"Gone is a citizen who though no peer [2]
Of those who disciplined the state of yore
In due submission to the bounds of right,
Yet in this age irreverent of law
Has played a noble part. Great was his power,
But freedom safe: when all the plebs was prone
To be his slaves, he chose the private gown;
So that the Senate ruled the Roman state,
The Senate's ruler: nought by right of arms
He e'er demanded: willing took he gifts   240
Yet from a willing giver: wealth was his
Vast, yet the coffers of the State he filled

---

[1] See line 709.
[2] This passage is described by Lord Macaulay as "a pure gem of rhetoric without one flaw, and, in my opinion, not very far from historical truth" (Trevelyan's "Life and Letters", vol. i., page 462.)

Beyond his own. He seized upon the sword,
Knew when to sheath it; war did he prefer
To arts of peace, yet armed loved peace the more.
Pleased took he power, pleased he laid it down:
Chaste was his home and simple, by his wealth
Untarnished. Mid the peoples great his name
And venerated: to his native Rome[1]
He wrought much good. True faith in liberty   250
Long since with Marius and Sulla fled:
Now when Pompeius has been reft away
Its counterfeit has perished. Now unshamed
Shall seize the despot on Imperial power,
Unshamed shall cringe the Senate. Happy he
Who with disaster found his latest breath
And met the Pharian sword prepared to slay.
Life might have been his lot, in despot rule,
Prone at his kinsman's throne. Best gift of all
The knowledge how to die; next, death compelled.   260
If cruel Fortune doth reserve for me
An alien conqueror, may Juba be
As Ptolemaeus. So he take my head
My body grace his triumph, if he will."
More than had Rome resounded with his praise
Words such as these gave honour to the shade
Of that most noble dead.

          Meanwhile the crowd
Weary of warfare, since Pompeius' fall,
Broke into discord, as their ancient chief   270
Cilician called them to desert the camp.
But Cato hailed them from the furthest beach:
"Untamed Cilician, is thy course now set
For Ocean theft again; Pompeius gone,
Once more a pirate?" Thus he spake, and gazed
At all the stirring throng; but one whose mind
Was fixed on flight, thus answered, "Pardon, chief,

---

[1] "... Clarum et venembile nomen   Gentibus, et multum nostrae quod pro-
fuit urbi," quoted by Mr. Burke, and applied to Lord Chatham, in his Speech
on American taxation.

'Twas love of Magnus, not of civil war,
That led us to the fight: his side was ours:
With him whom all the world preferred to peace,   280
Our cause is perished. Let us seek our homes
Long since unseen, our children and our wives.
If nor the rout nor dread Pharsalia's field
Nor yet Pompeius' death shall close the war,
Whence comes the end? The vigour of a life
For us is vanished: in our failing years
Give us at least some pious hand to speed
The parting soul, and light the funeral pyre.
Scarce even to its captains civil strife
Concedes due burial. Nor in our defeat   290
Does Fortune threaten us with the savage yoke
Of distant nations. In the garb of Rome
And with her rights, I leave thee. Who had been
Second to Magnus living, he shall be
My first hereafter: to that sacred shade
Be the prime honour. Chance of war appoints
My lord but not my leader. Thee alone
I followed, Magnus; after thee the fates.
Nor hope we now for victory, nor wish;
For all our Thracian army is fled   300
In Caesar's victory, whose potent star
Of fortune rules the world, and none but he
Has power to keep or save. That civil war
Which while Pompeius lived was loyalty
Is impious now. If in the public right
Thou, patriot Cato, find'st thy guide, we seek
The standards of the Consul." Thus he spake
And with him leaped into the ship a throng
Of eager comrades.

       Then was Rome undone,   310
For all the shore was stirring with a crowd
Athirst for slavery. But burst these words
From Cato's blameless breast: "Then with like vows
As Caesar's rival host ye too did seek
A lord and master! not for Rome the fight,
But for Pompeius! For that now no more
Ye fight for tyranny, but for yourselves,

Not for some despot chief, ye live and die;
Since now 'tis safe to conquer and no lord
Shall rob you, victors, of a world subdued --   320
Ye flee the war, and on your abject necks
Feel for the absent yoke; nor can endure
Without a despot! Yet to men the prize
Were worth the danger. Magnus might have used
To evil ends your blood; refuse ye now,
With liberty so near, your country's call?
Now lives one tyrant only of the three;
Thus far in favour of the laws have wrought
The Pharian weapons and the Parthian bow;
Not you, degenerate! Begone, and spurn   330
This gift of Ptolemaeus. [1] Who would think
Your hands were stained with blood? The foe will deem
That you upon that dread Thessalian day
First turned your backs. Then flee in safety, flee!
By neither battle nor blockade subdued
Caesar shall give you life! O slaves most base,
Your former master slain, ye seek his heir!
Why doth it please you not yet more to earn
Than life and pardon? Bear across the sea
Metellus' daughter, Magnus' weeping spouse,   340
And both his sons; outstrip the Pharian gift,
Nor spare this head, which, laid before the feet
Of that detested tyrant, shall deserve
A full reward. Thus, cowards, shall ye learn
In that ye followed me how great your gain.
Quick to your task and purchase thus with blood
Your claim on Caesar. Dastardly is flight
Which crime commends not."

           Cato thus recalled
The parting vessels. So when bees in swarm   350
Desert their waxen cells, forget the hive
Ceasing to cling together, and with wings
Untrammelled seek the air, nor slothful light
On thyme to taste its bitterness -- then rings

---

[1] That is, liberty, which by the murder of Pompeius they had obtained.

227

The Phrygian gong -- at once they pause aloft
Astonied; and with love of toil resumed
Through all the flowers for their honey store
In ceaseless wanderings search; the shepherd joys,
Sure that th' Hyblaean mead for him has kept
His cottage store, the riches of his home.   360

Now in the active conduct of the war
Were brought to discipline their minds, untaught
To bear repose; first on the sandy shore
Toiling they learned fatigue: then stormed thy walls,
Cyrene; prizeless, for to Cato's mind
'Twas prize enough to conquer. Juba next
He bids attack, though Nature on the path
Had placed the Syrtes; which his sturdy heart
Aspired to conquer. Either at the first
When Nature gave the universe its form   370
She left this region neither land nor sea;
Not wholly shrunk, so that it should receive
The ocean flood; nor firm enough to stand
Against its buffets -- all the pathless coast
Lies in uncertain shape; the land by earth
Is parted from the deep; on sandy banks
The seas are broken, and from shoal to shoal
The waves advance to sound upon the shore.
Nature, in spite, thus left her work undone,
Unfashioned to men's use -- Or else of old   380
A foaming ocean filled the wide expanse,
But Titan feeding from the briny depths
His burning fires (near to the zone of heat)
Reduced the waters; and the sea still fights
With Phoebus' beams, which in the length of time
Drank deeper of its fountains.

            When the main
Struck by the oars gave passage to the fleet,
Black from the sky rushed down a southern gale
Upon his realm, and from the watery plain   390
Drave back th' invading ships, and from the shoals
Compelled the billows, and in middle sea
Raised up a bank. Forth flew the bellying sails

Beyond the prows, despite the ropes that dared
Resist the tempest's fury; and for those
Who prescient housed their canvas to the storm,
Bare-masted they were driven from their course.
Best was their lot who gained the open waves
Of ocean; others lightened of their masts
Shook off the tempest; but a sweeping tide   400
Hurried them southwards, victor of the gale.
Some freed of shallows on a bank were forced
Which broke the deep: their ship in part was fast,
Part hanging on the sea; their fates in doubt.
Fierce rage the waves till hems [1] them in the land;
Nor Auster's force in frequent buffets spent
Prevails upon the shore. High from the main
By seas inviolate one bank of sand,
Far from the coast arose; there watched in vain
The storm-tossed mariners, their keel aground,   410
No shore descrying. Thus in sea were lost
Some portion, but the major part by helm
And rudder guided, and by pilots' hands
Who knew the devious channels, safe at length
Floated the marsh of Triton loved (as saith
The fable) by that god, whose sounding shell [2]
All seas and shores re-echo; and by her,
Pallas, who springing from her father's head
First lit on Libya, nearest land to heaven,
(As by its heat is proved); here on the brink   420
She stood, reflected in the placid wave
And called herself Tritonis. Lethe's flood
Flows silent near, in fable from a source
Infernal sprung, oblivion in his stream;
Here, too, that garden of the Hesperids
Where once the sleepless dragon held his watch,
Shorn of its leafy wealth. Shame be on him
Who calls upon the poet for the proof
Of that which in the ancient days befell;

---

[1] Reading "saepit", Hosius. The passage seems to be corrupt.
[2] "Scaly Triton's winding shell", (Comus, 878). He was Neptune's son and
trumpeter. That Pallas sprang armed from the head of Jupiter is well known.

But here were golden groves by yellow growth   430
Weighed down in richness, here a maiden band
Were guardians; and a serpent, on whose eyes
Sleep never fell, was coiled around the trees,
Whose branches bowed beneath their ruddy load.
But great Alcides stripped the bending boughs,
And bore their shining apples (thus his task
Accomplished) to the court of Argos' king.

Driven on the Libyan realms, more fruitful here,
Pompeius [1] stayed the fleet, nor further dared
In Garamantian waves. But Cato's soul   440
Leaped in his breast, impatient of delay,
To pass the Syrtes by a landward march,
And trusting to their swords, 'gainst tribes unknown
To lead his legions. And the storm which closed
The main to navies gave them hope of rain;
Nor biting frosts they feared, in Libyan clime;
Nor suns too scorching in the falling year.

Thus ere they trod the deserts, Cato spake:
"Ye men of Rome, who through mine arms alone
Can find the death ye covet, and shall fall   450
With pride unbroken should the fates command,
Meet this your weighty task, your high emprise
With hearts resolved to conquer. For we march
On sterile wastes, burnt regions of the world;
Scarce are the wells, and Titan from the height
Burns pitiless, unclouded; and the slime
Of poisonous serpents fouls the dusty earth.
Yet shall men venture for the love of laws
And country perishing, upon the sands
Of trackless Libya; men who brave in soul   460
Rely not on the end, and in attempt
Will risk their all. 'Tis not in Cato's thoughts
On this our enterprise to lead a band
Blind to the truth, unwitting of the risk.
Nay, give me comrades for the danger's sake,

_____

[1] Cnaeus.

230

Whom I shall see for honour and for Rome
Bear up against the worst. But whose needs
A pledge of safety, to whom life is sweet,
Let him by fairer journey seek his lord.
First be my foot upon the sand; on me   470
First strike the burning sun; across my path
The serpent void his venom; by my fate
Know ye your perils. Let him only thirst
Who sees me at the spring: who sees me seek
The shade, alone sink fainting in the heat;
Or whoso sees me ride before the ranks
Plodding their weary march: such be the lot
Of each, who, toiling, finds in me a chief
And not a comrade. Snakes, thirst, burning sand
The brave man welcomes, and the patient breast   480
Finds happiness in labour. By its cost
Courage is sweeter; and this Libyan land
Such cloud of ills can furnish as might make
Men flee unshamed." 'Twas thus that Cato spake,
Kindling the torch of valour and the love
Of toil: then reckless of his fate he strode
The desert path from which was no return:
And Libya ruled his destinies, to shut
His sacred name within a narrow tomb.

One-third of all the world, [1] if fame we trust,   490
Is Libya; yet by winds and sky she yields
Some part to Europe; for the shores of Nile
No more than Scythian Tanais are remote
From furthest Gades, where with bending coast,
Yielding a place to Ocean, Europe parts
From Afric shores. Yet falls the larger world
To Asia only. From the former two
Issues the Western wind; but Asia's right
Touches the Southern limits and her left
The Northern tempest's home; and of the East   500

---

[1] Compare Herodotus, ii., 16: "For they all say that the earth is divided into
three parts, Europe, Asia and Libya." (And see Bunbury's "Ancient Geogra-
phy", i., 145, 146, for a discussion of this subject.)

She's mistress to the rising of the Sun.
All that is fertile of the Afric lands
Lies to the west, but even here abound
No wells of water: though the Northern wind,
Infrequent, leaving us with skies serene,
Falls there in showers. Not gold nor wealth of brass
It yields the seeker: pure and unalloyed
Down to its lowest depths is Libyan soil.
Yet citron forests to Maurusian tribes
Were riches, had they known; but they, content,   510
Lived 'neath the shady foliage, till gleamed
The axe of Rome amid the virgin grove,
To bring from furthest limits of the world
Our banquet tables and the fruit they bear. [1]
But suns excessive and a scorching air
Burn all the glebe beside the shifting sands:
There die the harvests on the crumbling mould;
No root finds sustenance, nor kindly Jove
Makes rich the furrow nor matures the vine.
Sleep binds all nature and the tract of sand   520
Lies ever fruitless, save that by the shore
The hardy Nasamon plucks a scanty grass.
Unclothed their race, and living on the woes
Worked by the cruel Syrtes on mankind;
For spoilers are they of the luckless ships
Cast on the shoals: and with the world by wrecks
Their only commerce.

       Here at Cato's word
His soldiers passed, in fancy from the winds
That sweep the sea secure: here on them fell   530
Smiting with greater strength upon the shore,
Than on the ocean, Auster's tempest force,
And yet more fraught with mischief: for no crags
Repelled his strength, nor lofty mountains tamed
His furious onset, nor in sturdy woods
He found a bar; but free from reining hand,

---

[1] Citron tables were in much request at Rome. (Comp. "Paradise Regained",
Book iv., 115; and see Book X., line 177.)

Raged at his will o'er the defenceless earth.
Nor did he mingle dust and clouds of rain
In whirling circles, but the earth was swept
And hung in air suspended, till amazed   540
The Nasamon saw his scanty field and home
Reft by the tempest, and the native huts
From roof to base were hurried on the blast.
Not higher, when some all-devouring flame
Has seized upon its prey, in volumes dense
Rolls up the smoke, and darkens all the air.
Then with fresh might he fell upon the host
Of marching Romans, snatching from their feet
The sand they trod. Had Auster been enclosed
In some vast cavernous vault with solid walls   550
And mighty barriers, he had moved the world
Upon its ancient base and made the lands
To tremble: but the facile Libyan soil
By not resisting stood, and blasts that whirled
The surface upwards left the depths unmoved.
Helmet and shield and spear were torn away
By his most violent breath, and borne aloft
Through all the regions of the boundless sky;
Perchance a wonder in some distant land,
Where men may fear the weapons from the heaven   560
There falling, as the armour of the gods,
Nor deem them ravished from a soldier's arm.
'Twas thus on Numa by the sacred fire
Those shields descended which our chosen priests [1]
Bear on their shoulders; from some warlike race
By tempest rapt, to be the prize of Rome.

Fearing the storm prone fell the host to earth
Winding their garments tight, and with clenched hands
Gripping the earth: for not their weight alone

---

[1] Alluding to the shield of Mars which fell from heaven on Numa at sacrifice.
Eleven others were made to match it ("Dict. Antiq.") While Horace speaks of
them as chief objects of a patriot Roman's affection ("Odes" iii., 5, 9), Lucan
discovers for them a ridiculous origin. They were in the custody of the priests
of Mars. (See Book I., 666.)

Withstood the tempest which upon their frames   570
Piled mighty heaps, and their recumbent limbs
Buried in sand. At length they struggling rose
Back to their feet, when lo! around them stood,
Forced by the storm, a growing bank of earth
Which held them motionless. And from afar
Where walls lay prostrate, mighty stones were hurled,
Thus piling ills on ills in wondrous form:
No dwellings had they seen, yet at their feet
Beheld the ruins. All the earth was hid
In vast envelopment, nor found they guide   580
Save from the stars, which as in middle deep
Flamed o'er them wandering: yet some were hid
Beneath the circle of the Libyan earth
Which tending downwards hid the Northern sky.

When warmth dispersed the tempest-driven air,
And rose upon the earth the flaming day,
Bathed were their limbs in sweat, but parched and dry
Their gaping lips; when to a scanty spring
Far off beheld they came, whose meagre drops
All gathered in the hollow of a helm   590
They offered to their chief. Caked were their throats
With dust, and panting; and one little drop
Had made him envied. "Wretch, and dost thou deem
Me wanting in a brave man's heart?" he cried,
"Me only in this throng? And have I seemed
Tender, unfit to bear the morning heat?
He who would quench his thirst 'mid such a host,
Doth most deserve its pangs." Then in his wrath
Dashed down the helmet, and the scanty spring,
Thus by their leader spurned, sufficed for all.   600

Now had they reached that temple which possess
Sole in all Libya, th' untutored tribes
Of Garamantians. Here holds his seat
(So saith the story) a prophetic Jove,
Wielding no thunderbolts, nor like to ours,
The Libyan Hammen of the curved horn.
No wealth adorns his fane by Afric tribes
Bestowed, nor glittering hoard of Eastern gems.

Though rich Arabians, Ind and Ethiop
Know him alone as Jove, still is he poor   610
Holding his shrine by riches undefiled
Through time, and god as of the olden days
Spurns all the wealth of Rome. That here some god
Dwells, witnesses the only grove
That buds in Libya -- for that which grows
Upon the arid dust which Leptis parts
From Berenice, knows no leaves; alone
Hammon uprears a wood; a fount the cause
Which with its waters binds the crumbling soil.
Yet shall the Sun when poised upon the height   620
Strike through the foliage: hardly can the tree
Protect its trunk, and to a little space
His rays draw in the circle of the shade.
Here have men found the spot where that high band
Solstitial divides in middle sky [1]
The zodiac stars: not here oblique their course,
Nor Scorpion rises straighter than the Bull,
Nor to the Scales does Ram give back his hours,
Nor does Astraea bid the Fishes sink
More slowly down: but watery Capricorn   630
Is equal with the Crab, and with the Twins
The Archer; neither does the Lion rise
Above Aquarius. But the race that dwells
Beyond the fervour of the Libyan fires
Sees to the South that shadow which with us
Falls to the North: slow Cynosure sinks [2]
For them below the deep; and, dry with us,
The Wagon plunges; far from either pole,
No star they know that does not seek the main,
But all the constellations in their course   640
Whirl to their vision through the middle sky.

Before the doors the Eastern peoples stood
Seeking from horned Jove to know their fates:
Yet to the Roman chief they yielded place,

---

[1] I.e. Where the equinoctial circle cuts the zodiac in its centre. -- Haskins.
[2] Compare Book III., 288.

Whose comrades prayed him to entreat the gods
Famed through the Libyan world, and judge the voice
Renowned from distant ages. First of these
Was Labienus: [1] "Chance," he said, "to us
The voice and counsel of this mighty god
Has offered as we march; from such a guide   650
To know the issues of the war, and learn
To track the Syrtes. For to whom on earth
If not to blameless Cato, shall the gods
Entrust their secrets? Faithful thou at least,
Their follower through all thy life hast been;
Now hast thou liberty to speak with Jove.
Ask impious Caesar's fates, and learn the laws
That wait our country in the future days:
Whether the people shall be free to use
Their rights and customs, or the civil war   660
For us is wasted. To thy sacred breast,
Lover of virtue, take the voice divine;
Demand what virtue is and guide thy steps
By heaven's high counsellor."

                    But Cato, full
Of godlike thoughts borne in his quiet breast,
This answer uttered, worthy of the shrines:
"What, Labienus, dost thou bid me ask?
Whether in arms and freedom I should wish
To perish, rather than endure a king?   670
Is longest life worth aught? And doth its term
Make difference? Can violence to the good
Do injury? Do Fortune's threats avail
Outweighed by virtue? Doth it not suffice
To aim at deeds of bravery? Can fame
Grow by achievement? Nay! No Hammen's voice
Shall teach us this more surely than we know.
Bound are we to the gods; no voice we need;
They live in all our acts, although the shrine
Be silent: at our birth and once for all   680
What may be known the author of our being

---

[1] See Book V., 400.

Revealed; nor Chose these thirsty sands to chaunt
To few his truth, whelmed in the dusty waste.
God has his dwelling in all things that be,
In earth and air and sea and starry vault,
In virtuous deeds; in all that thou can'st see,
In all thy thoughts contained. Why further, then,
Seek we our deities? Let those who doubt
And halting, tremble for their coming fates,
Go ask the oracles. No mystic words,   690
Make sure my heart, but surely-coming Death.
Coward alike and brave, we all must die.
Thus hath Jove spoken: seek to know no more."

Thus Cato spake, and faithful to his creed
He parted from the temple of the god
And left the oracle of Hammon dumb.

Bearing his javelin, as one of them
Before the troops he marched: no panting slave
With bending neck, no litter bore his form.
He bade them not, but showed them how to toil.   700
Spare in his sleep, the last to sip the spring
When at some rivulet to quench their thirst
The eager ranks pressed onward, he alone
Until the humblest follower might drink
Stood motionless. If for the truly good
Is fame, and virtue by the deed itself,
Not by sucoessful issue, should be judged,
Yield, famous ancestors! Fortune, not worth
Gained you your glory. But such name as his
Who ever merited by successful war   710
Or slaughtered peoples? Rather would I lead
With him his triumph through the pathless sands
And Libya's bounds, than in Pompeius' car
Three times ascend the Capitol, [1] or break
The proud Jugurtha. [1] Rome! in him behold

---

[1] 1st. For his victories in Sicily and Africa, B.C. 81; 2nd. For the conquest of Sertorius, B.C. 71; 3rd. For his Eastern triumphs, B.C. 61. (Compare Book II., 684, &c.)

His country's father, worthiest of thy vows;
A name by which men shall not blush to swear,
Whom, should'st thou break the fetters from thy neck,
Thou may'st in distant days decree divine.

Now was the heat more dense, and through that clime   720
Than which no further on the Southern side
The gods permit, they trod; and scarcer still
The water, till in middle sands they found
One bounteous spring which clustered serpents held
Though scaroe the space sufficed. By thirsting snakes
The fount was thronged and asps pressed on the marge.
But when the chieftain saw that speedy fate
Was on the host, if they should leave the well
Untasted, "Vain," he cried, "your fear of death.
Drink, nor delay: 'tis from the threatening tooth   730
Men draw their deaths, and fatal from the fang
Issues the juice if mingled with the blood;
The cup is harmless." Then he sipped the fount,
Still doubting, and in all the Libyan waste
There only was he first to touch the stream.

Why fertile thus in death the pestilent air
Of Libya, what poison in her soil
Her several nature mixed, my care to know
Has not availed: but from the days of old
A fabled story has deceived the world.   740

Far on her limits, where the burning shore
Admits the ocean fervid from the sun
Plunged in its waters, lay Medusa's fields
Untilled; nor forests shaded, nor the plough
Furrowed the soil, which by its mistress' gaze
Was hardened into stone: Phorcus, her sire.
Malevolent nature from her body first
Drew forth these noisome pests; first from her jaws
Issued the sibilant rattle of serpent tongues;
Clustered around her head the poisonous brood   750

---

[1] Over whom Marius triumphed.

Like to a woman's hair, wreathed on her neck
Which gloried in their touch; their glittering heads
Advanced towards her; and her tresses kempt
Dripped down with viper's venom. This alone
Thou hast, accursed one, which men can see
Unharmed; for who upon that gaping mouth
Looked and could dread? To whom who met her glance,
Was death permitted? Fate delayed no more.
But ere the victim feared had struck him down:
Perished the limbs while living, and the soul   760
Grew stiff and stark ere yet it fled the frame.
Men have been frenzied by the Furies' locks,
Not killed; and Cerberus at Orpheus' song
Ceased from his hissing, and Alcides saw
The Hydra ere he slew. This monster born
Brought horror with her birth upon her sire
Phorcus, in second order God of Waves,
And upon Ceto and the Gorgon brood, [1]
Her sisters. She could threat the sea and sky
With deadly calm unknown, and from the world   770
Bid cease the soil. Borne down by instant weight
Fowls fell from air, and beasts were fixed in stone.
Whole Ethiop tribes who tilled the neighbouring lands
Rigid in marble stood. The Gorgon sight
No creature bore and even her serpents turned
Back from her visage. Atlas in his place
Beside the Western columns, by her look
Was turned to rocks; and when on snakes of old
Phlegraean giants stood and frighted heaven,
She made them mountains, and the Gorgon head   780
Borne on Athena's bosom closed the war.
Here born of Danae and the golden shower,
Floating on wings Parrhasian, by the god
Arcadian given, author of the lyre
And wrestling art, came Perseus, down from heaven
Swooping. Cyllenian Harp [1] did he bear

---

[1] Phoreus and Ceto were the parents of the Gorgons -- Stheno, Euryale. and Medusa, of whom the latter alone was mortal, (Hesiod. "Theogony", 276.) Phorcus was a son of Pontus and Gaia (sea and land), ibid, 287.

Still crimson from another monster slain,
The guardian of the heifer loved by Jove.
This to her winged brother Pallas lent
Price of the monster's head: by her command   790
Upon the limits of the Libyan land
He sought the rising sun, with flight averse,
Poised o'er Medusa's realm; a burnished shield
Of yellow brass upon his other arm,
Her gift, he bore: in which she bade him see
The fatal face unscathed. Nor yet in sleep
Lay all the monster, for such total rest
To her were death -- so fated: serpent locks
In vigilant watch, some reaching forth defend
Her head, while others lay upon her face   800
And slumbering eyes. Then hero Perseus shook
Though turned averse; trembled his dexter hand:
But Pallas held, and the descending blade
Shore the broad neck whence sprang the viper brood.
What visage bore the Gorgon as the steel
Thus reft her life! what poison from her throat
Breathed! from her eyes what venom of death distilled!
The goddess dared not look, and Perseus' face
Had frozen, averse, had not Athena veiled
With coils of writhing snakes the features dead.   810
Then with the Gorgon head the hero flew
Uplifted on his wings and sought the sky.
Shorter had been his voyage through the midst
Of Europe's cities; but Athena bade
To spare her peoples and their fruitful lands;
For who when such an airy courser passed
Had not looked up to heaven? Western winds
Now sped his pinions, and he took his course
O'er Libya's regions, from the stars and suns
Veiled by no culture. Phoebus' nearer track   820

---

[1] The scimitar lent by Hermes (or Mercury) to Perseus for the purpose; with
which had been slain Argus the guardian of Io (Conf. "Prometheus vinctus",
579.) Hermes was born in a cave in Mount Cyllene in Arcadia.

BOOK IX

There burns the soil, and loftiest on the sky [1]
There fails the night, to shade the wandering moon,
If o'er forgetful of her course oblique,
Straight through the stars, nor bending to the North
Nor to the South, she hastens. Yet that earth,
In nothing fertile, void of fruitful yield,
Drank in the poison of Medusa's blood,
Dripping in dreadful dews upon the soil,
And in the crumbling sands by heat matured.

First from the dust was raised a gory clot [2]   830
In guise of Asp, sleep-bringing, swollen of neck:
Full was the blood and thick the poison drop
That were its making; in no other snake
More copious held. Greedy of warmth it seeks
No frozen world itself, nor haunts the sands
Beyond the Nile; yet has our thirst of gain
No shame nor limit, and this Libyan death,
This fatal pest we purchase for our own.
Haemorrhois huge spreads out his scaly coils,
Who suffers not his hapless victims' blood   840
To stay within their veins. Chersydros sprang
To life, to dwell within the doubtful marsh
Where land nor sea prevails. A cloud of spray
Marked fell Chelyder's track: and Cenchris rose
Straight gliding to his prey, his belly tinged
With various spots unnumbered, more than those
Which paint the Theban [3] marble; horned snakes

---

[1] The idea seems to be that the earth, bulging at the equator, casts its shadow highest on the sky: and that the moon becomes eclipsed by it whenever she follows a straight path instead of an oblique one, which may happen from her forgetfulness (Mr. Haskins' note).
[2] This catalogue of snakes is alluded to in Dante's "Inferno", 24.   "I saw a crowd within   Of serpents terrible, so strange of shape   And hideous that remembrance in my veins   Yet shrinks the vital current. Of her sands Let Libya vaunt no more: if Jaculus,   Pareas, and Chelyder be her brood, Cenchris and Amphisbaena, plagues so dire   Or in such numbers swarming ne'er she showed."
        -- Carey.   (See also Milton's "Paradise Lost", Book X., 520-530.)
[3] The Egyptian Thebes.

With spines contorted: like to torrid sand
Ammodytes, of hue invisible:
Sole of all serpents Scytale to shed   850
In vernal frosts his slough; and thirsty Dipsas;
Dread Amphisbaena with his double head
Tapering; and Natrix who in bubbling fount
Fuses his venom. Greedy Prester swells
His foaming jaws; Pareas, head erect
Furrows with tail alone his sandy path;
Swift Jaculus there, and Seps [1] whose poisonous juice
Makes putrid flesh and frame: and there upreared
His regal head, and frighted from his track
With sibilant terror all the subject swam,   860
Baneful ere darts his poison, Basilisk [2]
In sands deserted king. Ye serpents too
Who in all other regions harmless glide
Adored as gods, and bright with golden scales,
In those hot wastes are deadly; poised in air
Whole herds of kine ye follow, and with coils
Encircling close, crush in the mighty bull.
Nor does the elephant in his giant bulk,
Nor aught, find safety; and ye need no fang
Nor poison, to compel the fatal end.   870

Amid these pests undaunted Cato urged
His desert journey on. His hardy troops
Beneath his eyes, pricked by a scanty wound,
In strangest forms of death unnumbered fall.
Tyrrhenian Aulus, bearer of a flag,
Trod on a Dipsas; quick with head reversed
The serpent struck; no mark betrayed the tooth:

---

[1] "... All my being   Like him whom the Numidian Seps did thaw   Into a
dew with poison, is dissolved,   Sinking through its foundations."
           --Shelley, "Prometheus Unbound", Act iii, Scene 1.
[2] The glance of the eye of the basilisk or cockatrice, was supposed to be dead-
ly. (See "King Richard III", Act i., Scene 2: --   Gloucester: Thine eyes,
sweet lady, have infected
           mine.   Anne: Would they were basilisks, to strike
           thee dead!) The word is also used for a big cannon. ("1 King
Henry IV", Act ii., Scene 3.)

The aspect of the wound nor threatened death,
Nor any evil; but the poison germ
In silence working as consuming fire 880
Absorbed the moisture of his inward frame,
Draining the natural juices that were spread
Around his vitals; in his arid jaws
Set flame upon his tongue: his wearied limbs
No sweat bedewed; dried up, the fount of tears
Fled from his eyelids. Tortured by the fire
Nor Cato's sternness, nor of his sacred charge
The honour could withhold him; but he dared
To dash his standard down, and through the plains
Raging, to seek for water that might slake 890
The fatal venom thirsting at his heart.
Plunge him in Tanais, in Rhone and Po,
Pour on his burning tongue the flood of Nile,
Yet were the fire unquenched. So fell the fang
Of Dipsas in the torrid Libyan lands;
In other climes less fatal. Next he seeks
Amid the sands, all barren to the depths,
For moisture: then returning to the shoals
Laps them with greed -- in vain -- the briny draught
Scarce quenched the thirst it made. Nor knowing yet 900
The poison in his frame, he steels himself
To rip his swollen veins and drink the gore.
Cato bids lift the standard, lest his troops
May find in thirst a pardon for the deed.

But on Sabellus' yet more piteous death
Their eyes were fastened. Clinging to his skin
A Seps with curving tooth, of little size,
He seized and tore away, and to the sands
Pierced with his javelin. Small the serpent's bulk;
None deals a death more horrible in form. 910
For swift the flesh dissolving round the wound
Bared the pale bone; swam all his limbs in blood;
Wasted the tissue of his calves and knees:
And all the muscles of his thighs were thawed
In black distilment, and file membrane sheath
Parted, that bound his vitals, which abroad
Flowed upon earth: yet seemed it not that all

His frame was loosed, for by the venomous drop
Were all the bands that held his muscles drawn
Down to a juice; the framework of his chest 920
Was bare, its cavity, and all the parts
Hid by the organs of life, that make the man.
So by unholy death there stood revealed
His inmost nature. Head and stalwart arms,
And neck and shoulders, from their solid mass
Melt in corruption. Not more swiftly flows
Wax at the sun's command, nor snow compelled
By southern breezes. Yet not all is said:
For so to noxious humours fire consumes
Our fleshly frame; but on the funeral pyre 930
What bones have perished? These dissolve no less
Than did the mouldered tissues, nor of death
Thus swift is left a trace. Of Afric pests
Thou bear'st the palm for hurtfulness: the life
They snatch away, thou only with the life
The clay that held it.

            Lo! a different fate,
Not this by melting! for a Prester's fang
Nasidius struck, who erst in Marsian fields
Guided the ploughshare. Burned upon his face 940
A redness as of flame: swollen the skin,
His features hidden, swollen all his limbs
Till more than human: and his definite frame
One tumour huge concealed. A ghastly gore
Is puffed from inwards as the virulent juice
Courses through all his body; which, thus grown,
His corselet holds not. Not in caldron so
Boils up to mountainous height the steaming wave;
Nor in such bellying curves does canvas bend
To Eastern tempests. Now the ponderous bulk 950
Rejects the limbs, and as a shapeless trunk
Burdens the earth: and there, to beasts and birds
A fatal feast, his comrades left the corse
Nor dared to place, yet swelling, in the tomb.

But for their eyes the Libyan pests prepared
More dreadful sights. On Tullus great in heart,

244

And bound to Cato with admiring soul,
A fierce Haemorrhois fixed. From every limb, [1]
(As from a statue saffron spray is showered
In every part) there spouted forth for blood   960
A sable poison: from the natural pores
Of moisture, gore profuse; his mouth was filled
And gaping nostrils, and his tears were blood.
Brimmed full his veins; his very sweat was red;
All was one wound.

       Then piteous Levus next
In sleep was victim, for around his heart
Stood still the blood congealed: no pain he felt
Of venomous tooth, but swift upon him fell
Death, and he sought the shades; more swift to kill   970
No draught in poisonous cups from ripened plants
Of direst growth Sabaean wizards brew.

Lo! Upon branchless trunk a serpent, named
By Libyans Jaculus, rose in coils to dart
His venom from afar. Through Paullus' brain
It rushed, nor stayed; for in the wound itself
Was death. Then did they know how slowly flies,
Flung from a sling, the stone; how gently speed
Through air the shafts of Scythia.

          What availed,   980
Murrus, the lance by which thou didst transfix
A Basilisk? Swift through the weapon ran
The poison to his hand: he draws his sword
And severs arm and shoulder at a blow:
Then gazed secure upon his severed hand
Which perished as he looked. So had'st thou died,
And such had been thy fate!

       Whoe'er had thought
A scorpion had strength o'er death or fate?
Yet with his threatening coils and barb erect   990

---

[1] See Book III., 706.

He won the glory of Orion [1] slain;
So bear the stars their witness. And who would fear
Thy haunts, Salpuga? [2] Yet the Stygian Maids
Have given thee power to snap the fatal threads.

Thus nor the day with brightness, nor the night
With darkness gave them peace. The very earth
On which they lay they feared; nor leaves nor straw
They piled for couches, but upon the ground
Unshielded from the fates they laid their limbs,
Cherished beneath whose warmth in chill of night   1000
The frozen pests found shelter; in whose jaws
Harmless the while, the lurking venom slept.
Nor did they know the measure of their march
Accomplished, nor their path; the stars in heaven
Their only guide. "Return, ye gods," they cried,
In frequent wail, "the arms from which we fled.
Give back Thessalia. Sworn to meet the sword
Why, lingering, fall we thus? In Caesar's place
The thirsty Dipsas and the horned snake
Now wage the warfare. Rather let us seek   1010
That region by the horses of the sun
Scorched, and the zone most torrid: let us fall
Slain by some heavenly cause, and from the sky
Descend our fate! Not, Africa, of thee
Complain we, nor of Nature. From mankind
Cut off, this quarter, teeming thus with pests
She gave to snakes, and to the barren fields
Denied the husbandman, nor wished that men
Should perish by their venom. To the realms
Of serpents have we come. Hater of men,   1020
Receive thy vengeance, whoso of the gods
Severed this region upon either hand,
With death in middle space. Our march is set
Through thy sequestered kingdom, and the host
Which knows thy secret seeks the furthest world.

---

[1] According to one story Orion, for his assault on Diana, was killed by the
Scorpion, who received his reward by being made into a constellation.
[2] A sort of venomous ant.

BOOK IX

Perchance some greater wonders on our path
May still await us; in the waves be plunged
Heaven's constellations, and the lofty pole
Stoop from its height. By further space removed
No land, than Juba's realm; by rumour's voice   1030
Drear, mournful. Haply for this serpent land
There may we long, where yet some living thing
Gives consolation. Not my native land
Nor European fields I hope for now
Lit by far other suns, nor Asia's plains.
But in what land, what region of the sky,
Where left we Africa? But now with frosts
Cyrene stiffened: have we changed the laws
Which rule the seasons, in this little space?
Cast from the world we know, 'neath other skies   1040
And stars we tread; behind our backs the home
Of southern tempests: Rome herself perchance
Now lies beneath our feet. Yet for our fates
This solace pray we, that on this our track
Pursuing Caesar with his host may come."

Thus was their stubborn patience of its plaints
Disburdened. But the bravery of their chief
Forced them to bear their toils. Upon the sand,
All bare, he lies and dares at every hour
Fortune to strike: he only at the fate   1050
Of each is present, flies to every call;
And greatest boon of all, greater than life,
Brought strength to die. To groan in death was shame
In such a presence. What power had all the ills
Possessed upon him? In another's breast
He conquers misery, teaching by his mien
That pain is powerless.

        Hardly aid at length
Did Fortune, wearied of their perils, grant.
Alone unharmed of all who till the earth,   1060
By deadly serpents, dwells the Psyllian race.
Potent as herbs their song; safe is their blood,
Nor gives admission to the poison germ
E'en when the chant has ceased. Their home itself

247

Placed in such venomous tract and serpent-thronged
Gained them this vantage, and a truce with death,
Else could they not have lived. Such is their trust
In purity of blood, that newly born
Each babe they prove by test of deadly asp
For foreign lineage. So the bird of Jove   1070
Turns his new fledglings to the rising sun
And such as gaze upon the beams of day
With eyes unwavering, for the use of heaven
He rears; but such as blink at Phoebus' rays
Casts from the nest. Thus of unmixed descent
The babe who, dreading not the serpent touch,
Plays in his cradle with the deadly snake.
Nor with their own immunity from harm
Contented do they rest, but watch for guests
Who need their help against the noisome plague.   1080

Now to the Roman standards are they come,
And when the chieftain bade the tents be fixed,
First all the sandy space within the lines
With song they purify and magic words
From which all serpents flee: next round the camp
In widest circuit from a kindled fire
Rise aromatic odours: danewort burns,
And juice distils from Syrian galbanum;
Then tamarisk and costum, Eastern herbs,
Strong panacea mixt with centaury   1090
From Thrace, and leaves of fennel feed the flames,
And thapsus brought from Eryx: and they burn
Larch, southern-wood and antlers of a deer
Which lived afar. From these in densest fumes,
Deadly to snakes, a pungent smoke arose;
And thus in safety passed the night away.
But should some victim feel the fatal fang
Upon the march, then of this magic race
Were seen the wonders, for a mighty strife
Rose 'twixt the Psyllian and the poison germ.   1100
First with saliva they anoint the limbs
That held the venomous juice within the wound;
Nor suffer it to spread. From foaming mouth
Next with continuous cadence would they pour

Unceasing chants -- nor breathing space nor pause --
Else spreads the poison: nor does fate permit
A moment's silence. Oft from the black flesh
Flies forth the pest beneath the magic song:
But should it linger nor obey the voice,
Repugmant to the summons, on the wound   1110
Prostrate they lay their lips and from the depths
Now paling draw the venom. In their mouths,
Sucked from the freezing flesh, they hold the death,
Then spew it forth; and from the taste shall know
The snake they conquer.

     Aided thus at length
Wanders the Roman host in better guise
Upon the barren fields in lengthy march. [1]
Twice veiled the moon her light and twice renewed;
Yet still, with waning or with growing orb   1120
Saw Cato's steps upon the sandy waste.
But more and more beneath their feet the dust
Began to harden, till the Libyan tracts
Once more were earth, and in the distance rose
Some groves of scanty foliage, and huts
Of plastered straw unfashioned: and their hearts
Leaped at the prospect of a better land.
How fled their sorrow! how with growing joy
They met the savage lion in the path!
In tranquil Leptis first they found retreat: 1130
And passed a winter free from heat and rain. [2]

When Caesar sated with Emathia's slain

---

[1] No other author gives any details of this march; and those given by Lucan
are unreliable. The temple of Hammon is far from any possible line of route
taken from the Lesser Syrtes to Leptis. Dean Merivale states that the inhospi-
table sands extended for seven days' journey, and ranks the march as one of
the greatest exploits in Roman military history. Described by the names
known to modern geography, it was from the Gulf of Cabes to Cape Africa.
Pope, in a letter to Henry Cromwell, dated November 11, 1710, makes some
caustic remarks on the geography of this book. (See "Pope's Works", Vol. vi.,
109; by Elwin & Courthope.)
[2] See Line 444.

Forsook the battlefield, all other cares
Neglected, he pursued his kinsman fled,
On him alone intent: by land his steps
He traced in vain; then, rumour for his guide,
He crossed the sea and reached the Thracian strait
For love renowned; where on the mournful shore
Rose Hero's tower, and Helle born of cloud [1]
Took from the rolling waves their former name.   1140
Nowhere with shorter space the sea divides
Europe from Asia; though Pontus parts
By scant division from Byzantium's hold
Chalcedon oyster-rich: and small the strait
Through which Propontis pours the Euxine wave.
Then marvelling at their ancient fame, he seeks
Sigeum's sandy beach and Simois' stream,
Rhoeteum noble for its Grecian tomb,
And all the hero's shades, the theme of song.
Next by the town of Troy burnt down of old   1150
Now but a memorable name, he turns
His steps, and searches for the mighty stones
Relics of Phoebus' wall. But bare with age
Forests of trees and hollow mouldering trunks
Pressed down Assaracus' palace, and with roots
Wearied, possessed the temples of the gods.
All Pergamus with densest brake was veiled
And even her stones were perished. He beheld
Thy rock, Hesione; the hidden grove,
Anchises' nuptial chamber; and the cave   1160
Where sat the arbiter; the spot from which
Was snatched the beauteous youth; the mountain lawn
Where played Oenone. Not a stone but told
The story of the past. A little stream
Scarce trickling through the arid plain he passed,
Nor knew 'twas Xanthus: deep in grass he placed,
Careless, his footstep; but the herdsman cried
"Thou tread'st the dust of Hector." Stones confused
Lay at his feet in sacred shape no more:
"Look on the altar of Jove," thus spake the guide,   1170

---

[1] See Book IV., 65.

"God of the household, guardian of the home."

O sacred task of poets, toil supreme,
Which rescuing all things from allotted fate
Dost give eternity to mortal men!
Grudge not the glory, Caesar, of such fame.
For if the Latian Muse may promise aught,
Long as the heroes of the Trojan time
Shall live upon the page of Smyrna's bard,
So long shall future races read of thee
In this my poem; and Pharsalia's song   1180
Live unforgotten in the age to come.

When by the ancient grandeur of the place
The chieftain's sight was filled, of gathered turf
Altars he raised: and as the sacred flame
Cast forth its odours, these not idle vows
Gave to the gods, "Ye deities of the dead,
Who watch o'er Phrygian ruins: ye who now
Lavinia's homes inhabit, and Alba's height:
Gods of my sire Aeneas, in whose fanes
The Trojan fire still burns: pledge of the past   1190
Mysterious Pallas, [1] of the inmost shrine,
Unseen of men! here in your ancient seat,
Most famous offspring of Iulus' race,
I call upon you and with pious hand
Burn frequent offerings. To my emprise
Give prosperous ending! Here shall I replace
The Phrygian peoples, here with glad return
Italia's sons shall build another Troy,
Here rise a Roman Pergamus."

        This said,   1200
He seeks his fleet, and eager to regain
Time spent at Ilium, to the favouring breeze
Spreads all his canvas. Past rich Asia borne,
Rhodes soon he left while foamed the sparkling main

---

[1] The "Palladium" or image of Pallas, preserved in the temple of Vesta. (See Book I., 659.)

Beneath his keels; nor ceased the wind to stretch
His bending sails, till on the seventh night
The Pharian beam proclaimed Egyptian shores.
But day arose, and veiled the nightly lamp
Ere rode his barks on waters safe from storm.
Then Caesar saw that tumult held the shore,   1210
And mingled voices of uncertain sound
Struck on his ear: and trusting not himself
To doubtful kingdoms, of uncertain troth,
He kept his ships from land.
                              But from the king
Came his vile minion forth upon the wave,
Bearing his dreadful gift, Pompeius' head,
Wrapped in a covering of Pharian wool.
First took he speech and thus in shameless words
Commends the murder: "Conqueror of the world,   1220
First of the Roman race, and, what as yet
Thou dost not know, safe by thy kinsman slain;
This gift receive from the Pellaean king,
Sole trophy absent from the Thracian field,
To crown thy toils on lands and on the deep.
Here in thine absence have we placed for thee
An end upon the war. Here Magnus came
To mend his fallen fortunes; on our swords
Here met his death. With such a pledge of faith
Here have we bought thee, Caesar; with his blood   1230
Seal we this treaty. Take the Pharian realm
Sought by no bloodshed, take the rule of Nile,
Take all that thou would'st give for Magnus' life:
And hold him vassal worthy of thy camp
To whom the fates against thy son-in-law
Such power entrusted; nor hold thou the deed
Lightly accomplished by the swordsman's stroke,
And so the merit. Guest ancestral he
Who was its victim; who, his sire expelled,
Gave back to him the sceptre. For a deed   1240
So great, thou'lt find a name -- or ask the world.
If 'twas a crime, thou must confess the debt
To us the greater, for that from thy hand
We took the doing."

Then he held and showed
Unveiled the head. Now had the hand of death
Passed with its changing touch upon the face:
Nor at first sight did Caesar on the gift
Pass condemnation; nor avert his gaze,
But dwelt upon the features till he knew   1250
The crime accomplished. Then when truth was sure
The loving father rose, and tears he shed
Which flowed at his command, and glad in heart
Forced from his breast a groan: thus by the flow
Of feigned tears and grief he hoped to hide
His joy else manifest: and the ghastly boon
Sent by the king disparaging, professed
Rather to mourn his son's dissevered head,
Than count it for a debt. For thee alone,
Magnus, he durst not fail to find a tear: 1260
He, Caesar, who with mien unaltered spurned
The Roman Senate, and with eyes undimmed
Looked on Pharsalia's field. O fate most hard!
Didst thou with impious war pursue the man
Whom 'twas thy lot to mourn? No kindred ties
No memory of thy daughter and her son
Touch on thy heart. Didst think perchance that grief
Might help thy cause 'mid lovers of his name?
Or haply, moved by envy of the king,
Griev'st that to other hands than thine was given   1270
To shed the captive's life-blood? and complain'st
Thy vengeance perished and the conquered chief
Snatched from thy haughty hand? Whate'er the cause
That urged thy grief, 'twas far removed from love.
Was this forsooth the object of thy toil
O'er lands and oceans, that without thy ken
He should not perish? Nay! but well was reft
From thine arbitrament his fate. What crime
Did cruel Fortune spare, what depth of shame
To Roman honour! since she suffered not,   1280
Perfidious traitor, while yet Magnus lived,
That thou should'st pity him!

Thus by words he dared,
To gain their credence in his sembled grief:

253

"Hence from my sight with thy detested gift,
Thou minion, to thy King. Worse does your crime
Deserve from Caesar than from Magnus' hands.
The only prize that civil war affords
Thus have we lost -- to bid the conquered live.
If but the sister of this Pharian king   1290
Were not by him detested, by the head
Of Cleopatra had I paid this gift.
Such were the fit return. Why did he draw
His separate sword, and in the toil that's ours
Mingle his weapons? In Thessalia's field
Gave we such right to the Pellaean blade?
Magnus as partner in the rule of Rome
I had not brooked; and shall I tolerate
Thee, Ptolemaeus? In vain with civil wars
Thus have we roused the nations, if there be   1300
Now any might but Caesar's. If one land
Yet owned two masters, I had turned from yours
The prows of Latium; but fame forbids,
Lest men should whisper that I did not damn
This deed of blood, but feared the Pharian land.
Nor think ye to deceive; victorious here
I stand: else had my welcome at your hands
Been that of Magnus; and that neck were mine
But for Pharsalia's chance. At greater risk
So seems it, than we dreamed of, took we arms;   1310
Exile, and Magnus' threats, and Rome I knew,
Not Ptolemaeus. But we spare the boy:
Pass by the murder. Let the princeling know
We give no more than pardon for his crime.
And now in honour of the mighty dead,
Not merely that the earth may hide your guilt,
Lay ye the chieftain's head within the tomb;
With proper sepulture appease his shade
And place his scattered ashes in an urn.
Thus may he know my coming, and may hear   1320
Affection's accents, and my fond complaints.
Me sought he not, but rather, for his life,
This Pharian vassal; snatching from mankind
The happy morning which had shown the world
A peace between us. But my prayers to heaven

254

No favouring answer found; that arms laid down
In happy victory, Magnus, once again
I might embrace thee, begging thee to grant
Thine ancient love to Caesar, and thy life.
Thus for my labours with a worthy prize   1330
Content, thine equal, bound in faithful peace,
I might have brought thee to forgive the gods
For thy disaster; thou had'st gained for me
From Rome forgiveness."

          Thus he spake, but found
No comrade in his tears; nor did the host
Give credit to his grief. Deep in their breasts
They hide their groans, and gaze with joyful front
(O famous Freedom!) on the deed of blood:
And dare to laugh when mighty Caesar wept.   1340

BOOK X

CAESAR IN EGYPT

When Caesar, following those who bore the head,
First trod the shore accursed, with Egypt's fates
His fortunes battled, whether Rome should pass
In crimson conquest o'er the guilty land,
Or Memphis' arms should ravish from the world
Victor and vanquished: and the warning shade
Of Magnus saved his kinsman from the sword.

First, by the crime assured, his standards borne
Before, he marched upon the Pharian town;
But when the people, jealous of their laws,   10
Murmured against the fasces, Caesar knew
Their minds were adverse, and that not for him
Was Magnus' murder wrought. And yet with brow
Dissembling fear, intrepid, through the shrines
Of Egypt's gods he strode, and round the fane
Of ancient Isis; bearing witness all
To Macedon's vigour in the days of old.
Yet did nor gold nor ornament restrain
His hasting steps, nor worship of the gods,
Nor city ramparts: but in greed of gain   20

He sought the cave dug out amid the tombs. [1]
The madman offspring there of Philip lies
The famed Pellaean robber, fortune's friend,
Snatched off by fate, avenging so the world.
In sacred sepulchre the hero's limbs,
Which should be scattered o'er the earth, repose,
Still spared by Fortune to these tyrant days:
For in a world to freedom once recalled,
All men had mocked the dust of him who set
The baneful lesson that so many lands   30
Can serve one master. Macedon he left
His home obscure; Athena he despised
The conquest of his sire, and spurred by fate
Through Asia rushed with havoc of mankind,
Plunging his sword through peoples; streams unknown
Ran red with Persian and with Indian blood.
Curse of all earth and thunderbolt of ill
To every nation! On the outer sea [2]
He launched his fleet to sail the ocean wave:
Nor flame nor flood nor sterile Libyan sands   40
Stayed back his course, nor Hammon's pathless shoals;
Far to the west, where downward slopes the world
He would have led his armies, and the poles
Had compassed, and had drunk the fount of Nile:
But came his latest day; such end alone
Could nature place upon the madman king,
Who jealous in death as when he won the world
His empire with him took, nor left an heir.
Thus every city to the spoiler's hand
Was victim made: Yet in his fall was his   50
Babylon; and Parthia feared him. Shame on us
That eastern nations dreaded more the lance
Of Macedon than now the Roman spear.
True that we rule beyond where takes its rise
The burning southern breeze, beyond the homes

---

[1] The body of Alexander was embalmed, and the mummy placed in a glass
case. The sarcophagus which enclosed them is stated to be now in the British
Museum.
[2] See Book III., 268.

Of western winds, and to the northern star;
But towards the rising of the sun, we yield
To him who kept the Arsacids in awe;
And puny Pella held as province sure
The Parthia fatal to our Roman arms.   60

Now from the stream Pelusian of the Nile,
Was come the boyish king, taming the rage
Of his effeminate people: pledge of peace;
And Caesar safely trod Pellaean halls;
When Cleopatra bribed her guard to break
The harbour chains, and borne in little boat
Within the Macedonian palace gates,
Caesar unknowing, entered: Egypt's shame;
Fury of Latium; to the bane of Rome
Unchaste. For as the Spartan queen of yore   70
By fatal beauty Argos urged to strife
And Ilium's homes, so Cleopatra roused
Italia's frenzy. By her drum [1] she called
Down on the Capitol terror (if to speak
Such word be lawful); mixed with Roman arms
Coward Canopus, hoping she might lead
A Pharian triumph, Caesar in her train;
And 'twas in doubt upon Leucadian [2] waves
Whether a woman, not of Roman blood,
Should hold the world in awe. Such lofty thoughts   80
Seized on her soul upon that night in which
The wanton daughter of Pellaean kings
First shared our leaders' couches. Who shall blame
Antonius for the madness of his love,
When Caesar's haughty breast drew in the flame?
Who red with carnage, 'mid the clash of arms,
In palace haunted by Pompeius' shade,
Gave place to love; and in adulterous bed,
Magnus forgotten, from the Queen impure,

---

[1] The kettledrum used in the worship of Isis. (See Book VIII, line 974.)
[2] At the Battle of Actium. The island of Leucas, close to the promontory of Actium, is always named by Lucan when he refers to this battle. (See also Virgil, "Aeneid", viii., 677.)

To Julia gave a brother: on the bounds,   90
Of furthest Libya permitting thus
His foe to gather: he in dalliance base
Waited upon his mistress, and to her
Pharos would give, for her would conquer all.

Then Cleopatra, trusting to her charms,
Tearless approached him, though in form of grief;
Her tresses loose as though in sorrow torn,
So best becoming her; and thus began:
"If, mighty Caesar, aught to noble birth
Be due, give ear. Of Lagian race am I   100
Offspring illustrious; from my father's throne
Cast forth to banishment; unless thy hand
Restore to me the sceptre: then a Queen
Falls at thy feet embracing. To our race
Bright star of justice thou! Nor first shall I
As woman rule the cities of the Nile;
For, neither sex preferring, Pharos bows
To queenly governance. Of my parted sire
Read the last words, by which 'tis mine to share
With equal rights the kingdom and the bed.   110
And loves the boy his sister, were he free;
But his affections and his sword alike
Pothinus orders. Nor wish I myself
To wield my father's power; but this my prayer:
Save from this foul disgrace our royal house,
Bid that the king shall reign, and from the court
Remove this hateful varlet, and his arms.
How swells his bosom for that his the hand
That shore Pompeius' head! And now he threats
Thee, Caesar, also; which the Fates avert!   120
'Twas shame enough upon the earth and thee
That of Pothinus Magnus should have been
The guilt or merit."

       Caesar's ears in vain
Had she implored, but aided by her charms
The wanton's prayers prevailed, and by a night
Of shame ineffable, passed with her judge,
She won his favour.

When between the pair [1]
Caesar had made a peace, by costliest gifts   130
Purchased, a banquet of such glad event
Made fit memorial; and with pomp the Queen
Displayed her luxuries, as yet unknown
To Roman fashions. First uprose the hall
Like to a fane which this corrupted age
Could scarcely rear: the lofty ceiling shone
With richest tracery, the beams were bound
In golden coverings; no scant veneer
Lay on its walls, but built in solid blocks
Of marble, gleamed the palace. Agate stood   140
In sturdy columns, bearing up the roof;
Onyx and porphyry on the spacious floor
Were trodden 'neath the foot; the mighty gates
Of Maroe's throughout were formed,
He mere adornment; ivory clothed the hall,
And fixed upon the doors with labour rare
Shells of the tortoise gleamed, from Indian seas,
With frequent emeralds studded. Gems of price
And yellow jasper on the couches shone.
Lustrous the coverlets; the major part   150
Dipped more than once within the vats of Tyre
Had drunk their juice: part feathered as with gold;
Part crimson dyed, in manner as are passed
Through Pharian leash the threads. There waited slaves
In number as a people, some in ranks
By different blood distinguished, some by age;
This band with Libyan, that with auburn hair
Red so that Caesar on the banks of Rhine
None such had witnessed; some with features scorched
By torrid suns, their locks in twisted coils   160
Drawn from their foreheads. Eunuchs too were there,
Unhappy race; and on the other side
Men of full age whose cheeks with growth of hair
Were hardly darkened.

---

[1] Between Cleopatra and her brother.

BOOK X

Upon either hand

Lay kings, and Caesar in the midst supreme.
There in her fatal beauty lay the Queen
Thick daubed with unguents, nor with throne content
Nor with her brother spouse; laden she lay
On neck and hair with all the Red Sea spoils,   170
And faint beneath the weight of gems and gold.
Her snowy breast shone through Sidonian lawn
Which woven close by shuttles of the east
The art of Nile had loosened. Ivory feet
Bore citron tables brought from woods that wave [1]
On Atlas, such as Caesar never saw
When Juba was his captive. Blind in soul
By madness of ambition, thus to fire
By such profusion of her wealth, the mind
Of Caesar armed, her guest in civil war!   180
Not though he aimed with pitiless hand to grasp
The riches of a world; not though were here
Those ancient leaders of the simple age,
Fabricius or Curius stern of soul,
Or he who, Consul, left in sordid garb
His Tuscan plough, could all their several hopes
Have risen to such spoil. On plates of gold
They piled the banquet sought in earth and air
And from the deepest seas and Nilus' waves,
Through all the world; in craving for display,   190
No hunger urging. Frequent birds and beasts,
Egypt's high gods, they placed upon the board:
In crystal goblets water of the Nile
They handed, and in massive cups of price
Was poured the wine; no juice of Mareot grape [2]
But noble vintage of Falernian growth
Which in few years in Meroe's vats had foamed,
(For such the clime) to ripeness. On their brows
Chaplets were placed of roses ever young
With glistening nard entwined; and in their locks   200

---

[1] See Book IX., 507.
[2] Yet the Mareot grape was greatly celebrated. (See Professor Rawlinson's note to Herodotus. ii., 18.)

Was cinnamon infused, not yet in air
Its fragrance perished, nor in foreign climes;
And rich amomum from the neighbouring fields.
Thus Caesar learned the booty of a world
To lavish, and his breast was shamed of war
Waged with his son-in-law for meagre spoil,
And with the Pharian realm he longed to find
A cause of battle.

       When of wine and feast
They wearied and their pleasure found an end,   210
Caesar drew out in colloquy the night
Thus with Achoreus, on the highest couch
With linen ephod as a priest begirt:
"O thou devoted to all sacred rites,
Loved by the gods, as proves thy length of days,
Tell, if thou wilt, whence sprang the Pharian race;
How lie their lands, the manners of their tribes,
The form and worship of their deities.
Expound the sculptures on your ancient fanes:
Reveal your gods if willing to be known: 220
If to th' Athenian sage your fathers taught
Their mysteries, who worthier than I
To bear in trust the secrets of the world?
True, by the rumour of my kinsman's flight
Here was I drawn; yet also by your fame:
And even in the midst of war's alarms
The stars and heavenly spaces have I conned;
Nor shall Eudoxus' year [1] excel mine own.
But though such ardour burns within my breast,
Such zeal to know the truth, yet my chief wish   230
To learn the source of your mysterious flood
Through ages hidden: give me certain hope
To see the fount of Nile -- and civil war
Then shall I leave."

---

[1] The calendar introduced by Caesar, in B.C. 45, was founded on the Egyptian or solar year. (See Herodotus, ii., 4.) Eudoxus seems to have dealt with this year and to have corrected it. He is probably alluded to by Virgil, "Eclogue" iii., 41.

He spake, and then the priest:
"The secrets, Caesar, of our mighty sires [1]
Kept from the common people until now
I hold it right to utter. Some may deem
That silence on these wonders of the earth

Were greater piety. But to the gods   240
I hold it grateful that their handiwork
And sacred edicts should be known to men.

"A different power by the primal law,
Each star possesses: [2] these alone control
The movement of the sky, with adverse force
Opposing: while the sun divides the year,
And day from night, and by his potent rays
Forbids the stars to pass their stated course.
The moon by her alternate phases sets
The varying limits of the sea and shore.   250
'Neath Saturn's sway the zone of ice and snow
Has passed; while Mars in lightning's fitful flames
And winds abounds' beneath high Jupiter
Unvexed by storms abides a temperate air;
And fruitful Venus' star contains the seeds
Of all things. Ruler of the boundless deep
The god [3] Cyllenian: whene'er he holds
That part of heaven where the Lion dwells
With neighbouring Cancer joined, and Sirius star
Flames in its fury; where the circular path   260
(Which marks the changes of the varying year)
Gives to hot Cancer and to Capricorn
Their several stations, under which doth lie
The fount of Nile, he, master of the waves,

---

[1] Herodotus was less fortunate. For he says "Concerning the nature of the river I was not able to gain any information either from the priests or others." (ii., 19.)
[2] It was supposed that the Sun and Moon and the planets (Saturn, Jupiter, Mars, Mercury, and Venus) were points which restrained the motion of the sky in its revolution. (See Book VI., 576.)
[3] Mercury. (See Book IX., 777.)

Strikes with his beam the waters. Forth the stream
Brims from his fount, as Ocean when the moon
Commands an increase; nor shall curb his flow
Till night wins back her losses from the sun. [1]

"Vain is the ancient faith that Ethiop snows [2]
Send Nile abundant forth upon the lands.   270
Those mountains know nor northern wind nor star.
Of this are proof the breezes of the South,
Fraught with warm vapours, and the people's hue
Burned dark by suns: and 'tis in time of spring,
When first are thawed the snows, that ice-fed streams
In swollen torrents tumble; but the Nile
Nor lifts his wave before the Dog star burns;
Nor seeks again his banks, until the sun
In equal balance measures night and day.
Nor are the laws that govern other streams   280
Obeyed by Nile. For in the wintry year
Were he in flood, when distant far the sun,
His waters lacked their office; but he leaves
His channel when the summer is at height,
Tempering the torrid heat of Egypt's clime.
Such is the task of Nile; thus in the world
He finds his purpose, lest exceeding heat
Consume the lands: and rising thus to meet
Enkindled Lion, to Syene's prayers
By Cancer burnt gives ear; nor curbs his wave   290
Till the slant sun and Meroe's lengthening shades
Proclaim the autumn. Who shall give the cause?
'Twas Parent Nature's self which gave command
Thus for the needs of earth should flow the Nile.

"Vain too the fable that the western winds [1]

---

[1] That is, at the autumnal equinox. The priest states that the planet Mercury
causes the rise of the Nile. The passage is difficult to follow; but the idea
would seem to be that this god, who controlled the rise and fall of the waves
of the sea, also when he was placed directly over the Nile caused the rise of
that river.
[2] So also Herodotus, Book ii., 22. Yet modern discoveries have proved the
snows.

BOOK X

Control his current, in continuous course
At stated seasons governing the air;
Or hurrying from Occident to South
Clouds without number which in misty folds
Press on the waters; or by constant blast,   300
Forcing his current back whose several mouths
Burst on the sea; -- so, forced by seas and wind,
Men say, his billows pour upon the land.
Some speak of hollow caverns, breathing holes
Deep in the earth, within whose mighty jaws
Waters in noiseless current underneath
From northern cold to southern climes are drawn:
And when hot Meroe pants beneath the sun,
Then, say they, Ganges through the silent depths
And Padus pass: and from a single fount   310
The Nile arising not in single streams
Pours all the rivers forth. And rumour says
That when the sea which girdles in the world [2]
O'erflows, thence rushes Nile, by lengthy course,
Softening his saltness. More, if it be true
That ocean feeds the sun and heavenly fires,
Then Phoebus journeying by the burning Crab
Sucks from its waters more than air can hold
Upon his passage -- this the cool of night
Pours on the Nile.   320

       "If, Caesar, 'tis my part
To judge such difference, 'twould seem that since
Creation's age has passed, earth's veins by chance
Some waters hold, and shaken cast them forth:
But others took when first the globe was formed
A sure abode; by Him who framed the world
Fixed with the Universe.

       "And, Roman, thou,
In thirsting thus to know the source of Nile

---

[1] So, too, Herodotus, Book ii., 20, who attributes the theory to Greeks who
wish to get a reputation for cleverness.
[2] See on Book V., 709. Herodotus mentions this theory also, to dismiss it.

Dost as the Pharian and Persian kings   330

And those of Macedon; nor any age
Refused the secret, but the place prevailed
Remote by nature. Greatest of the kings
By Memphis worshipped, Alexander grudged [1]
To Nile its mystery, and to furthest earth
Sent chosen Ethiops whom the crimson zone
Stayed in their further march, while flowed his stream
Warm at their feet. Sesostris [2] westward far
Reached, to the ends of earth; and necks of kings
Bent 'neath his chariot yoke: but of the springs   340
Which fill your rivers, Rhone and Po, he drank.
Not of the fount of Nile. Cambyses king
In madman quest led forth his host to where
The long-lived races dwell: then famine struck,
Ate of his dead [3] and, Nile unknown, returned.
No lying rumour of thy hidden source
Has e'er made mention; wheresoe'er thou art
Yet art thou sought, nor yet has nation claimed
In pride of place thy river as its own.
Yet shall I tell, so far as has the god,   350
Who veils thy fountain, given me to know.
Thy progress. Daring to upraise thy banks
'Gainst fiery Cancer's heat, thou tak'st thy rise
Beneath the zenith: straight towards the north
And mid Bootes flowing; to the couch
Bending, or to the risings, of the sun
In sinuous bends alternate; just alike

---

[1] The historians state that Alexander made an expedition to the temple of Jupiter Hammon and consulted the oracle. Jupiter assisted his march, and an army of crows pointed out the path (Plutarch). It is, however stated, in a note in Langhorne's edition, that Maximus Tyrius informs us that the object of the journey was the discovery of the sources of the Nile.
[2] Sesostris, the great king, does not appear to have pushed his conquests to the west of Europe.
[3] See Herodotus, iii., 17. These Ethiopian races were supposed to live to the age of 120 years, drinking milk, and eating boiled flesh. On Cambyses's march his starving troops cast lots by tens for the one man who was to be eaten.

To Araby's peoples and to Libyan sands.
By Seres [1] first beheld, yet know they not

Whence art thou come; and with no native stream   360
Strik'st thou the Ethiop fields. Nor knows the world
To whom it owes thee. Nature ne'er revealed
Thy secret origin, removed afar.
Nor did she wish thee to be seen of men
While still a tiny rivulet, but preferred
Their wonder to their knowledge. Where the sun
Stays at his limit, dost thou rise in flood
Untimely; such try right: to other lands
Bearing try winter: and by both the poles
Thou only wanderest. Here men ask thy rise   370
And there thine ending. Meroe rich in soil
And tilled by swarthy husbandmen divides
Thy broad expanse, rejoicing in the leaves
Of groves of ebony, which though spreading far
Their branching foliage, by no breadth of shade
Soften the summer sun -- whose rays direct
Pass from the Lion to the fervid earth. [2]
Next dost thou journey onwards past the realm
Of burning Phoebus, and the sterile sands,
With equal volume; now with all thy strength   380
Gathered in one, and now in devious streams
Parting the bank that crumbles at thy touch.
Then by our kingdom's gates, where Philae parts
Arabian peoples from Egyptian fields
The sluggish bosom of thy flood recalls
Try wandering currents, which through desert wastes
Flow gently on to where the merchant track
Divides the Red Sea waters from our own.
Who, gazing, Nile, upon thy tranquil flow,
Could picture how in wild array of foam   390

---

[1] The Seres are, of course, the Chinese. The ancients seem to have thought that the Nile came from the east. But it is possible that there was another tribe of this name dwelling in Africa.
[2] A passage of difficulty. I understand it to mean that at this spot the summer sun (in Leo) strikes the earth with direct rays.

(Where shelves the earth) thy billows shall be plunged
Down the steep cataracts, in fuming wrath
That rocks should bar the passage of thy stream
Free from its source? For whirled on high the spray
Aims at the stars, and trembles all the air
With rush of waters; and with sounding roar
The foaming mass down from the summit pours
In hoary waves victorious. Next an isle
In all our ancient lore "untrodden" named
Stems firm thy torrent; and the rocks we call   400
Springs of the river, for that here are marked
The earliest tokens of the coming flood.
With mountain shores now nature hems thee in
And shuts thy waves from Libya; in the midst
Hence do thy waters run, till Memphis first
Forbids the barrier placed upon thy stream
And gives thee access to the open fields."

Thus did they pass, as though in peace profound,
The nightly watches. But Pothinus' mind,
Once with accursed butchery imbued,   410
Was frenzied still; since great Pompeius fell
No deed to him was crime; his rabid soul
Th' avenging goddesses and Magnus' shade
Stirred to fresh horrors; and a Pharian hand
No less was worthy, as he deemed, to shed
That blood which Fortune purposed should bedew
The conquered fathers: and the fell revenge
Due to the senate for the civil war
This hireling almost snatched. Avert, ye fates,
Far hence the shame that not by Brutus' hand   420
This blow be struck! Shall thus the tyrant's fall
Just at our hands, become a Pharian crime,
Reft of example? To prepare a plan
(Fated to fail) he dares; nor veils in fraud
A plot for murder, but with open war
Attacks th' unconquered chieftain: from his crimes
He gained such courage as to send command
To lop the head of Caesar, and to join
In death the kinsmen chiefs.

These words by night   430
His faithful servants to Achillas bear,
His foul associate, whom the boy had made
Chief of his armies, and who ruled alone
O'er Egypt's land and o'er himself her king:
"Now lay thy limbs upon the sumptuous couch
And sleep in luxury, for the Queen hath seized
The palace; nor alone by her betrayed,
But Caesar's gift, is Pharos. Dost delay
Nor hasten to the chamber of thy Queen?
Thou only? Married to the Latian chief,   440
The impious sister now her brother weds
And hurrying from rival spouse to spouse
Hath Egypt won, and plays the bawd for Rome.
By amorous potions she has won the man:
Then trust the boy! Yet give him but a night
In her enfondling arms, and drunk with love
Thy life and mine he'll barter for a kiss.
We for his sister's charms by cross and flame
Shall pay the penalty: nor hope of aid;
Here stands adulterous Caesar, here the King   450
Her spouse: how hope we from so stern a judge
To gain acquittal? Shall she not condemn
Those who ne'er sought her favours? By the deed
We dared together and lost, by Magnus' blood
Which wrought the bond between us, be thou swift
With hasty tumult to arouse the war:
Dash in with nightly band, and mar with death
Their shameless nuptials: on the very bed
With either lover smite the ruthless Queen.
Nor let the fortunes of the Western chief   460
Make pause our enterprise. We share with him
The glory of his empire o'er the world.
Pompeius fallen makes us too sublime.
There lies the shore that bids us hope success:
Ask of our power from the polluted wave,
And gaze upon the scanty tomb which holds
Not all Pompeius' ashes. Peer to him
Was he whom now thou fearest. Noble blood
True, is not ours: what boots it? Nor are realms
Nor wealth of peoples given to our command.   470

Yet have we risen to a height of power
For deeds of blood, and Fortune to our hands
Attracts her victims. Lo! a nobler now
Lies in our compass, and a second death
Hesperia shall appease; for Caesar's blood,
Shed by these hands, shall give us this, that Rome
Shall love us, guilty of Pompeius' fall.
Why fear these titles, why this chieftain's strength?
For shorn of these, before your swords he lies
A common soldier. To the civil war   480
This night shall bring completion, and shall give
To peoples slain fit offerings, and send
That life the world demands beneath the shades.
Rise then in all your hardihood and smite
This Caesar down, and let the Roman youths
Strike for themselves, and Lagos for its King.
Nor do thou tarry: full of wine and feast
Thou'lt fall upon him in the lists of love;
Then dare the venture, and the heavenly gods
Shall grant of Cato's and of Brutus' prayers   490
To thee fulfilment."

       Nor was Achillas slow
To hear the voice that counselled him to crime.
No sounding clarion summoned, as is wont,
His troops to arms; nor trumpet blare betrayed
Their nightly march: but rapidly he seized
All needed instruments of blood and war.
Of Latian race the most part of his train,
Yet to barbarian customs were their minds
By long forgetfulness of Rome debased: 500
Else had it shamed to serve the Pharian King;
But now his vassal and his minion's word
Compel obedience. Those who serve in camps
Lose faith and love of kin: their pittance earned [1]
Makes just the deed: and for their sordid pay,
Not for themselves, they threaten Caesar's life.
Where finds the piteous destiny of the realm

---

[1] Reading "ibi fas ubi proxima merees", with Hosius.

270

Rome with herself at peace? The host withdrawn
From dread Thessalia raves on Nilus' banks
As all the race of Rome. What more had dared,   510
With Magnus welcomed, the Lagean house?
Each hand must render to the gods their due,
Nor son of Rome may cease from civil war;
By Heaven's command our state was rent in twain;
Nor love for husband nor regard for sire
Parted our peoples. 'Twas a slave who stirred
Afresh the conflict, and Achillas grasped
In turn the sword of Rome: nay more, had won,
Had not the fates adverse restrained his hand
From Caesar's slaughter.   520

      For the murderous pair
Ripe for their plot were met; the spacious hall
Still busied with the feast. So might have flowed
Into the kingly cups a stream of gore,
And in mid banquet fallen Caesar's head.
Yet did they fear lest in the nightly strife
(The fates permitting) some incautious hand --
So did they trust the sword -- might slay the King.
Thus stayed the deed, for in the minds of slaves
The chance of doing Caesar to the death   530
Might bear postponement: when the day arose
Then should he suffer; and a night of life
Thus by Pothinus was to Caesar given.

Now from the Casian rock looked forth the Sun
Flooding the land of Egypt with a day
Warm from its earliest dawn, when from the walls
Not wandering in disorder are they seen,
But drown in close array, as though to meet
A foe opposing; ready to receive
Or give the battle. Caesar, in the town   540
Placing no trust, within the palace courts
Lay in ignoble hiding place, the gates
Close barred: nor all the kingly rooms possessed,
But in the narrowest portion of the space
He drew his band together. There in arms
They stood, with dread and fury in their souls.

He feared attack, indignant at his fear.
Thus will a noble beast in little cage
Imprisoned, fume, and break upon the bars
His teeth in frenzied wrath; nor more would rage   550
The flames of Vulcan in Sicilian depths
Should Etna's top be closed. He who but now
By Haemus' mount against Pompeius chief,
Italia's leaders and the Senate line,
His cause forbidding hope, looked at the fates
He knew were hostile, with unfaltering gaze,
Now fears before the crime of hireling slaves,
And in mid palace trembles at the blow:
He whom nor Scythian nor Alaun [1] had dared
To violate, nor the Moor who aims the dart   560
Upon his victim slain, to prove his skill.
The Roman world but now did not suffice
To hold him, nor the realms from furthest Ind
To Tyrian Gades. Now, as puny boy,
Or woman, trembling when a town is sacked,
Within the narrow corners of a house
He seeks for safety; on the portals closed
His hope of life; and with uncertain gait
He treads the hails; yet not without the King;
In purpose, Ptolemaeus, that thy life   570
For his shall give atonement; and to hurl
Thy severed head among the servant throng
Should darts and torches fail. So story tells
The Colchian princess [2] with sword in hand,
And with her brother's neck bared to the blow,
Waited her sire, avenger of his realm
Despoiled, and of her flight. In the imminent risk
Caesar, in hopes of peace, an envoy sent
To the fierce vassals, from their absent lord
Bearing a message, thus: "At whose command   580
Wage ye the war?" But not the laws which bind

---

[1] See Book VIII., 253.
[2] Medea, who fled from Colchis with her brother, Absyrtus. Pursued by her father Aeetes, she killed her brother and strewed the parts of his body into the sea. The king paused to collect them.

All nations upon earth, nor sacred rights,
Availed to save or messenger of peace,
Or King's ambassador; or thee from crime
Such as befitted thee, thou land of Nile
Fruitful in monstrous deeds: not Juba's realm
Vast though it be, nor Pontus, nor the land
Thessalian, nor the arms of Pharnaces,
Nor yet the tracts which chill Iberus girds,
Nor Libyan coasts such wickedness have dared,   590
As thou, with all thy luxuries. Closer now
War hemmed them in, and weapons in the courts,
Shaking the innermost recesses, fell.
Yet did no ram, fatal with single stroke,
Assail the portal, nor machine of war;
Nor flame they called in aid; but blind of plan
They wander purposeless, in separate bands
Around the circuit, nor at any spot
With strength combined attempt to breach the wall.
The fates forbad, and Fortune from their hands   600
Held fast the palace as a battlement.
Nor failed they to attack from ships of war
The regal dwelling, where its frontage bold
Made stand apart the waters of the deep:
There, too, was Caesar's all-protecting arm;
For these at point of sword, and those with fire [1]
He forces back, and though besieged he dares
To storm th' assailants: and as lay the ships
Joined rank to rank, bids drop upon their sides
Lamps drenched with reeking tar. Nor slow the fire   610
To seize the hempen cables and the decks
Oozing with melting pitch; the oarsman's bench
All in one moment, and the topmost yards
Burst into flame: half merged the vessels lay
While swam the foemen, all in arms, the wave;
Nor fell the blaze upon the ships alone,
But seized with writhing tongues the neighbouring homes,
And fanned to fury by the Southern breeze

---

[1] It was in this conflagration that a large part of the library of the Ptolemies was destroyed. 400,000 volumes are stated to have perished.

273

Tempestuous, it leaped from roof to roof;
Not otherwise than on its heavenly track,   620
Unfed by matter, glides the ball of light,
By air alone aflame.

          This pest recalled
Some of the forces to the city's aid
From the besieged halls. Nor Caesar gave
To sleep its season; swifter than all else
To seize the crucial moment of the war.
Quick in the darkest watches of the night
He leaped upon his ships, and Pharos [1] seized,
Gate of the main; an island in the days   630
Of Proteus seer, now bordering the walls
Of Alexander's city. Thus he gained
A double vantage, for his foes were pent
Within the narrow entrance, which for him
And for his aids gave access to the sea.

Nor longer was Pothinus' doom delayed,
Yet not with cross or flame, nor with the wrath
His crime demanded; nor by savage beasts
Torn, did he suffer; but by Magnus' death,
Alas the shame! he fell; his head by sword   640
Hacked from his shoulders. Next by frauds prepared
By Ganymede her base attendant, fled
Arsinoe [2] from the Court to Caesar's foes;
There in the absence of the King she ruled
As of Lagean blood: there at her hands,
The savage minion of the tyrant boy,
Achillas, fell by just avenging sword.
Thus did another victim to thy shade
Atone, Pompeius; but the gods forbid
That this be all thy vengeance! Not the king 650

---

[1] The island of Pharos, which lay over against the port of Alexandria, had been connected with the mainland in the middle by a narrow causeway. On it stood the lighthouse. (See Book IX, 1191.) Proteus, the old man of the sea, kept here his flock of seals, according to the Homeric story. ("Odyssey", Book IV, 400.)
[2] Younger sister of Cleopatra.

Nor all the stock of Lagos for thy death
Would make fit sacrifice! So Fortune deemed;
And not till patriot swords shall drink the blood
Of Caesar, Magnus, shalt thou be appeased.
Still, though was slain the author of the strife,
Sank not their rage: with Ganymede for chief
Again they rush to arms; in deeds of fight
Again they conquer. So might that one day
Have witnessed Caesar's fate; so might its fame
Have lived through ages.   660

                    As the Roman Chief,
Crushed on the narrow surface of the mole,
Prepared to throw his troops upon the ships,
Sudden upon him the surrounding foes
With all their terrors came. In dense array
Their navy lined the shores, while on the rear
The footmen ceaseless charged. No hope was left,
For flight was not, nor could the brave man's arm
Achieve or safety or a glorious death.
Not now were needed for great Caesar's fall,   670
Caught in the toils of nature, routed host
Or mighty heaps of slain: his only doubt
To fear or hope for death: while on his brain
Brave Scaeva's image flashed, now vainly sought,
Who on the wall by Epidamnus' fields
Earned fame immortal, and with single arm
Drove back Pompeius as he trod the breach....

The Gracchi Marius and Sulla Epochs Of Ancient History - with original maps and sidenotes as sub headings
A. H. Beesley
Benediction Classics, 2011
178 pages
ISBN: 978-1-84902-417-4

Available from www.amazon.com, www.amazon.co.uk

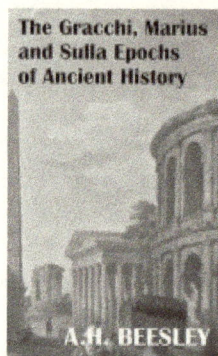

Epochs of ancient history, the Gracchi, Marius and Sulla was written by A.H. Beesley in 1921. It is a historical text, describing a time of crisis in the Roman Empire, which eventually culminated in its demise. Beesley sought to provide the most a consistent and faithful account of the leaders and legislation of this era. He drew on Long's 'History of the Decline of the Roman Republic' and Mommsen's 'History of Rome'. This edition comes complete with the original maps and the sidenotes have been converted into sub-headings.

The Poetical Works of Elizabeth Barrett Browning - Volume IV
Elizabeth Barrett Browning
Benediction Classics, 2011
212 pages
ISBN: 978-1-78139-027-6

Available from www.amazon.com,
www.amazon.co.uk

Elizabeth Barrett Browning (6 March 1806 -
29 June 1861) was an English poet and one of
the most prominent poets of her time. During her lifetime her po-
etry gained great applaud both in England and in the United
States. She suffered from ill health all her life and was amazed that
Robert Browning fell in love with her and wished to marry her.
She was eight years his senior and an invalid. The marriage result-
ed in her being disinherited by her father and the Brownings lived
in Italy for most of their married life. After she died, Robert
Browning published her later poems. This Volume contains the
following poems, including "How do I love thee? Let me count the
ways": Poems A Child's Grave At Florence. Catarina To Camoens
Life And Love. A Denial. Proof And Disproof. Question And Answer.
Inclusions. Insufficiency. Sonnets From The Portuguese Casa Guidi
Windows. Poems Before Congress Napoleon Iii. In Italy. The
Dance. A Tale Of Villafranca. Told In Tuscany. A Court Lady. An
August Voice. Christmas Gifts. Italy And The World. A Curse For A
Nation. Prologue. The Curse. Last Poems Little Mattie. A False Step.
Void In Law. Lord Walter's Wife. Bianca Among The Nightingales.
My Kate. A Song For The Ragged School Of London. Written In
Rome. May's Love. Amy's Cruelty. My Heart And I. The Best Thing
In The World. Where's Agnes?

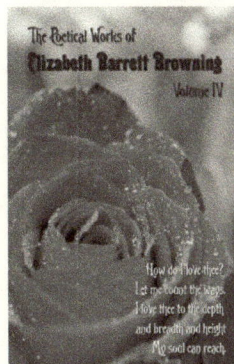

Enamels and Cameos and other Poems
Théophile Gautier
Benediction Classics, 2012
122 pages
ISBN: 978-1-78139-135-8

Available from www.amazon.com,
www.amazon.co.uk

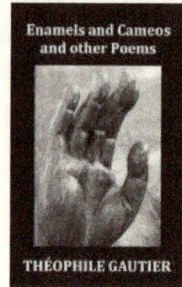

Pierre Jules Théophile Gautier (1811 - 1872) was a French writer and critic. In his youth Gautier was an adherent of Romanticism, but later his work became difficult to classify and he remains a point of reference for many subsequent literary traditions such as Parnassianism, Symbolism, Decadence and Modernism. He rejected bourgeois everyday life saying that it is a kingdom of vulgar men and hucksters. He despised petit bourgeois moralizing and democratic ideological content in literature. This book of poems - Enamels and Cameos - is his last and some consider his most important work. It focusses on the beauty of everyday life, his poetry becoming compact and Gautier's poetry changes profoundly, becoming compact and stark, as Gautier explained, "treating tiny subjects in a severely formal way." He was widely esteemed by writers as diverse as Balzac, Baudelaire, the Goncourt brothers, Flaubert, Proust and Oscar Wilde.

The Song of Hiawatha - An Epic Poem; also with: The Skeleton in Armor, The Wreck of the Hesperus, The Luck of Edenhall, The Elected Knight, and The Children of the Lord's Supper
Henry Wadsworth Longfellow
Benediction Classics, 2011
220 pages
ISBN: 978-1-84902-340-5

Available from www.amazon.com,
www.amazon.co.uk

The Song of Hiawatha is an epic poem, written in 1855 by Henry Wadsworth Longfellow. This version comes with copious illustrations and with line numbers, it also comprises five other poems: The Skeleton in Armor, The Wreck of the Hesperus, The Luck of Edenhall, The Elected Knight, and The Children of the Lord's Supper. The Song of Hiawatha is about an Indian hero who is based on the legends of the Ojibwe and other Native American peoples. Longfellow's work is a saga in the genre of American Romantic literature, and is not representative of Native American oral tradition. Longfellow had originally planned to call his hero Manabozho, which was the name of a Ojibwe folklore trickster-transformer . However, in his journal entry on June 28th, 1854, he wrote, "Work at 'Manabozho;' or, as I think I shall call it, 'Hiawatha'-that being another name for the same personage." Longfellow was mistaken about this, Hiawatha was probably an Iroquois hero. But as a result of the popularity of the poem, "Hiawatha" was used as a common name for everything, from towns to a telephone company, in the region of the western Great Lakes, where no Iroquois live.

Also from Benediction Books ...
Wandering Between Two Worlds: Essays on Faith and Art
Anita Mathias
Benediction Books, 2007
152 pages
ISBN: 0955373700

Available from www.amazon.com, www.amazon.co.uk

In these wide-ranging lyrical essays, Anita Mathias writes, in lush, lovely prose, of her naughty Catholic childhood in Jamshedpur, India; her large, eccentric family in Mangalore, a sea-coast town converted by the Portuguese in the sixteenth century; her rebellion and atheism as a teenager in her Himalayan boarding school, run by German missionary nuns, St. Mary's Convent, Nainital; and her abrupt religious conversion after which she entered Mother Teresa's convent in Calcutta as a novice. Later rich, elegant essays explore the dualities of her life as a writer, mother, and Christian in the United States-- Domesticity and Art, Writing and Prayer, and the experience of being "an alien and stranger" as an immigrant in America, sensing the need for roots.

About the Author

Anita Mathias is the author of *Wandering Between Two Worlds: Essays on Faith and Art.* She has a B.A. and M.A. in English from Somerville College, Oxford University, and an M.A. in Creative Writing from the Ohio State University, USA. Anita won a National Endowment of the Arts fellowship in Creative Nonfiction in 1997. She lives in Oxford, England with her husband, Roy, and her daughters, Zoe and Irene.

Anita's website:
    http://www.anitamathias.com, and
Anita's blog Dreaming Beneath the Spires:
    http://dreamingbeneaththespires.blogspot.com

The Church That Had Too Much
Anita Mathias
Benediction Books, 2010
52 pages
ISBN: 9781849026567

Available from www.amazon.com, www.amazon.co.uk

The Church That Had Too Much was very well-intentioned. She
wanted to love God, she wanted to love people, but she was both ham-
pered by her muchness and the abundance of her possessions, and
beset by ambition, power struggles and snobbery. Read about the sur-
prising way The Church That Had Too Much began to resolve her
problems in this deceptively simple and enchanting fable.

About the Author

Anita Mathias is the author of *Wandering Between Two Worlds: Es-
says on Faith and Art*. She has a B.A. and M.A. in English from
Somerville College, Oxford University, and an M.A. in Creative Writ-
ing from the Ohio State University, USA. Anita won a National
Endowment of the Arts fellowship in Creative Nonfiction in 1997.
She lives in Oxford, England with her husband, Roy, and her daugh-
ters, Zoe and Irene.

Anita's website:
    http://www.anitamathias.com, and
Anita's blog Dreaming Beneath the Spires:
    http://dreamingbeneaththespires.blogspot.com

www.ingramcontent.com/pod-product-compliance
Lightning Source LLC
Chambersburg PA
CBHW030522100426
42813CB00001B/116